Red Hat Linux 5.2

The Red Hat Linux Installation Guide

Red Hat Software, Inc.

Research Triangle Park, North Carolina

Revision: Inst-5.2-Print-MDP (10/98)

Red Hat Software, Inc.
4201 Research Commons, Suite 100
79 T. W. Alexander Drive
P. O. Box 13588
Research Triangle Park, NC 27709
(919) 547-0012
redhat@redhat.com
http://www.redhat.com

Contents

Introduction to the Macmillan Digital Publishing Edition

(**Editor's Note:** This manual is derived from the original Red Hat Linux 5.2 Official Installation Guide produced by Red Hat Software, Inc. This introduction has been added by Macmillan Digital Publishing to document features that are unique to our version of Red Hat Linux, or to stress issues of particular importance, particularly to first-time Linux users.)

Thanks for purchasing the *Complete Red Hat Linux 5.2 Operating System*! This award-winning operating system brings true multi-tasking and the power of a UNIX workstation to your Intel-processor PC.

Please Note: Linux is not an add-on to DOS. It is a complete operating system, so it's *very important* that you read this manual *before* installing the software. While Red Hat Linux is the easiest version of Linux to install, it is not like installing Windows or DOS on your machine. So if you've never installed Linux before, please take the time to read the installation-related chapters before starting to install Red Hat Linux.

Minimum System Requirements

Before you install Red Hat Linux, make sure your computer has the following minimum hardware and software requirements. Note that your experience using Red Hat Linux will be substantially more enjoyable if your system exceeds these minimum requirements, particularly in the areas of RAM and free hard drive space.

- IBM-compatible PC
- Intel-compatible '386, '486, Pentium, Pentium Pro, or Pentium II processor
- SCSI or IDE CD-ROM drive

- 8MB RAM (16MB or more highly recommended)
- 3.5 inch diskette drive (as drive A)
- 100MB hard drive space
- Internet connection required for Internet software

Please Note: Red Hat Linux supports the widest possible range of PC hardware, including sound cards, video cards (and monitors), laser (and dot-matrix) printers, Ethernet network cards, and other specialized peripherals. To ensure compatibility with your PC's hardware, check the hardware compatibility list at
`http://www.redhat.com/support/docs/hardware.html`.

New to Linux?

Please Note: If you are new to Linux and this is your first installation, you should read this section; otherwise, you can skip ahead to the "Electronic Resource Library" section on page xi.

Many new users who install Linux the first time wonder, "Where are the .EXE files?" You'll find that Linux does not use file extensions like DOS or Windows does. All programs reside in the various `bin` directories on your hard drive (`/bin`, `/usr/bin`, and `/usr/X11R6/bin` are but a few of these directories). These directories contain the binary executables that run when you enter their name as a command. For example, the `ls` command runs `/bin/ls`, while the `less` command runs `/usr/bin/less`, and so on.

Another important item that confuses new users – Linux is case sensitive. For example, if you see a program called `Lynx` and you want to run it, you must type it exactly the way it appears – `lynx`, `LYNX`, or other variations will not work.

With MS-DOS, directories are separated with the backward slash character: `\`. For example, the `System` subdirectory of the `Windows` directory would be `\Windows\System`. However, with Linux, you must use the forward slash character: `/`. For example, the `local` subdirectory of the `usr` directory would be `/usr/local`.

When you need to read a CD-ROM, you must first *mount* the CD-ROM. The `mount` command makes the CD-ROM available to the Linux system. With DOS, Windows, and Macintosh systems, CD-ROMs automatically mount when you insert them in the drive. This manual and the electronic books contain more information on mounting CD-ROM and hard drives. However, here's a quick overview:

You must first have a directory that will serve as your CD-ROM's *mount point*. You can create a directory with the `mkdir` command. For example:

```
mkdir /mnt/cdrom
```

Next, you would issue a `mount` command to mount the CD-ROM on the mount point:

```
mount /dev/cdrom /mnt/cdrom
```

Please Note: The device specification /dev/cdrom used above may not correspond to your system's CD-ROM drive. If you have a SCSI CD-ROM drive, you should use /dev/scd0. If you have an ATAPI (also known as IDE) CD-ROM drive, your device name will be /dev/hdX, where X is a single letter (normally in the range a through d). You can use the dmesg command to see the device name given to your CD-ROM drive when the Linux kernel booted.

After you mount the CD-ROM, you can view its contents by looking in the mount point
(/mnt/cdrom in our example). You'll need to use the umount command to unmount the CD-ROM in order to change discs (for example, umount /mnt/cdrom). Note that if you changed directory "into" the CD-ROM, the umount command will fail with a device is busy error. If this happens, simply change directory "out" of the CD-ROM (for instance, cd /).

Another hint that will save you time typing is to use the [Tab] key to automatically complete commands and filenames. For example, if the file you want to run is xloadimage, all you need to do is type the beginning of the filename, followed by [Tab]. If the system can unambiguously identify the filename, the complete filename will appear; otherwise, the system will beep at you, prompting you to enter more of the filename.

The X Window System

If you are new to Linux, your enjoyment of the operating system will be heightened by installing the X Window System. X is a graphical user interface that uses windows (not to be confused with Microsoft ® Windows®) that may be moved and resized on your screen. However, like Microsoft Windows, the X Window System allows you to operate in a graphical point-and-click environment. Red Hat Linux uses a version of X known as XFree86.

Please Note: While an X session looks similar to a Windows session, X does not act the same as Windows. For example:

- When typing in a text box, some X configurations will require you to first click on the window, while other configurations only require the pointer to be placed within the window.

- X, in general, does not support Drag and Drop operations, or associating file extensions with specific applications. Therefore, double-clicking on a spreadsheet file may not do what you'd expect.

Electronic Resource Library

A number of Sams Publishing books have been provided in electronic format on your Red Hat Linux CD-ROM. The books are in Adobe Acrobat format, and may be read with the included Acrobat reader described below.

Adobe Acrobat Reader

To view the Acrobat versions of the electronic books, you must install the Adobe Acrobat Reader, which is located on CD-ROM, in the file:

```
/ebooks/acroread_linux_30.tar.gz
```

After creating a temporary directory on your hard drive, use cd to change directory into that temporary directory, and issue the following command:

```
tar zxvf /ebooks/acroread_linux_30.tar.gz
```

Read the newly-created file INSTGUID.TXT, and follow the directions carefully to complete the installation. After you install the software, the reader will typically be named
/usr/local/Acrobat3/bin/acroread. While running the X Window System, type the complete filename (with path) to start the reader.

Using the Acrobat Reader

If you haven't used Adobe Acrobat before, here are a few tips to help you get started.

The Acrobat Reader allows you to easily navigate through documents, search for words in the document, and jump from the table of contents to the area of interest using hyperlinks. The Acrobat buttons on the tool bar are there to help you control the reader's basic operation (See Figure 1 on page xiii).

You'll notice that the buttons are divided into six groups. Let's take a look at these button groups, from left to right:

- The first three buttons control the Acrobat Reader's screen layout. Only one of these buttons may be depressed at a given time. They produce the following layouts:
  - **Page image only** – The screen will contain the page image of the Acrobat document being displayed.
  - **Browser and page image** – The screen will consist of two panes: On the left, a hierarchical browser, allowing you to quickly find the desired section of the Acrobat document being displayed. The right-hand pane contains the page image.
  - **Thumbnail and page image** – The screen will consist of two panes: On the left, thumbnail images of each page in the Acrobat document being displayed. The right-hand pane contains the current page.

Figure 1: Adobe Acrobat Reader

The next three buttons control how you can interact with the Acrobat Reader. Only one of these buttons may be depressed at a given time:

- **"Hand" scrolling** – When depressed, this button allows you to scroll (vertically and horizontally) using your mouse. Simply point at the part of the document you'd like to "grasp", press the primary mouse button, and drag. The document will scroll in the direction you drag.

- **Magnification control** – When depressed, this button allows you to set the magnification applied to the document. Simply point at the part of the document you'd like to magnify, and press the primary mouse button. The document will be magnified, with the point you selected at the center of the screen.

- **Text selection** – When depressed, this button allows you to select text for copying using the mouse. Simply point at the part of the document you'd like to select, and press the primary mouse button. Drag to the end of the text you'd like to copy, and release the primary mouse button. You may then paste the selected text into another window (Under X, this is most often done using the center mouse button on a three-button mouse, or by pressing both mouse buttons simultaneously on a two-button mouse).

The next group of buttons control navigation through the Acrobat document being displayed:

- **First page** – This button will take you directly to the first page of the Acrobat document being displayed.

- **Previous page** – This button will take you to the previous page of the document.

- **Next page** – This button will take you to the next page of the Acrobat document being displayed.
- **Last page** – This button will take you directly to the last page of the document.

The next group of buttons allow you to retrace your steps through the document:

- **Previous historical page** – This button will take you to the page that you had displayed last.
- **Next historical page** – This button will take you to the next page in your list of pages displayed. This button is only active if you've used the **Previous historical page** button at least once.

The next group of three buttons control how each page is to be displayed on your screen:

- **Actual size** – This button causes each page to be displayed at its actual size.
- **Fit page** – This button causes each page to be displayed at the largest size that can fit entirely within the Acrobat Reader's window.
- **Fit width** – This button causes each page to be displayed at the largest size that can fit within the width of the Acrobat Reader's window.

The last button (in a group of its own) allows you to search the document for the occurrence of any text you specify. A dialog box will appear allowing you to enter the search string, as well as to control case sensitivity, whole-word matching, and the like.

Additional help is available within the Acrobat Reader.

Introduction

Preface

Welcome! And thanks for your interest in Red Hat Linux. We have what we think is the best Linux distribution on the market today, and we work hard to keep it that way. Red Hat Linux 5.2 is the latest in a long line of software from Red Hat Software. We hope you like it, and that you enjoy using Red Hat Linux as much as we've enjoyed making it for you.

It's interesting to note that, while Linux is popular and well-known by a certain segment of the computer-using population, there are many people out there that are only now hearing about Linux. For this group of people, the following section should provide enough background to help you get acquainted with Linux and Red Hat Software.

What is Linux?

Back in August of 1991, a student from Finland began a post to the `comp.os.minix` newsgroup with the words:

```
Hello everybody out there using minix -
I'm doing a (free) operating system (just a hobby,
won't be big and professional like gnu) for
386(486) AT clones.
```

The student was Linus Torvalds, and the "hobby" he spoke of eventually became what we know today as Linux.

A full-featured POSIX-like operating system, Linux has been developed not just by Linus, but by hundreds of programmers around the world. The interesting thing about this is that this massive, world-wide development effort is largely uncoordinated. Sure, Linus calls the shots where the kernel is concerned, but Linux is more than just the kernel. There's no management infrastructure; a student in Russia gets a new motherboard, and writes a driver to support a neat feature the motherboard has. A system administrator in Maryland needs backup software, writes it, and gives it away to anyone that needs it. The right things just seem to happen at the right time.

Another interesting thing is that Linux can be obtained for absolutely no money. That's right, most of the software is available (at no charge) to anyone with the time and inclination to download it. But not everyone has that much time...

What is Red Hat Linux?

Enter a group of programmers based in North Carolina. Their goal was to make it easier for people to give Linux a try. Like many other such groups, their approach was to bundle all the necessary bits and pieces into a cohesive *distribution*, relieving "newbies" from some of the more esoteric aspects of bootstrapping a new operating system on their PCs.

However, unlike other distributions, this one was fundamentally different. The difference? Instead of being a snapshot of a hard disk that had a working copy of Linux on it, or a set of diskettes from which different parts of the operating system could be dumped, this distribution was based on *packages*.

Each package provided a different piece of software, fully tested, configured, and ready to run. Want to try a new editor? Download the package and install it. In seconds, you can give it a try. Don't like it? Issue a single command, and the package is removed.

If that was all there was to it, this distribution would be pretty nifty. But being package-based meant there was one additional advantage:

This Linux distribution could be easily upgraded.

Software development in the Linux world is fast-paced, so new versions of old software come out continually. With other distributions, upgrading software was painful – a complete upgrade usually meant deleting everything on your hard drive and starting over.

By now you've probably guessed that the group of programmers in North Carolina is Red Hat Software, and the package-based distribution is Red Hat Linux.

Since Red Hat Linux's introduction in the summer of 1994, Linux and Red Hat Software have grown by leaps and bounds. Much has changed; support for more esoteric hardware, huge increases in reliability, and the growing use of Linux by companies around the world.

But much still remains the same. Linux is still developed by people world-wide; Linus is still involved. Red Hat Software is still located in North Carolina; still trying to make Linux easier for people to use.

And Red Hat Linux is still package-based; always has been, always will be.

We make Red Hat Linux available by unrestricted FTP from our site and many mirror sites on the Internet. Red Hat Linux is also available on CD-ROM. For current information on our product offerings and links to other Linux resources please check Red Hat Software's web site at
http://www.redhat.com.

On most systems, Red Hat Linux is easy to install; the installation program can walk you through the process in as little as 15 minutes. The system itself is very flexible. With RPM, you can install and uninstall individual software packages with minimal effort. Because of RPM, Red Hat Linux is also easy to maintain – package installations can be verified and corrected, and packages can be installed and uninstalled simply and reliably. Furthermore, Red Hat Linux is easy to administer. Included are a rich set of administrative tools which reduce the hassle of everyday system administration. Complete source code is provided for the freely distributable components of the system.

An Overview of This Manual

This manual is organized to guide you through the process of installing Red Hat Linux quickly and easily. Toward that goal, let's take a quick look at each chapter to help you get acclimated:

Chapter 1, *New Features Of Red Hat Linux 5.2* contains information concerning new functionality that has been added to Red Hat Linux 5.2.

Chapter 2, *Before You Begin* contains information on tasks you should perform prior to starting the Red Hat Linux installation.

Chapter 3, *Starting the Installation* contains detailed instructions for starting the Red Hat Linux installation process.

Chapter 4, *Continuing the Installation* contains instructions on the main part of the installation process.

Chapter 5, *Finishing the Installation* contains instructions on the last steps required to complete the installation process.

Chapter 6, *What Do I Do Now?* contains information on logging in, performing system shutdowns, and configuring the more popular system components (such as X).

Chapters 7 – 11 explain how to find documentation on your system, and how to use the various system management and administration tools which accompany Red Hat Linux. They also include an explanation of what's special about your Red Hat Linux system, including where special files live and more.

Appendixes contain extra information about Red Hat Linux, including an explanation on Red Hat Software's support offerings, frequently asked questions, etc.

Quick Start Information

Those of you that have installed Red Hat Linux/Intel before and are in a hurry to get started need only boot from a boot diskette (or the Red Hat Linux/Intel CD-ROM, if your computer supports booting directly from CD-ROM). Next, select the desired installation method. If you are installing from an FTP site, a hard disk, or you'll be using a PCMCIA card during the installation, you'll be prompted to insert a supplemental diskette[1]. In either case, answer all questions as they are presented.

Upgrading from a Prior Version of Red Hat Linux

The installation process for Red Hat Linux 5.2 includes the ability to upgrade from prior versions of Red Hat Linux (2.0 through 5.0, inclusive) which are based on RPM technology. Upgrading your system installs the modular 2.0.x kernel as well as updated versions of the packages that are installed on your machine. The upgrade process preserves existing configuration files using a .rpmsave extension (e.g., sendmail.cf.rpmsave) and leaves a log telling what actions it took in /tmp/upgrade.log. As software evolves, configuration file formats can change, so you should carefully compare your original configuration files to the new files before integrating your changes.

A Word From the Developers

We would like to thank all our beta testers for entrusting their systems to early versions of Red Hat Linux and for taking the time to submit bug reports from the front, especially those of you who have been with Red Hat since the "Halloween" release and earlier. We would also like to thank Linus Torvalds and the hundreds of developers around the world for creating, truly, one of the wonders of distributed development.

And, again, we'd like to thank *you* for your interest in Red Hat Linux!

The Red Hat Development Team

Notes from the Editor

Our evolutionary process of expanding the scope of this Installation Guide continues. As before, we've updated the chapters related to the actual installation process. We've also updated the New Features chapter to reflect all the good stuff that's been added to Red Hat Linux 5.2. We consider this to be "business as usual".

We've also made some changes as a direct result of customer feedback. Some people have expressed confusion over all the different terms and acronyms that seem to surround computer technology in general, and Linux in particular. For those people, we've added a glossary. While it's not our goal to include a complete data

---

[1] If you need a supplemental diskette, you'll need to create one. Section 2.5 on page 16 describes how a supplemental diskette is created.

processing dictionary with every copy of Red Hat Linux, if you think a particular word should be present but is not, feel free to let us know via docs@redhat.com.

As the linuxconf system configuration tool continues to mature, we've created a new system configuration chapter containing task-based linuxconf documentation, as well as those vestiges of the control-panel tools that still remain. Our goal is to continue adding linuxconf documentation; what you see here is just a first step in that process.

We've also worked on the Frequently Asked Questions section of the Installation Guide, adding more of the "timeless" questions that seem to persist from release to release, while weeding out version-specific questions that, if you think about it, will always be somewhat dated, given the nature of printed documentation.

The package list has proven to be quite popular; this time we've improved it by adding icons showing whether a given package is part of one of several pre-defined sets of packages.

All of this has resulted in the Installation Guide putting on a little weight – 100 pages, to be exact. This is a trend that we expect to continue, which leads us right into the next subject. . .

We Need Feedback!

If you spot a typo in the Installation Guide, or if you've thought of a way to make this manual better, we'd love to hear from you! Please send mail to:

docs@redhat.com

Be sure to mention the manual's identifier:

Inst-5.2-Print-MDP (10/98)

That way we'll know exactly which version of the guide you have. If you have a suggestion, try to be as specific as possible when describing it. If you've found an error, please include the section number and some of the surrounding text so we can find it easily. We may not be able to respond to every message sent to us, but you can be sure that we'll be reading them all!

I Couldn't Have Done it Without. . .

Thanks go out to the past authors of this manual. A great deal of their work is still here. A great, big "Thank You" is also owed to the Red Hat Linux 5.2 development team for putting up with the many questions, comments, and pleading requests for reviews of this manual. Without them, I wouldn't be here writing this, you wouldn't be there reading this, and things wouldn't be nearly as much fun. Thanks, guys!

Thanks are also due to all the readers of past Installation Guides that took the time to send corrections, suggestions, and even the occasional "well done". I've tried to incorporate as much of your feedback as possible (pagecount and deadlines permitting). Keep the feedback coming – it's the only way I know whether you're getting what you need from our documentation!

Thanks to Paul Gerwe (one of our new writers) for his hard work documenting linuxconf. Thanks also go to Support Genius Stephen Smoogen for his work on the new FAQ. It's been a pleasure working with you both.

Last but far from least is the support group at Red Hat Software. They have given many insightful suggestions regarding this manual, based on extensive experience with thousands of Red Hat Linux customers. So if you find yourself breezing through the installation chapters, it's due in no small part to their input. I thank them.

Edward C. Bailey

1

New Features Of Red Hat Linux 5.2

This chapter describes features that are new to Red Hat Linux 5.2.

1.1 Installation-Related Enhancements

There have been many changes made to make the Red Hat Linux installation process easier. Here's a list:

- New installation classes
- Improved Installation Guide
- Support for multiple SCSI adapters
- Disk Druid supported on all platforms

Let's take a look at each one in a bit more detail.

1.1.1 New Installation Classes

The Red Hat Linux 5.2 installation program now includes pre-defined installation classes. Workstation and server modes automatically handle partitioning and basic defaults. The installation program's previous behavior has been retained as the custom class, and can be used for complete control over the installation process.

For more information on the installation classes, please refer to section 2.6 on page 17.

1.1.2   Improved Installation Guide

The Red Hat Linux Installation Guidehas been improved with:

- **Additional Linuxconf Documentation** – Chapter 8 contains more in-depth descriptions of using Linuxconf to configure your Red Hat Linux system.

- **Improved Installation Chapters** – The chapters covering the installation of Red Hat Linux have been expanded to include more detailed information in a more streamlined form.

- **Glossary** – Appendix E contains a glossary of words some people might find confusing.

- **All-New FAQ** – Appendix D contains a newly updated set of frequently asked questions. If you run into problems (before *or* after the installation), check it out...

1.1.3   Support for Multiple SCSI Adapters

The Red Hat Linux 5.2 installation program now supports systems with more than one SCSI adapter.

1.1.4   Disk Druid Supported on All Platforms

Disk Druid is now supported on the SPARC and Alpha versions of Red Hat Linux.

1.2   System Administration-Related Enhancemen*

Red Hat Linux 5.2 has these features for system administrators:

- Linux 2.2 ready — ?
- Traffic shaping support
- Enhanced sound support
- Enhanced printer support
- Updated PCMCIA support

1.2.1   Linux 2.2 Ready

Red Hat Linux 5.2 has been engineered to be ready for the latest stable kernel (version 2.2.x) when it is finally released. Red Hat Software will make 2.2-based kernel packages available as soon as the kernel has been released.

For those of you looking for more excitement in your lives, this also means that the 2.1 development kernels may also be easily installed.

1.2.2   Traffic Shaping Support

Red Hat Linux 5.2 also includes both kernel support and utilities for traffic shaping. This is great for Internet service providers that need more complete control over their bandwidth utilization. If you're interested in this feature, make sure you install the `shapecfg` package; you will then be able to run the traffic shaping configuration tool located in `/sbin/shapecfg`.

1.2.3   Enhanced Sound Support

The `sndconfig` sound configuration utility now recognizes more sound cards, as well as the standard sound hardware present in SPARC systems.

1.2.4   Enhanced Printer Support

The `printtool` printer configuration utility now supports the configuration of NetWare-based remote printers.

1.2.5   Updated PCMCIA Support

Red Hat Linux 5.2 has updated PCMCIA support. Some of the latest PCMCIA cards may now be used.

1.3   Miscellaneous New Features

These new features defy categorization:

- Window Maker window manager included
- Apache 1.3 included
- GIMP 1.0.1 included

1.3.1   Window Maker Included

The popular Window Maker window manager is now included with Red Hat
Linux 5.2. If you're interested in using Window Maker, run the script
`/usr/X11R6/bin/wmaker.inst` (you should just be able to type `wmaker.inst`).
When asked for the name of the script to be updated, simply press (Enter). The
script will create the necessary files in your login directory. Then, make sure the
new script file is executable by using this command:

```
chmod +x .xinitrc
```

Now, the next time you start X, you'll be running Window Maker.

1.3.2   Apache 1.3 Included

Version 1.3 of the popular Apache web server software is included with Red Hat
Linux 5.2.

1.3.3   GIMP 1.0.1 Included

Version 1.0.1 of the GNU Image Manipulation Program (GIMP to its friends) is
included with Red Hat Linux 5.2.

2

Before You Begin

While installing Red Hat Linux is a straightforward process, taking some time prior to starting the installation can make things go much more smoothly. In this chapter, we'll discuss the steps that should be performed before you start the installation.

Please Note: If you are currently running a version 2.0 (or greater) Red Hat Linux system, you can perform an upgrade. Skim this chapter to review the basic issues relating to installation, and read the following chapters in order, following the directions as you go. The upgrade procedure starts out identically to the installation procedure; you will be directed to choose an installation or upgrade after booting the installation program and answering a few questions.

There are five things you should do prior to installing Red Hat Linux:

1. Make sure you have sufficient documentation to effectively use your Red Hat Linux system after the installation.

2. Make sure you have access to the Red Hat Linux components required for installation.

3. Make sure you know your computer's hardware configuration and networking information.

4. Decide, based on the first two tasks, what method you will use to install Red Hat Linux.

5. Determine where on your hard drive(s) Red Hat Linux will reside.

Let's start by making sure you have the documentation you'll need after you install Red Hat Linux.

2.1   Getting Documentation

Red Hat Linux is a powerful, full-featured operating system. Unless you're a Linux wizard, you're going to need documentation to make the most of your Red Hat Linux system. Everyone should review Chapter 7 on page 99 for more information on available Linux documentation. While many people find the resources described in chapter 7 to be very helpful, people who are just starting to use Linux will likely need additional information. The information that will be most helpful to you depends on your level of Linux expertise:

New To Linux – If this is your first time using Linux (or any Linux-like operating system, for that matter), you'll need solid introductory information on basic Unix concepts. For example, O'Reilly and Associates (http://www.ora.com/) produce a wide variety of Linux and Unix-related books. Give their more general titles a try.

Some Linux Experience – If you've used other Linux distributions (or a Linux-like operating system), you'll probably find what you're looking for in some of the more in-depth reference material available. Red Hat Software's *Linux Undercover* and *Linux Complete Command Reference* are great for overall documentation, while O'Reilly's more specialized titles are valuable when you need a lot of information on a particular subject.

Old Timer – If you're a long-time Red Hat Linux user, you probably don't need us telling you what documentation to read. Thanks for reading this far!

We also discuss the issue of additional documentation in Chapter 6 on page 81.

2.2   Getting the Right Red Hat Linux Components

If you've purchased the Red Hat Linux boxed set, you're ready to go! However, mistakes occasionally happen, so now is a good time to double-check the contents of your boxed set. If you haven't purchased a Red Hat Linux boxed set, skip to Section 2.2.3 on page 8.

2.2.1   Contents of the Red Hat Linux Boxed Set

The Red Hat Linux boxed set contains the following items:

- The Red Hat Linux Installation Guide

- Red Hat Linux CDs 1 and 2.

- Boot diskette.

- License and Registration information.

Let's take a quick look at each item:

Installation Guide

The Red Hat Linux Installation Guideis what you're currently reading. It contains the information necessary to install Red Hat Linux. In addition, it contains information about aspects of the operating system that are unique to Red Hat Linux.

CDs 1 and 2

These two Compact Discs contain the entire Red Hat Linux distribution, including source code. CD 1 contains all the binary packages . CD 2 contains the source packages that were used to build the binary packages on CD 1.

Boot Diskette

This diskette is used to start the installation process for Red Hat Linux/Intel. Depending on your computer's configuration and the type of installation you select, you may or may not need the boot diskette. In addition, you may require a *supplemental* diskette, again depending on your system's hardware configuration, and the installation method you choose. When we discuss the different installation methods later in this chapter, we'll explain which diskettes are needed for each type of installation, and give you instructions for producing any diskettes you require.

License and Registration Information

The CD-ROM case includes the the license terms for Red Hat Linux, in addition to the license terms for any commercial software that may be included on the Red Hat Linux CD.

2.2.2 Missing Something?

If you've purchased the Official Red Hat Linux boxed set from Red Hat Software, (or one of its distributors) and you're missing one or more of the items listed above, please let us know!

One thing to keep in mind is that Red Hat Software partners with companies (international and domestic) so that we can make Red Hat Linux available to you in the most convenient form. Because of this, you might find that your Red Hat Linux boxed set may not have been actually produced by Red Hat Software.

Not sure how to identify our official boxed set? Here's how: The bottom of our box has an ISBN number next to one of the bar codes. That ISBN number should be in the form:

$$1\text{-}888172\text{-}xx\text{-}y$$

(Where xx and y may vary.) If your box has an ISBN number in this form, and you're missing something, feel free to call us at 1-888-733-4281 (+1-919-547-0012 outside the USA), or to send mail to sales@redhat.com.

If your box has a different ISBN number (or none at all), you'll need to contact the company that produced your boxed set. Normally, third-party producers will include their logo and/or contact information on the outside of the box; an official Red Hat Linux boxed set has only our name and contact info on the outside...

If your Red Hat Linux boxed set is complete, please skip ahead to section 2.2.4.

2.2.3   No Boxed Set? No Problem!

Of course, not everyone purchases a Red Hat Linux boxed set. It's entirely possible to install Red Hat Linux using a CD created by another company, or even via FTP. In these cases, you may need to create one or more diskettes to get started.

For people installing Red Hat Linux/Intel, you'll need a boot diskette, and optionally, a supplemental diskette. It may also be possible to start the installation directly from the CD, under certain conditions. We'll discuss this in more detail when we outline the various installation methods available.

2.2.4   Checking for Updated Diskette Images

From time to time, we find that the installation may fail, and that a revised diskette image is required in order for the installation to work properly. In these cases, we make special images available via the Red Hat Linux Errata.

Since this is a relatively rare occurrence, you will in general save time if you try to use the standard diskette images first, and then review the Errata only if you experience any problems completing the installation.

There are two ways to review the Errata:

1. **World Wide Web** – By pointing your web browser at http://www.redhat.com/errata, you can read the Errata on-line, and download diskette images easily.

2. **Electronic Mail** – By sending an empty mail message to errata@redhat.com, you will receive a mail message containing the complete Errata. Also included are URLs to each updated package and diskette image in the Errata. By using these URLs, you can then download any necessary diskette images. Remember to use binary mode when transferring a diskette image!

For now, concentrate only on the Errata entries that include new diskette images (the filenames always end in .img). If you find an entry that seems to apply to your problem, get a copy of the diskette images, and create them using the instructions in Appendix A on page 213.

2.3   Things You Should Know

In order to prevent any surprises during the installation, you should collect some information before attempting to install Red Hat Linux. You can find most of this information in the documentation that came with your system, or from the system's vendor or manufacturer.

Please Note: The most recent list of hardware supported by Red Hat Linux can be found at Red Hat Software's World Wide Web site at http://www.redhat.com/hardware. It's a good idea to check your hardware against this list before proceeding.

2.3.1   Basic Hardware Configuration

You should have a basic understanding of the hardware installed in your computer, including:

- **hard drive(s)** – Specifically, the number, size, and type. If you have more than one, it's helpful to know which one is first, second, and so on. It is also good to know if your drives are IDE or SCSI. If you have IDE drives, you should check your computer's BIOS to see if you are accessing them in *LBA* mode.

- **memory** – The amount of RAM installed in your computer.

- **CD-ROM** – Most importantly, the unit's interface type (IDE, SCSI, or other interface) and, for non-IDE, non-SCSI CD-ROMs, the make and model number. IDE CD-ROMs (also known as ATAPI) are the most common type in recently manufactured, PC-compatible computers.

- **SCSI adapter (if one is present)** – The adapter's make and model number.

- **network card (if one is present)** – The card's make and model number.

- **mouse** – The mouse's type (serial, PS/2, or bus mouse), protocol (Microsoft, Logitech, MouseMan, etc.), and number of buttons; also, for serial mice, the serial port it is connected to.

On many newer systems, the installation program is able to automatically identify most hardware. However, it's a good idea to collect this information anyway, just to be sure.

Learning About Your Hardware With Windows®

If your computer is already running Windows 9x, you can use the following procedure to get additional configuration information:

- With Windows running, click on the "My Computer" icon using the secondary (normally the right) mouse button. A popup menu should appear.

- Select "Properties". The "System Properties" window should appear (See Figure 2.1). Note the information listed under "Computer:" – in particular the amount of RAM listed.

Figure 2.1: Windows System Properties Window

- Click on the "Device Manager" tab. You will then see a graphical representation of your computer's hardware configuration. Make sure the "View devices by type" button is selected.

At this point, you can either double-click on the icons (or single-click on the plus sign ⊕) to look at each entry in more detail (See Figure 2.2 on the next page). Look under the following icons for more information:

Figure 2.2: Device Manager Under Windows 95

- **Disk drives** – You will find the type (IDE or SCSI) of hard drive here. (IDE drives will normally include the word "IDE", while SCSI drives won't.)

- **Hard disk controllers** – You can get more information about your hard drive controller here.

- **CDROM** – Here is where you'll find out about any CD-ROM drives connected to your computer.

  Please Note: In some cases, there may be no CD-ROM icon, yet your computer has a functioning CD-ROM drive. This is normal, depending on how Windows was originally installed. In this case, you may be able to glean additional information by looking at the CD-ROM driver loaded in your computer's `config.sys` file.

- **Mouse** – The type of mouse present on your computer can be found here.

- **Display adapters** – If you're interested in running the X Window System, you should write down the information you find here.

- **Sound, video and game controllers** – If your computer has sound capabilities, you'll find more information about that here.

- **Network adapters** – Here you'll find additional info on your computer's network card (if you have one).

- **SCSI controllers** – If your computer uses SCSI peripherals, you'll find additional info on the SCSI controller here.

While this method is not a complete substitute for opening your computer's case and physically examining each component, in many cases it can provide sufficient information to continue with the installation.

Please Note: This information can also be printed by clicking on the "Print..." button. A second window will appear, allowing you to choose the printer, as well as the type of report (The "All Devices and System Summary" report type is the most complete).

2.3.2   Video Configuration

If you will be installing the X Window System, you should also be familiar with the following:

- **your video card** – The card's make and model number (or the video chipset it uses), and the amount of video RAM it has. (Most PCI-based cards are auto-detected by the installation program.)
- **your monitor** – The unit's make and model number, along with allowable ranges for horizontal and vertical refresh rates.

2.3.3   Network-related Information

If you will be connected to a network, be sure you know your:

- **IP address** – Usually represented as a set of four numbers separated by dots, such as
  `10.0.2.15`.
- **netmask** – Another set of four numbers separated by dots. An example netmask would be `255.255.248.0`.
- **gateway IP address** – Yet another set of four dot-separated numbers. For instance,
  `10.0.2.254`.
- **one or more name server IP addresses** – One or more sets of dot-separated numbers. `10.0.2.1` might be the address of a name server.
- **domain name** – The name given to your organization. For instance, Red Hat Software has a domain name of `redhat.com`.
- **hostname** – The name of your computer. A computer might be named `pooh`, for instance.

Please Note: The information given above is an example only! Do *not* use it when you install Red Hat Linux! If you don't know the proper values for your network, ask your network administrator.

2.4   Installation Methods

You can install or upgrade Red Hat Linux via any of several different methods. Each method works best in different situations, and has different requirements. But before we discuss each installation method, let's take a look at an issue that may affect some of you.

2.4.1   PCMCIA Support During the Installation

This section is specific to Intel-based computers only

Most Intel-based laptop computers support PCMCIA (also known as PC Card). Computers that support PCMCIA devices contain a controller having one or more slots in which a PCMCIA device can be installed. These devices may be modems, LAN adapters, SCSI adapters, and so on.

When installing Red Hat Linux/Intel on a PCMCIA-capable computer, it is important to note if a PCMCIA device will be used during installation. For example, if you want to install Red Hat Linux/Intel from a CD-ROM, and your CD-ROM drive is connected to a PCMCIA adapter, the installation program will require PCMCIA support. Likewise, if you are going to use one of the network-based installation methods, you will need PCMCIA support if your network adapter is PCMCIA-based.

Please Note: You don't need install-time PCMCIA support if you're installing Red Hat Linux on a laptop, and using the laptop's built-in CD-ROM drive.

PCMCIA support is dependent on two things:

1. The type of PCMCIA controller in your computer system.

2. The type of PCMCIA device that you wish to use during the installation.

While nearly every PCMCIA controller and most popular PCMCIA devices are supported, there are some exceptions. For more information, please consult the Red Hat Linux Hardware Compatibility List at http://www.redhat.com/hardware.

The main thing to keep in mind is that if you require install-time PCMCIA support, you will need a supplemental diskette. We'll show you how to do this after you've determined which installation method is best for you.

2.4.2   Installing From a CD-ROM

If you have a Red Hat Linux CD-ROM, and your computer has a supported CD-ROM drive, you should consider this installation method. Installing directly from CD-ROM is the most straightforward approach. When installing from CD-ROM, the packages you select are read from the CD-ROM, and are installed on your hard drive.

How To Do It

As the name implies, you'll need a Red Hat Linux CD-ROM, a supported CD-ROM drive, and a means of starting the installation program.

Intel systems will need to use the boot diskette (and the supplemental diskette if PCMCIA support is required). There is an alternate method of installing from CD-ROM that uses no diskettes, but requires that the system be running DOS. We'll discuss this approach (known as *autoboot*) in Section 3.2.1 on page 32. For now, note that PCMCIA support is not available when using *autoboot*.

Please Note: The Red Hat Linux/Intel CD-ROM can also be booted by newer computers that support bootable CD-ROMs. Not all computers support this feature, so if yours can't boot from CD-ROM, you'll have to use a boot diskette (or autoboot from DOS) to get things started. Note that you may need to change BIOS settings in your computer to enable this feature.

If you've determined that this installation method is most applicable to your situation, please skip ahead to Section 2.5 on page 16.

2.4.3   Installing From an FTP Site

If you don't have a Red Hat Linux CD-ROM or a CD-ROM drive, but you do have network access, then an FTP installation may be for you. When installing via FTP, the Red Hat Linux packages you select are downloaded (using FTP) across the network to your computer, and are installed on your hard drive.

How To Do It

When doing an FTP install, you'll need LAN-based access to a network; a dialup connection via modem won't cut it. If your Local Area Network has Internet access, you can use one of the many FTP sites that mirror Red Hat Linux. You can find a list of mirror sites at
`ftp://ftp.redhat.com/pub/MIRRORS`.

If your LAN doesn't have Internet access, all is not lost. If there is a computer on your LAN that can accept anonymous FTP requests, simply put a copy of the Red Hat Linux distribution on that system, and you're ready to go.

Please Note: Your FTP server must be able to handle long filenames.

For an FTP installation, you must use both the boot and supplemental diskettes. You will need to have a valid nameserver configured or you must specify the IP address of the FTP server you will be using. You will also need the path to the Red Hat Linux directory on the FTP server.

If you've determined that this installation method is most applicable to your situation, please skip ahead to Section 2.5 on page 16.

2.4.4   Installing From an NFS Server

If your system doesn't have a CD-ROM drive, but you do have network access, then an NFS installation may be for you. When installing via NFS, the Red Hat Linux packages you select are NFS-served to your computer from an NFS server system. The packages are then installed on your hard drive.

How To Do It

If you wish to perform an NFS installation, you will need to mount the Red Hat Linux CD-ROM on a machine that supports ISO-9660 file systems with Rock Ridge extensions. The machine must also support NFS. Export the CD-ROM file system via NFS. You will need to have a nameserver configured, or know the NFS server's IP address, as well as the path to the exported CD-ROM.

Please Note: Your NFS server must be able to handle long filenames.

For an NFS installation, you'll need a boot diskette only.

If you've determined that this installation method is most applicable to your situation, please skip ahead to Section 2.5 on the next page.

2.4.5   Installing From an SMB Shared Volume

If your system doesn't have a CD-ROM drive, but you do have network access, then installing Red Hat Linux using an SMB shared volume may be for you. When performing an SMB installation, your computer accesses the Red Hat Linux packages using a DOS-style network drive. The packages you select are then installed on your hard drive.

How To Do It

If you wish to install from an SMB shared volume, you will need to mount the Red Hat Linux CD-ROM on a Microsoft Windows NT or Windows 95 server that supports shared volumes. You will need to have nameservices configured; you will also need the name of the shared volume containing the Red Hat Linux CD-ROM and the account and password information required to access the volume.

Please Note: The Windows system's Microsoft Networking name must be identical to the system's DNS hostname. For example, given a Microsoft Networking name of windows1, the system's DNS hostname must be windows1.whatever.your.domain.is.

For an SMB installation, you'll need boot and supplemental diskettes.

If you've determined that this installation method is most applicable to your situation, please skip ahead to Section 2.5 on the following page.

2.4.6   Installing From a Hard Drive

If none of the other installation methods will work for you, but you have some means of getting the Red Hat Linux package files written to your system's hard drive, you can install from your hard drive. In this installation method, the Red Hat Linux packages you select are read from one partition on a hard drive, and are installed on another partition (or set of partitions).

How To Do It

The hard drive installation method requires a bit of up-front effort on your part, as you must copy all the necessary files to a partition before starting the Red Hat Linux installation program. You must first create a RedHat directory at the top level of your directory tree. Everything you will install should be placed in that directory. First copy the base subdirectory and its contents.

Next, copy the packages you want to install to another subdirectory called RPMS. You can use available space on an existing DOS partition or a Linux partition that is not required in the install procedure (for example, a partition that would be used for data storage on the installed system).

If you are using a DOS filesystem, you will not be able to use the full Linux file-names for the RPM packages. The installation process does not care what the file-names look like, but it is a good idea that you keep track of them.

You'll need a boot and supplemental diskette when installing from a hard drive.

2.5   Need a Supplemental Diskette?

This section is specific to Intel-based computers only. If you are using an Alpha or SPARC computer, please skip ahead to 2.7 on page 19.

Here's a checklist that you can use to see if you'll need to create a supplemental diskette:

- **Installing From a PCMCIA-Connected CD-ROM** – If you'll be installing Red Hat Linux from a CD-ROM, and your CD-ROM drive is attached to your computer through a PCMCIA card, you'll need a supplemental diskette.

- **Installing using a PCMCIA Network Card** – If you will be using a PCM-CIA network adapter during the installation, you'll need a supplemental diskette.

- **FTP Install** – If you want to install Red Hat Linux via FTP, you'll need a supplemental diskette.

- **Hard Drive Install** – If you'll be performing an install from a hard drive, you'll need a supplemental diskette.

- **SMB Install** – If you want to install from an SMB shared drive, you'll need a supplemental diskette.

If you've determined you'll need a supplemental diskette, you'll have to make one. The supplemental diskette image file is supp.img, and is located in the images directory on your Red Hat Linux/Intel CD. Please turn to Appendix A on page 213 and follow the instructions there. Then, return here, and read on.

2.6 Installation Classes

Red Hat Linux includes defines three different classes, or types of installations. They are:

- **Workstation**
- **Server**
- **Custom**

These classes give you the option of simplifying the installation process (with some loss of configuration flexibility), or retaining complete flexibility with a slightly more complex installation process. Let's take a look at each class in more detail, so you can see which one is right for you.

2.6.1 The Workstation-Class Installation

A workstation-class installation is most appropriate for you if you're new to the world of Linux, and would like to give it a try. By answering very few installation questions, you can be up and running Red Hat Linux in no time!

What Does It Do?

A workstation-class installation removes any linux-related partitions (and uses all free unpartitioned disk space) to create the following partitions:

- A 32MB swap partition.
- A 16MB partition (mounted as /boot) in which the Linux kernel and related files reside.
- A larger (the exact size is dependent on available disk space) partition (mounted as /) in which all other files are stored.

This approach to disk partitioning results in the simplest, filesystem configuration possible.

Please Note: You will need approximately 600MB of free disk space in order to perform a workstation-class installation.

If your system already runs Windows, a workstation-class installation will automatically configure your system to dual-boot using LILO.

2.6.2   The Server-Class Installation

A server-class installation is most appropriate for you if you'd like your system to function as a Linux-based server, and you don't want to heavily customize your system configuration.

What Does It Do?

A server-class installation removes *all* existing partitions on your system, so choose this installation class only if you're sure you have nothing you want saved! When the installation is complete, you'll find the following partitions:

- A 64MB swap partition.

- A 16MB partition (mounted as /boot) in which the Linux kernel and related files are kept.

- A larger (the exact size is dependent on available disk space) partition (mounted as /) in which all other files are stored.

- A 256MB partition (mounted as /).

- A partition of at least 512MB (mounted as /usr).

- A partition of at least 512MB (mounted as /home).

- A 256MB partition (mounted as /var).

This approach to disk partitioning results in a reasonably flexible filesystem configuration for most server-class tasks.

Please Note: You will need approximately 1.6GB of free disk space in order to perform a server-class installation.

2.6.3   The Custom-Class Installation

As you might guess from the name, a custom-class installation puts the emphasis on flexibility. During a custom-class installation, it is up to *you* how disk space should be partitioned. You have complete control over the packages that will be installed on your system. You can also determine whether or not you'll use LILO to boot your system.

For those of you with prior Red Hat Linux installation experience, you've already done a custom-class installation – it is the same installation procedure we've used past versions of Red Hat Linux.

2.7   Disk Partitions

Please Note: If you intend to perform a workstation- or server-class installation, and you already have sufficient *unpartitioned* disk space available, you don't need to read this section, and may turn to Section 2.8 on page 25. Otherwise, please read this section in order to determine the best approach to freeing disk space for your Red Hat Linux installation.

In order to install Red Hat Linux, you must make disk space available for it. This disk space needs to be separate from the disk space used by other operating systems you may have installed on your computer, such as Windows, OS/2, or even a different version of Linux.

A disk can be divided into different *partitions*. Each partition can be accessed as if it was a separate disk. Furthermore, each partition has a *type* that is used to indicate how information is stored in the partition. For example, there are different partition types used by DOS, OS/2, and Linux.

Please Note: You must install Red Hat Linux to one or more partitions having a partition type of "Linux native". Red Hat Linux also requires a *swap* partition, which has a partition type of "Linux swap". This means that an installation of Red Hat Linux requires at least two partitions:

- One or more partitions of type "Linux native"

- A partition of type "Linux swap"

We will discuss partitioning issues in more detail below. For now, keep in mind that Red Hat Linux requires at least two dedicated partitions, and that you *cannot* install Red Hat Linux to a DOS/Windows partition!

Even if you will be installing Red Hat Linux on its own hard disk, or on a computer which contains no other operating system, you'll still need to create partitions for Red Hat Linux to use. In this case it's pretty easy, as there are no other partitions on the hard disk to worry about.

On the other hand, you may wish to install Red Hat Linux on a disk which already contains software or data from a different operating system. Things can get a little trickier in this situation, since a mistake can destroy your existing partitions, not to mention the data they contain!

During the installation process, you'll be given the chance to create partitions for Red Hat Linux. At this point, your main concern is making sure you have sufficient disk space available to create those partitions. Let's review the different ways to free up space for Red Hat Linux partitions.

2.7.1   Partition Naming Scheme

Linux refers to disk partitions using a combination of letters and numbers which may be confusing, particularly if you're used to the "C drive" way of referring to hard disks and their partitions. Red Hat Linux uses a naming scheme that is more flexible and conveys more information than the approach used by other operating systems. Here is a summary:

First Two Letters – The first two letters of the partition name indicate the type of device on which the partition resides. You'll normally see either hd (for IDE disks), or sd (for SCSI disks).

The Next Letter – This letter indicates which device the partition is on. For example,
/dev/hda (the first IDE hard disk) or /dev/sdb (the second SCSI disk).

The number The final number denotes the partition. The first four (primary or extended) partitions are numbered 1 through 4. Logical partitions start at 5. E.g., /dev/hda3 is the third primary or extended partition on the first IDE hard disk; /dev/sdb6 is the second logical partition on the second SCSI hard disk.

Keep this information in mind; it will make things easier to understand when you're setting up the partitions Red Hat Linux requires.

2.7.2   Repartitioning Strategies

There are three possible scenarios you may face when attempting to repartition your hard disk:

- Unpartitioned free space is available.

- An unused partition is available.

- Free space in an actively used partition is available.

Let's look at each scenario in order.

Using Unpartitioned Free Space

In this situation, the partitions already defined do not span the entire hard disk, leaving unallocated space that is not part of any defined partition. If you think about it, an unused hard disk also falls into this category; the only difference is that *all* the space is not part of any defined partition.

In this case, you can simply create the necessary partitions from the unused space.

Using Space From An Unused Partition

Last year you replaced that tiny 105MB hard drive on your Windows system with a 1.2GB monster. You partitioned it into two equal parts, figuring that you'd use the C: "drive" (really the drive's first partition) for Windows, and the D: "drive" (really the drive's second partition) for your collection of freeware programs downloaded from the Internet. Well, you'd been so used to using C: that you never put anything of substance on D:.

If you find yourself in this situation, you can use the space allocated to the unused partition. In this case, you'll first need to delete the partition, and then create the appropriate Linux partitions in its place. You can either delete the partition using DOS fdisk, or you'll be given the opportunity to do so during a custom-class installation.

Using Free Space From An Active Partition

This is the most common situation. It is also, unfortunately, the hardest to deal with. The main problem is that you have enough free space, but it's presently allocated to a partition that is in use. If you purchased a computer with pre-installed software, the hard disk most likely has one massive partition holding the operating system and data.

Aside from adding a new hard drive to your system, you have two choices:

Destructive Repartitioning – Basically, you delete the single large partition, and create several smaller ones. As you might imagine, any data you had in that partition is destroyed. This means that making a complete backup is necessary. For your own sake, make two backups, use verification (if available in your backup software), and try to read data from your backup *before* you delete the partition. Note also that if there was an operating system of some type installed on that partition, it will need to be reinstalled as well.

After creating a smaller partition for your existing software, you can reinstall any software, restore your data, and continue with your Red Hat Linux installation.

Non-Destructive Repartitioning – Here, you run a program that does the seemingly impossible; it makes a big partition smaller without losing any of the files stored in that partition. Many people have found this method to be reliable and trouble-free. What software should you use to perform this feat? There are several disk management software products on the market; you'll have to do some research to find the one that is best for your situation.

As a convenience to our customers, we provide the fips utility. This is a freely available program that can resize FAT (File Allocation Table) partitions. It's included on the Red Hat Linux/Intel CD-ROM in the `dosutils` directory.

Please Note: Many people have successfully used `fips` to repartition their hard drives. However, because of the nature of the operations carried out by `fips`, and the wide variety of hardware and software configurations under which it must run, Red Hat Software cannot guarantee that `fips` will work properly on your system. Therefore, no installation support whatsoever is available for `fips`; use it at your own risk.

That said, if you decide to repartition your hard drive with `fips`, it is *vital* that you do two things:

- **Perform a Backup** – Make two copies of all the important data on your computer. These copies should be to removable media (such as tape or diskettes), and you should make sure they are readable before proceeding.
- **Read the Documentation** – Completely read the `fips` documentation, located in the `/dosutils/fipsdocs` subdirectory on Red Hat Linux/Intel CD 1.

Should use decide to use `fips`, be aware that after fips runs you will be left with *two* partitions: the one you resized, and the one `fips` created out of the newly-freed space. If your goal is to use that space to install Red Hat Linux, you should delete the newly-created partition, either by using fdisk under your current operating system, or while setting up partitions during a custom-class installation.

2.7.3   Disk Partitions and Other Operating Systems

If your Red Hat Linux partitions will be sharing a hard disk with partitions used by other operating systems, most of the time you'll have no problems. However, there are certain combinations of Linux and other operating systems that require extra care. Information on creating disk partitions compatible with other operating systems is available in several HOWTOs and Mini-HOWTOs, available on the Red Hat Linux CD in the `doc/HOWTO` and `doc/HOWTO/mini` directories. In particular, the Mini-HOWTOs whose names start with `Linux+` are quite helpful.

If Red Hat Linux/Intel will coexist on your machine with OS/2, you must create your disk partitions with the OS/2 partitioning software—otherwise, OS/2 may not recognize the disk partitions. During the installation, do not create any new partitions, but do set the proper partition types for your Linux partitions using the Linux `fdisk`.

2.7.4   One Last Wrinkle: Using LILO

LILO (the LInux LOader) is the most commonly used method to boot Red Hat Linux on Intel-based systems. Being an operating system loader, LILO operates "outside" of any operating system, using only the Basic I/O System (or BIOS) built into the computer hardware itself. This section describes LILO's interactions with PC BIOSes, and is specific to Intel-compatible computers.

BIOS-Related Limitations Impacting LILO

LILO is subject to some limitations imposed by the BIOS in most Intel-based computers. Specifically, most BIOSes can't access more than two hard drives and they can't access any data stored beyond cylinder 1023 (the 1024th cylinder) of any drive. Note that some recent BIOSes do not have these limitations, but this is by no means universal.

All the data LILO needs to access at boot time (including the Linux kernel) are located in the /boot directory, which is normally part of the root partition (known as /). Here are the guidelines you must follow if you are going to use LILO to boot your Red Hat Linux system:

On First Two IDE Drives – If you have 2 IDE (or EIDE) drives, /boot must be located on one of them. Note that this two-drive limit also includes any IDE CD-ROM drives on your primary IDE controller. So, if you have one IDE hard drive, and one IDE CD-ROM on your primary controller, /boot must be located on the first hard drive *only*, even if you have other hard drives on your secondary IDE controller.

On First IDE Or First SCSI Drive – If you have one IDE (or EIDE) drive and one or more SCSI drives, /boot must be located either on the IDE drive or the SCSI drive at ID 0. No other SCSI IDs will work.

On First Two SCSI Drives – If you have only SCSI hard drives, /boot must be located on a drive at ID 0 or ID 1. No other SCSI IDs will work.

Partition *Completely* Below Cylinder 1023 – No matter which of the above configurations apply, the partition that holds /boot must be located entirely below cylinder 1023. If the partition holding /boot straddles cylinder 1023, you may face a situation where LILO will work initially (because all the necessary information is below cylinder 1023), but will fail if a new kernel is to be loaded, and that kernel resides above cylinder 1023.

As mentioned earlier, it is possible that some of the newer BIOSes may permit LILO to work with configurations that don't meet our guidelines. Likewise, some of LILO's more esoteric features may be used to get a Linux system started, even if the configuration doesn't meet our guidelines. However, due to the number of variables involved, Red Hat Software cannot support such extraordinary efforts.

Please Note: Disk Druid as well as the workstation- and server-class installs take these BIOS-related limitations into account. However, if you decide to use fdisk instead, it is your responsibility to ensure that you keep these limitations in mind.

2.7.5   How Many Partitions?

Although you can install Red Hat Linux in a single large partition (subject to any of the partitioning considerations we've mentioned so far), it's a much better idea to split things up a bit. We recommend the following layout as a compromise between single-partition simplicity, and multi-partition flexibility:

Please Note: If you plan to install all the software packages that come with Red Hat Linux, you will need to use the larger partitions sizes shown here. In fact, you may want to increase the sizes above our recommendations, to allow for future growth without needing to repartition.

A swap partition – Swap partitions are used to support virtual memory. If your computer has 16 MB of RAM or less, you *must* create a swap partition. Even if you have more memory, a swap partition is still recommended. The minimum size of your swap partition should be equal to your computer's RAM, or 16 MB (whichever is larger). The largest useable swap partition is roughly 127 MB, so making a swap partition larger than that will result in wasted space. Note, however, that you can create and use more than one swap partition (although this is usually only necessary for large server installations).

A root partition – The root partition is where / (the root directory) resides. It only needs to contain things necessary to boot your system, as well as system configuration files. A root partition of 50 MB to 100 MB works well for most systems.

Don't forget the LILO constraints we mentioned in Section 2.7.4 on page 22!

A /usr partition – The /usr partition is where much of the software on a Red Hat Linux system resides. This partition should be between 300 MB and 700 MB, depending on how many packages you plan to install. If at all possible, try to be generous with the /usr partition. Any RPM-based packages you install later will (in general) use more space from /usr than from any other partition.

A /home partition – This is where users' home directories go; the size of /home depends on how many users you plan to have on your Red Hat Linux system and what they might store in their home directories.

Additionally, your circumstances may warrant creating one of more of the following partitions:

A /usr/local partition – Traditionally, /usr/local has been used to hold things you wish to keep separate from the rest of your Red Hat Linux system, such as software that is not available as an RPM package. The size depends on the amount of such software you anticipate putting on your system.

A /usr/src partition – There are two things that normally are stored in /usr/src on a Red Hat Linux system:

Linux Kernel Sources – The complete sources for the Linux kernel are stored here, and new kernels are built here. At present, the kernel sources are approximately 30MB in size. Keep in mind that you'll want to have additional free space for building kernels, and you may want to keep more than one version of the kernel available.

Sources For RPM-Based Packages – If a source package file (aka SRPM) is installed, the files are stored here. Note that, unless specified otherwise, any packages built will also use a build directory located here.

Again, the size of this partition would depend on the amount of software you anticipate building.

A /tmp **partition** – As the name implies, the /tmp partition is for temporary files. Creating a partition dedicated to /tmp is a good idea for larger, multiuser systems or network server machines. The reason is that many active users can fill the root partition (/), which is where /tmp is located. It's not necessary to dedicate a partition to /tmp on single-user workstations.

A /var **partition** – Your Red Hat Linux system will write to log files in /var/log. Files queued for printing will normally be written to /var/spool. These are just two examples of data that is written to /var. Unless otherwise configured, /var will be part of the root filesystem, and normally will not have much available free space. If you anticipate a lot of print, mail, or log activity on your system, you might want to consider creating a partition dedicated to /var. In general, only multiuser or server systems would make effective use of a separate /var filesystem.

An /opt **partition** – Some third-party software is designed to install itself under /opt. Unless an /opt partition is created, software that attempts to install itself under /opt will end up on the root partition, which may not have sufficient free space. Of course, this is not the only way of solving the /opt problem; it is also possible to create an /opt symbolic link to another partition with more space (such as /usr).

A /boot **partition** – While many of the partitions mentioned here make sense only for very large, active systems, this partition might be very useful on a small system, where free space is tight. If you recall, back in Section 2.7.4 on page 22, we discussed the various limitatons imposed by the standard PC BIOS, and how these limitations impact the LILO bootloader. All the files LILO needs to access (at boot time) are in the /boot directory. Since the files (including the Linux kernel) in /boot only take up a megabyte or so, if you're having trouble finding space for a 100 MB root partition in a place where LILO can get at it, you might have better luck trying to squeeze in a 5-10 MB (generously oversized) partition for /boot. You'll still need to create a root partition, but it can now be located anywhere on your system – the BIOS restrictions only apply to the partition holding /boot.

2.8   A Note About Kernel Drivers

During installation of Red Hat Linux, there are some limits placed on the filesystems and other drivers supported by the kernel. However, after installation there is support for all file systems available under Linux. At install time the modularized kernel has support for (E)IDE devices, (including ATAPI CD-ROM drives), SCSI adapters, and network cards. Additionally, all mice, SLIP, CSLIP, PPP, PLIP, FPU emulation, console selection, ELF, SysV IPC, IP forwarding, firewalling and accounting, reverse ARP, QIC tape and parallel printers, are supported.

Please Note: Because Red Hat Linux supports installation on many different types of hardware, many drivers (including those for SCSI adapters, network cards, and many CD-ROMs) are not built into the Linux kernel used during installation; rather, they are available as *modules* and loaded as you need them during the installation process. If necessary, you will have the chance to specify options for these modules at the time they are loaded, and in fact these drivers will ignore any options you specify for them at the boot: prompt.

After the installation is complete you may want to rebuild a kernel that includes support for your specific hardware configuration. See Section 11.6 on page 193 for information on building a customized kernel. Note that, in most cases, a custombuilt kernel is not necessary.

2.9   If You Have Problems. . .

If you have problems before, during, or after the installation, check the list of Red Hat Linux Frequently Asked Questions in Appendix D on page 297. In many cases, a quick check of the FAQ can quickly get you back in action.

2.10   One Last Note

Please read all of the installation instructions *before* starting; this will prepare you for any decisions you need to make and should eliminate potential surprises.

3

Starting the Installation

This chapter explains how to start the Red Hat Linux installation process. We'll cover the following areas in this chapter:

- Getting familiar with the installation program's user interface.

- Starting the installation program.

- Selecting an installation method.

By the end of this chapter, the installation program will be running on your system, and the appropriate installation method will have been selected.

3.1   The Installation Program User Interface

The Red Hat Linux installation program uses a screen-based interface that includes most of the on-screen "widgets" commonly found on graphical user interfaces. They may look a little different than their more graphical counterparts; Figures 3.1 on page 29 and 3.2 on page 30 are included here to make them easier to identify. Here's a list of the most important widgets:

- **Window** – Windows (also referred to as *dialog boxes* in this manual) will appear on your screen throughout the installation process. At times, one window may overlay another; in these cases, you may only interact with the window on top. When finished with that window, it will disappear, allowing you to continue with the window that was underneath.

- **Text Input** – Text input lines are regions where you can enter information required by the installation program. When the cursor rests on a text input line, you may enter and/or edit information on that line.

- **Check Box** – Check boxes allow you to select or deselect a particular feature offered to you by the installation program. When the cursor rests within a check box, pressing Space causes the check box to toggle between a selected and unselected state.

- **Text Widget** – Text widgets are regions of the screen that are devoted to the display of text. At times, text widgets may also contain other widgets, such as check boxes. It is possible that a text widget may contain more information than could be displayed at one time. In these cases, the text widget will have a scroll bar next to it; if you position the cursor within the text widget, you can then use the ↑ and ↓ keys to scroll through all the information available.

- **Scroll Bar** – Scroll bars provide a visual indication of your relative position in the information being displayed in a text widget. Your current position is shown by a # character, which will move up and down the scroll bar as you scroll back and forth.

- **Button Widget** – Button widgets are the primary method of interacting with the installation program. By "pressing" these buttons, you will progress through the series of windows that make up the installation process. Buttons may be pressed when they are highlighted by the cursor.

- **Cursor** – Although not a widget, the cursor is used to select (and interact) with a particular widget. As the cursor is moved from widget to widget, it may cause the widget to change color, or you may only see the cursor itself positioned in or next to the widget. In Figure 3.1 on the facing page, the cursor is positioned on the **Ok** button. Figure 3.2 on page 30 shows the cursor on the first line of the text widget at the stop of the window.

As you might have guessed by our description of these widgets, the installation program is character-based, and does not use a mouse. This is due to the fact that the installation program must run on a wide variety of computers, some of which may not even have a mouse. The following section describes the keystrokes necessary to interact with the installation program.

3.1.1   Using the Keyboard to Navigate

You can navigate around the installation dialogs using a simple set of keystrokes. You will need to move the cursor around by using various keys such as ←, →, ↑, and ↓. You can also use Tab, and Alt-Tab to cycle forward or backward through each widget on the screen. In most cases, there is a summary of available function keys presented at the bottom of each screen.

Figure 3.1: Installation Program Widgets

To "press" a button, position the cursor over the button (using [Tab], for instance) and press [Space] (or [Enter]). To select an item from a list of items, move the cursor to the item you wish to select and press [Enter]. To select an item with a *check box*, move the cursor to the check box and press [Space] to select an item. To deselect, press [Space] a second time.

Pressing [F12] accepts the current values and proceeds to the next dialog; it is usually equivalent to pressing the **OK** button.

Please Note: Unless a dialog box is waiting for your input, do not press any keys during the installation process – it may result in unpredictable behavior.

3.1.2 A Note About Virtual Consoles

There is more to the Red Hat Linux installation program than the dialog boxes it presents as it guides you through the installation process. In fact, the installation program makes several different kinds of diagnostic messages available to you, in addition to giving you a way to enter commands from a shell prompt. It presents this information on five *virtual consoles* which you can switch between using a single keystroke. These virtual consoles can be very helpful if you encounter

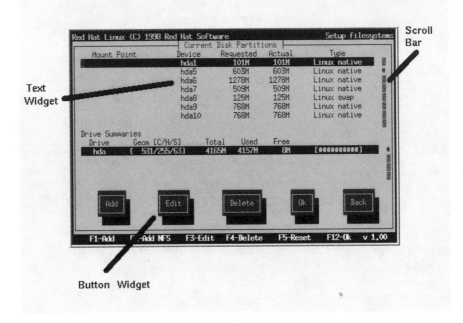

Figure 3.2: More Installation Program Widgets

a problem while installing Red Hat Linux. Messages displayed on the install or
system consoles can help pinpoint the problem. Please see Figure 3.3 for a listing
of the virtual consoles, the keystrokes to switch to them, and their contents.

Console	Keystroke	Contents
1	Alt-F1	installation dialog
2	Alt-F2	shell prompt
3	Alt-F3	install log (messages from install program)
4	Alt-F4	system log (messages from kernel, etc.)
5	Alt-F5	other messages

Figure 3.3: Virtual Console Information

In general, there should be no reason to leave virtual console #1 unless you are
attempting to diagnose installation problems. But if you are the curious type, feel
free to look around.

3.2   Starting the Installation Program

Now it's time to start installing Red Hat Linux. To start the installation, it is first necessary to boot the installation program. Before we start, please make sure you have all the resources you'll need for the installation. If you've already read through Chapter 2 on page 5, and followed the instructions, you should be ready.

3.2.1   Booting the Installation Program

To start installing Red Hat Linux, insert your boot diskette into your computer's first diskette drive and reboot (or boot from the Red Hat Linux CD-ROM, if your computer supports it). After a short delay, a screen containing the boot: prompt should appear. The screen contains information on a variety of boot options. Each boot option also has one or more help screens associated with it. To access a given help screen, press the appropriate function key as listed in the line at the bottom of the screen. You should keep two things in mind:

- The initial screen will automatically start the installation program if you take no action within the first minute. To disable this feature, press one of the help screen function keys.

- If you press a help screen function key, there will be a slight delay as the help screen is read from diskette.

Normally, you'll only need to press (Enter) to boot. Watch the boot messages to see whether the Linux kernel detects your hardware. If it does not properly detect your hardware, you may need to restart the installation in "expert" mode. Expert mode disables most hardware probing, and gives you the option of entering options for the drivers loaded during the installation. Expert mode can be entered using the following boot command:

```
boot: expert
```

Please Note: The initial boot messages will not contain any references to SCSI or network cards. These devices are supported by modules that are loaded during the installation process.

Options can also be passed to the kernel. For example, to instruct the kernel to use all the RAM in a 128 MB system, enter:

```
boot: linux mem=128M
```

After entering any options, press (Enter) to boot using those options. If you do need to specify boot options to identify your hardware, please make note of them – they will be needed later.

Installing Without Using a Boot Diskette The Red Hat Linux/Intel CD-ROM can also be booted by newer computers that support bootable CD-ROMs. Not all computers support this feature, so if yours can't boot from CD-ROM, there is one other way to start the installation without using a boot diskette. The following method is specific to Intel-based computers only.

If you have MS-DOS installed on your computer, you can boot the installation system directly from the CD without using any diskettes.

To do this, use the following commands (assuming your CD is drive d:):

```
C:\> d:
D:\> cd \dosutils
D:\dosutils> autoboot.bat
```

Note that this method will not work if run in a DOS window – the autoboot.bat file must be executed with DOS as the only operating system. In other words, Windows cannot be running.

If your computer can't boot directly from CD-ROM, and you can't use a DOS-based autoboot), you'll have to use a boot diskette to get things started.

3.3   Beginning the Installation

After booting, the installation program begins by displaying a welcome message. Press (Enter) to begin the installation. If you wish to abort the installation process at this time, simply eject the boot diskette now and reboot your machine.

3.3.1   Choosing a Language

After the welcome dialog, the installation program asks you to select the language to be used during the installation process (see Figure 3.4 on the facing page). Using the ⬆ and ⬇ keys, select the appropriate language. A scroll bar may appear to the right of the languages – if present, it indicates that there are more entries than can be displayed at one time. You'll be seeing scroll bars like this throughout the installation program.

3.3.2   Selecting a Keyboard Type

Next, the installation program gives you an opportunity to select a keyboard type (see Figure 3.5 on page 34). You may navigate this dialog box the same way you did with the language selection dialog.

After selecting the appropriate keyboard type, press (Enter); the keyboard type you select will be loaded automatically both for the remainder of the installation

Figure 3.4: Selecting a Language

process and each time you boot your Red Hat Linux system. If you wish to change your keyboard type after you have booted your Red Hat Linux system, you may use the /usr/sbin/kbdconfig command.

3.3.3 PCMCIA Support

Next, the installation program will probe your system to determine if your system requires PCMCIA (also known as PC Card) support. If a PCMCIA controller is found, you'll be asked if you require PCMCIA support during the installation. If you will be using a PCMCIA device during the installation (for example, you have a PCMCIA ethernet card and you'll be installing via NFS, or you have a PCMCIA SCSI card and will be installing from a SCSI CD), you should select **Yes**.

Please Note: This question applies *only* to PCMCIA support during the actual installation. Your installed Red Hat Linux system will still support PCMCIA, even if you say **No** here (assuming that you select the pcmcia-cs package during the subsequent installation).

If you require PCMCIA support, you will then be asked to insert the supplemental diskette – Select **OK** when you've done so.

The installation program will then display a progress bar as the supplemental diskette is loaded.

Please Note: If you are performing an installation in expert mode, you will be asked whether PCMCIA support is required. As you might imagine, you must answer **Yes** if the installation requires access to a PCMCIA device.

Figure 3.5: Selecting a Keyboard Type

3.4   Selecting an Installation Method

Next, you are asked what type of installation method you wish to use (see Figure 3.6 on the facing page). Highlight the appropriate choice and select **OK**, or press (Enter). You can install Red Hat Linux via any of five basic methods (see Section 2.4 on page 13), some of which require the use of a supplemental diskette. To summarize, you can install Red Hat Linux from:

CD-ROM – If you have a CD-ROM drive and the Red Hat Linux CD-ROM. Does not require a supplemental diskette. Please refer to Section 3.4.1 on the facing page to select the CD-ROM installation method.

NFS – If you are installing from an NFS server which is exporting the Red Hat Linux CD-ROM or a mirror image of Red Hat Linux. Does not require a supplemental diskette. Please refer to Section 3.4.2 on page 36 to select the NFS installation method.

Hard Drive – If you copied the Red Hat Linux files to a local hard drive. Requires a supplemental diskette. Please refer to Section 3.4.6 on page 39 to select the hard drive installation method.

FTP – If you are installing directly from an FTP server. Requires a supplemental diskette. Please refer to Section 3.4.7 on page 39 to select the FTP installation method.

SMB Image – If you are installing from a Windows "shared drive". Requires a supplemental diskette. Please refer to Section 3.4.8 on page 40 to select the SMB installation method.

Figure 3.6: Selecting an Installation Method

3.4.1   Installing From CD-ROM

If you are going to install Red Hat Linux from CD-ROM, select "CD-ROM", and select **Ok**. The installation program will then prompt you to insert your Red Hat Linux CD-ROM into your CD-ROM drive. When you've done so, select **Ok**, and press [Enter]. The installation program will then probe your system, and attempt to identify your CD-ROM drive. It will start by looking for an IDE (also known as ATAPI) CD-ROM drive. If one is found, the installation will continue. If the installation program cannot automatically detect your CD-ROM drive, you will be asked what type of CD-ROM you have. You can choose from the following types:

SCSI Select this if your CD-ROM is attached to a supported SCSI adapter; the installation program will then ask you to choose a SCSI driver. Choose the driver that most closely resembles your adapter. You may specify options for the driver if necessary; however, most drivers will detect your SCSI adapter automatically.

Other If your CD-ROM is neither an IDE nor a SCSI CD-ROM, it's an "other". Sound cards with proprietary CD-ROM interfaces are good examples of this CD-ROM type. The installation program presents a list of drivers for supported CD-ROMs – choose a driver and, if necessary, specify any driver options.

Please Note:A partial list of optional parameters for CD-ROMs can be found in Appendix C on page 291. If you have an ATAPI CD-ROM, and the installation program fails to find it (in other words, it asks you what type of CD-ROM you have), you must restart the installation, and enter linux hd$X$=cdrom. Replace the X with one of the following letters, depending on the interface the unit is connected to, and whether it is configured as master or slave:

- **a** – First IDE controller, master

- **b** – First IDE controller, slave

- **c** – Second IDE controller, master

- **d** – Second IDE controller, slave

(If you have a third and/or fourth controller, simply continue assigning letters in alphabetical order, going from controller to controller, and master to slave.)

Once your CD-ROM drive has been identified, you will be asked to insert the Red Hat Linux CD-ROM into your CD-ROM drive. Select **Ok** when you have done so. After a short delay, the next dialog box will appear. Turn to Chapter 4 on page 41 to continue installing Red Hat Linux.

3.4.2   Installing via NFS

If you are going to install Red Hat Linux from an NFS-served filesystem, highlight "NFS image" and select **OK**.

3.4.3   Network Driver Configuration

Next, the installation program will probe your system and attempt to identify your network card. Most of the time, the driver can locate the card automatically. If it is not able to identify your network card, you'll be asked to choose the driver that supports your network card and to specify any options necessary for the driver to locate and recognize it.

3.4.4   Configuring TCP/IP Networking

After the installation program has configured your network card, it presents several dialogs for configuring your system's TCP/IP networking. The first screen (shown in Figure 3.7 on the next page) allows you to select from one of three approaches to network configuration:

- **Static IP address** – You must supply all the necessary network-related information manually.

- **BOOTP** – The necessary network-related information is automatically provided using a `bootp` request.

- **DHCP** – The necessary network-related information is automatically provided using a `dhcp` request.

Figure 3.7: Selecting Method of Network Configuration

Please Note: The **BOOTP** and **DHCP** selections require an active, properly configured bootp (or dhcp) server running on your local area network.

If you choose **BOOTP** or **DHCP**, your network configuration will be set automatically, and you can skip the rest of this section.

If you've selected **Static IP address**, you'll need to specify all the networking information yourself. Figure 3.8 contains example networking information similar to what you'll be needing.

Field	Example Value
IP Address	10.0.2.15
Netmask	255.255.255.0
Default Gateway	10.0.2.254
Primary Nameserver	10.0.2.1
Domain Name	redhat.com
Hostname	pooh.redhat.com

Figure 3.8: Sample Networking Information

Please Note: The information in figure 3.8 is a sample only! You should obtain the proper information for your network from your network administrator.

The first dialog asks you for IP and other network addresses (see Figure 3.9 on the following page). Enter the **IP address** you are using during installation and press (Enter). The installation program attempts to guess your **Netmask** based on your IP address; you may change the netmask if it is incorrect. Press (Enter). The installation program guesses the **Default gateway** and **Primary nameserver** addresses from your IP address and netmask; you may change them if they are incorrect.

Figure 3.9: Configuring TCP/IP

In either case, choose **OK** to continue.

After the first dialog box, you may see a second one. It will prompt you for a domain name, a hostname, and other networking information (see Figure 3.10 on the next page). Enter the **Domain name** for your system and press Enter; the installation program carries the domain name down to the **Host name** field. Enter the hostname you are using in front of the domain name to form a fully qualified domain name (FQDN). If your network has more than one nameserver, you may enter IP addresses for additional nameservers in the **Secondary nameserver** and **Tertiary nameserver** fields. Choose **OK** to continue.

Please Note: If you're doing an FTP installation, head back to Section 4.6 on page 55, and pick up where you left off. If you're doing an SMB installation, head back to Section 4.7 on page 56, and continue from there. If you're doing an NFS installation, read on.

3.4.5   NFS Server Information

The next dialog requests information about the NFS server (see Figure 3.11 on page 40). Enter the name (which must be a fully-qualified domain name) or IP address of your NFS server, and the name of the exported directory that contains the Red Hat Linux CD. For example, if the NFS server has the Red Hat Linux CD mounted on /mnt/cdrom, enter /mnt/cdrom in **Red Hat directory**. If the NFS server is exporting a mirror of the Red Hat Linux installation tree instead of a CD, enter the directory which contains the RedHat directory. For example, if your NFS server contains the directory /mirrors/redhat/i386/RedHat, enter /mirrors/redhat/i386.

After a short delay, the next dialog box will appear. Turn to Chapter 4 on page 41

Figure 3.10: Configuring Networking

to continue installing Red Hat Linux.

3.4.6   Installing From a Hard Drive

If you are going to install Red Hat Linux from a locally-attached hard drive, high-light "hard drive" and select **OK**.

Before you started the installation program, you must first have copied all the nec-essary files to a partition on a locally-attached hard drive. If you haven't done this yet, please refer to Section 2.4.6 on page 16. Installing from a hard drive re-quires the supplemental diskette; when you are directed to, please insert it in your computer's diskette drive, and select **OK**. A progress bar will be displayed as the supplemental diskette is loaded.

Next, turn to Chapter 4 on page 41, and follow the directions there.

3.4.7   Installing via FTP

If you are going to install Red Hat Linux from an FTP site, highlight "FTP", and select **OK**. FTP installations require the supplemental diskette – when asked to in-sert it, do so, and select **OK**. The installation program will then display a progress bar as the supplemental diskette is loaded.

Next, turn to Chapter 4 on page 41, and follow the directions there.

Figure 3.11: Installing via NFS

3.4.8 Installing via SMB

If you would like to install Red Hat Linux from a disk shared by a Windows system (or by a Linux system running the Samba SMB connectivity suite), select "SMB image", and select **Ok**. SMB installations require a supplemental diskette – when asked to insert it, do so, and select **Ok**. The installation program will then display a progress bar as the supplemental diskette is loaded.

Next, turn to Chapter 4 on the next page, and follow the directions there.

4

Continuing the Installation

4.1   Upgrading or Installing

After you choose an installation method, the installation program prompts you to either *install* or *upgrade* (see Figure 4.1).

Figure 4.1: Upgrading or Installing

4.1.1   Installing

You usually install Red Hat Linux on a clean disk partition or set of partitions, or over another installation of Linux.

Please Note: Installing Red Hat Linux over another installation of Linux (including Red Hat Linux) does *not* preserve any information from the prior installation. Make sure you save any important files!

If you wish to perform a full install, choose **Install**, and skip to section 4.2.

4.1.2   Upgrading

The installation process for Red Hat Linux 5.2 includes the ability to upgrade from prior versions of Red Hat Linux (version 2.0 and later) which are based on RPM technology. Upgrading your system installs the modular 2.0.x kernel as well as updated versions of the packages which are currently installed on your machine. The upgrade process preserves existing configuration files by renaming them using a .rpmsave extension (e.g., sendmail.cf.rpmsave) and leaves a log telling what actions it took in /tmp/upgrade.log. As software evolves, configuration file formats can change, so you should carefully compare your original configuration files to the new files before integrating your changes.

If you wish to upgrade your Red Hat Linux system, choose **Upgrade**.

Please Note: Some upgraded packages may require that other packages are also installed for proper operation. The upgrade procedure takes care of these *dependencies*, but it may need to install additional packages. You will be shown the names of the required packages, and you may then decide to install them or not. You should install all such packages; otherwise, some of the upgraded packages may not work properly (or at all).

4.2   Installation Class

After you choose to perform an upgrade or a full install, the installation program will ask you to choose an installation class. You may choose from the following installation classes:

- **Workstation** – A workstation-class installation will automatically erase all Linux partitions from your computer's hard drive(s).

- **Server** – A server-class installation will automatically erase *all partitions* from your computer's hard drive(s).

- **Custom** – A custom-class installation gives you complete control over partitioning-related issues. If you have installed Red Hat Linux in the past, the custom-class installation is most similar to past installations.

Figure 4.2: Installation Class

Please Note: If you choose either **Workstation** or **Server**, part (or all) of your computer's stored data *will* be erased! You will be asked to confirm your decision; however, please keep in mind that once the installation program receives your confirmation, the erasure is irrevocable.

If you choose a workstation- or server-class installation, you should turn to one of the following sections, depending on the installation method you've selected:

- **CDROM** Turn to Chapter 5 on page 63.

- **NFS** – Turn to Chapter 5 on page 63.

- **Hard Drive** – Turn to Section 4.8 on page 57, follow the instructions there, then turn to Chapter 5 on page 63.

- **FTP** – Turn to Section 4.6 on page 55, follow the instructions there, then turn to Chapter 5 on page 63.

- **SMB** – Turn to Section 4.7 on page 56, follow the instructions there, then turn to Chapter 5 on page 63.

4.3 SCSI Support

After you choose the appropriate installation class, the installation program will probe your system for SCSI adapters. In some cases, the installation program will ask you whether you have any SCSI adapters. If you choose **Yes**, the following dialog presents a list of SCSI drivers. Choose the driver that most closely resembles your SCSI adapter. The installation program then gives you an opportunity to specify options for the SCSI driver you selected; most SCSI drivers should detect your hardware automatically, however.

4.4   Creating Partitions for Red Hat Linux

At this point, it's necessary to let the installation program know where it should install Red Hat Linux. This is done by defining *mount points* for one or more disk partitions in which Red Hat Linux will be installed. You may also need to create and/or delete partitions at this time.

Please Note: If you have not yet planned how you will set up your partitions, please turn to Section 2.7 on page 19, and review everything up to Section 2.8 on page 25. As a bare minimum, you'll need an appropriately-sized root partition, and a swap partition of at least 16 MB.

The installation program then presents a dialog box that allows you to choose from two disk partitioning tools (see Figure 4.3). The two choices you have are:

- **Disk Druid** – This is Red Hat Linux's install-time disk management utility. It can create and delete disk partitions according to user-supplied requirements, in addition to managing mount points for each partition.

- **fdisk** – This is the traditional Linux disk partitioning tool. While it is somewhat more flexible than Disk Druid, the downside is that fdisk assumes you have some experience with disk partitioning, and are comfortable with its somewhat terse user interface.

Figure 4.3: Selecting Disk Setup Method

With the exception of certain esoteric situations, Disk Druid can handle the partitioning requirements for a typical Red Hat Linux installation.

Select the disk partitioning tool you'd like to use, and press (Enter). If you choose Disk Druid, continue reading. If you'd rather use fdisk, please turn to Section 4.4.2 on page 51.

4.4.1 Using Disk Druid

If you selected Disk Druid, you will be presented with a screen that looks like figure 4.4. While it may look overwhelming at first, it really isn't. Let's go over each of Disk Druid's three sections.

Figure 4.4: Disk Druid Main Screen

The "Current Disk Partitions" Section

Each line in the "Current Disk Partitions" section represents a disk partition. You'll note that this section has a scroll bar to the right, which means that there might be more partitions than can be displayed at one time. If you use the (↑) and (↓) keys, you can see if there are any additional partitions there. Each line in this section has five different fields:

Mount Point – This field indicates where the partition will be mounted when Red Hat Linux is installed and running.

Device – This field displays the partition's device name.

Requested – The "Requested" field shows the minimum size requested when the partition was defined.

Actual – The "Actual" field shows the space currently allocated to the partition.

Type – This field shows the partition's type.

Another Type of Partition As you scroll through the "Current Disk Partitions" section, you might see an "Unallocated Requested Partitions" title bar, followed by one or more partitions. As the title implies, these are partitions that have been requested but, for one reason or another, have not been allocated. A common reason for having an unallocated partition is a lack of sufficient free space for the partition. In any case, the reason the partition remains unallocated will be displayed after the partition's mount point.

The "Drive Summaries" Section

Each line in the "Drive Summaries" section represents a hard disk on your system. Each line has the following fields:

Drive – This field shows the hard disk's device name.

Geom [C/H/S] – This field shows the hard disk's *geometry*. The geometry consists of three numbers representing the number of cylinders, heads, and sectors as reported by the hard disk.

Total – The "Total" field shows the total available space on the hard disk.

Used – This field shows how much of the hard disk's space is currently allocated to partitions.

Free – The "Free" field shows how much of the hard disk's space is still unallocated.

Bar Graph – This field presents a visual representation of the space currently used on the hard disk. The more pound signs there are between the square braces, the less free space there is. In Figure 4.4 on the page before, the bar graph shows no free space.

Please Note: The "Drive Summaries" section is displayed only to indicate your computer's disk configuration. It is not meant to be used as a means of specifying the target hard drive for a given partition. This is described more completely in Section 4.4.1 on the facing page.

Disk Druid's Buttons

These buttons control Disk Druid's actions. They are used to add and delete partitions, and to change partition attributes. In addition, there are buttons that are used to accept the changes you've made, or to exit Disk Druid entirely. Let's take a look at each button in order.

Add – The "Add" button is used to request a new partition. When selected, a dialog box will appear containing fields that must be filled in.

Edit – The "Edit" button is used to modify attributes of the partition currently highlighted in the "Current Disk Partitions" section. Selecting this button will cause a dialog box to appear. Some or all of the fields in the "Edit Partition" dialog box may be changed, depending on whether the partition information has already been written to disk or not.

Delete – The "Delete" button is used to delete the partition currently highlighted in the "Current Disk Partitions" section. Selecting this button will cause a dialog box to appear asking you to confirm the deletion.

Ok – The "Ok" button causes any changes made to your system's partitions to be written to disk. You will be asked to confirm your changes before Disk Druid rewrites your hard disk partition table(s). In addition, any mount points you've defined are passed to the installation program, and will eventually be used by your Red Hat Linux system to define the filesystem layout.

Back – This button causes Disk Druid to abort without saving any changes you've made. When this button is selected, the installation program will take you back to the previous screen, so you can start over.

Handy Function Keys

While there is some overlap between Disk Druid's buttons and the available functions keys, there are two function keys that have no corresponding buttons:

- F2 **(Add NFS)** – This function key is used to add a read-only NFS-served filesystem to the set of mount points on your Red Hat Linux system. When selected, a dialog box will appear containing fields that must be filled in.

- F5 **(Reset)** – This function key is used to discard all changes you may have made while in Disk Druid, and return the list of partitions to those read from the partition table(s) on your hard disk(s). When selected, you'll be asked to confirm whether you want the changes discarded or not. Note that any mount points you've specified will be lost, and will need to be reentered.

Please Note: You will need to dedicate at least one partition to Red Hat Linux, and optionally more. This is discussed more completely in Section 2.7.5 on page 24.

Now let's see how Disk Druid is used to set up partitions for your Red Hat Linux system.

Adding a Partition

To Add a new partition, select the **Add** button, and press Space or Enter. A dialog box entitled "Edit New Partition" will appear (see Figure 4.5 on the following page). It contains the following fields:

Figure 4.5: Creating a New Partition

- **Mount Point** – Highlight this field, and enter the partition's mount point. For example, if this partition should be the root partition, enter /, enter /usr for the usr partition, and so on.

- **Size (Megs)** – In this field, enter the size (in megabytes) of the partition. Note that this field starts with a "1" in it, meaning that unless you change it, you'll end up with a 1 MB partition. Delete it using the [Backspace] key, and enter the desired partition size.

- **Growable?** – This check box indicates whether the size you entered in the previous field is to be considered the partition's exact size, or its minimum size. Press [Space] to check and uncheck the box. When checked, the partition will grow to fill all available space on the hard disk. In this case, the partition's size will expand and contract as other partitions are modified. Note that you can make more than one partition growable; if you do so, the additional free space will be shared between all growable partitions.

- **Type** – This field contains a list of different partition types. Select the appropriate partition type by using the [↑] and [↓] keys.

- **Allowable Drives** – This field contains a list of the hard disks installed on your system, with a check box for each. If a hard disk's box is checked, then this partition may be created on that hard disk. If the box is *not* checked, then partition will *never* be created on that hard disk. By using different check box settings, you can direct Disk Druid to place partitions as you see fit, or let Disk Druid decide where partitions should go.

- **Ok** – Select this button and press [Space] when you are satisfied with the partition's settings, and wish to create it.

- **Cancel** – Select this button and press `Space` when you don't want to create the partition.

Problems When Adding a Partition If you attempt to add a partition and Disk Druid can't carry out your request, you'll see a dialog box like the one in Figure 4.6. In the box are listed any partitions that are currently unallocated, along with the reason they could not be allocated. Select the **Ok** button, and press `Space` to continue. Note that the unallocated partition(s) are also displayed on Disk Druid's main screen (though you may have to scroll the "Current Disk Partitions" section to see them).

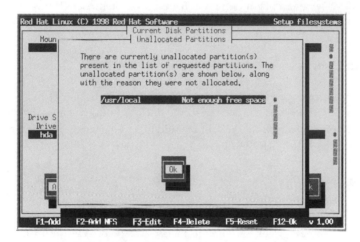

Figure 4.6: Unallocated Partition Warning

Deleting a Partition

To delete a partition, highlight the partition in the "Current Disk Partitions" section, select the **Delete** button, and press `Space`. You will be asked to confirm the deletion.

Editing a Partition

To change a partition's settings, highlight the partition in the "Current Disk Partitions" section, select the **Edit** button, and press `Space`. You will be presented with a dialog box very similar to the one shown in Figure 4.5 on the facing page. Make the appropriate changes, select **Ok**, and press `Space`.

Please Note: If the partition already existed on your hard disk, you will only be able to change the partition's mount point. If you want to make any other changes, you will need to delete the partition and recreate it.

Adding an NFS Mount

To add a read-only NFS-served filesystem, press ⟨F2⟩. If you have not selected a network-related installation method, you will be presented with several dialog boxes concerning network configuration (Turn back to Section 3.4.3 on page 36 for more information). Fill them in appropriately. You will then see a dialog box entitled, "Edit Network Mount Point" (similar to the one in Figure 4.11 on page 54). In this dialog box you will need to enter the NFS server name, the path to the exported filesystem, and the mount point for the filesystem. Select the **Ok** or **Cancel** button as appropriate, and press ⟨Space⟩.

Starting Over

If you'd like to abandon any changes you've made while in Disk Druid, and would rather use fdisk instead, you can select the **Back** button, and press ⟨Space⟩. If you want to continue using Disk Druid, but would like to start over, press ⟨F5⟩, and Disk Druid will be reset to its initial state.

When You're Finished...

Once you've finished configuring partitions and entering mount points, your screen should look something like the one in Figure 4.7. Select **OK**, and press ⟨Space⟩. Then turn to Section 4.5 on page 53.

Figure 4.7: Partitions and Mount Points Defined

4.4.2 Using `fdisk`

If you'd rather use `fdisk` to manage partitions, this is the section for you. Once you've selected `fdisk`, you'll be presented with a dialog box entitled "Partition Disks" (see Figure 4.8). In this box is a list of every disk on your computer. Move the highlight to the disk you'd like to partition, select **Edit**, and press ⌈Space⌋. You will then enter `fdisk` and can partition the disk you selected. Repeat this process for each disk you want to partition. When you're done, select "Done".

Figure 4.8: Selecting a Disk for Partitioning

An Overview of `fdisk`

`fdisk` includes online help which is terse but useful. Here are a few tips:

- The command for help is `m`.
- To list the current partition table, use the `p` command (see Figure 4.9 on the following page).
- To add a new partition, use `n`.
- Linux `fdisk` creates partitions of type `Linux native` by default. When you create a swap partition, don't forget to change it to type `Linux swap` using the `t` command. The value for the `Linux swap` type is `82`. For other partition types, use the `l` command to see a list of partition types and values.
- Linux allows up to four (4) partitions on one disk. If you wish to create more than that, one (and only one) of the four may be an *extended* partition, which acts as a container for one or more *logical* partitions. Since it acts as a container, the extended partition must be at least as large as the total size of all the logical partitions it is to contain.

- It's a good idea to write down which partitions (e.g., /dev/hda2) are meant for which filesystems (e.g., /usr) as you create each one.

- **Please Note:** None of the changes you make take effect until you save them and exit fdisk using the w command. You may quit fdisk at any time without saving changes by using the q command.

```
This is the fdisk program for partitioning your drive. It is running
on /dev/hda.

Command (m for help): p

Disk /tmp/hda: 128 heads, 63 sectors, 620 cylinders
Units = cylinders of 8064 * 512 bytes

   Device Boot    Begin    Start     End    Blocks   Id  System
/tmp/hda1            1        1       21     84640+  83  Linux native
/tmp/hda2           22       22      148    512064   83  Linux native
/tmp/hda3          149      149      620   1903104    5  Extended
/tmp/hda5          149      149      275    512032+  83  Linux native
/tmp/hda6          276      276      402    512032+  83  Linux native
/tmp/hda7          403      403      419     68512+  82  Linux swap
/tmp/hda8          420      420      620    810400+  83  Linux native

Command (m for help):
```

Figure 4.9: Sample Output From fdisk

Changing the Partition Table

When you are finished partitioning your disks, press **Done**; you may see a message indicating that the installation program needs to reboot. This is a normal occurrence after changing a disk's partition data; it usually happens if you created, changed, or deleted any extended partitions. After you press **OK**, your machine will reboot. Follow the same installation steps you did up until **Partitioning Disks**; then simply choose **Done**.

4.4.3   Filesystem Configuration

The next dialog box contains a list of all disk partitions with filesystems readable by Red Hat Linux, including partitions for MS-DOS or Windows. This gives you the opportunity to assign these partitions to different parts of your Red Hat Linux filesystem. The partitions you assign will be automatically mounted when your Red Hat Linux system boots. Select the partition you wish to assign and press (Enter) (or choose **Edit**); then enter the *mount point* for that partition, e.g., /usr (see Figure 4.10 on the next page).

Figure 4.10: Filesystem Configuration

If you are performing an upgrade, the installation program tries to find your root partition automatically; if it does, it obtains all this information automatically, and goes on to the next step.

Adding an NFS Mount

Red Hat Linux also allows you to mount read-only NFS volumes when your system boots; this allows directory trees to be shared across a network. To do so, press F2. If you have not selected a network-related installation method, you will be presented with several dialog boxes concerning network configuration (Turn back to Section 3.4.4 on page 36 for more information). Fill them in appropriately. You will then see a dialog box entitled "Edit Network Mount Point". Enter the NFS server's hostname, the path to the NFS volume, and the local mount point for that volume (see Figure 4.11 on the next page).

4.5 Initializing Swap Space

After you've created partitions for Red Hat Linux, the installation program looks for swap partitions (see Figure 4.12 on the following page). If it finds any, it asks whether you want to initialize them. Select the partition(s) you wish to initialize as swap space using Space; if you wish to check the partitions for bad blocks, make sure the **Check for bad blocks during format** box is checked. Choose **OK**, and press Space.

If the installation program can't find a swap partition and you're sure one exists, make sure you have set the partition type to Linux swap; see Section 4.4

Figure 4.11: Adding an NFS Mount

Figure 4.12: Initializing Swap Space

on page 44 for information on how this is done with Disk Druid or fdisk.

4.6   For FTP Installations Only...

If you are *not* performing an FTP installation, please skip ahead to Section 4.7 on the following page.

If you *are* performing an FTP installation, please mark this place in the manual, because you'll be returning here later. Turn to Section 3.4.3 on page 36. This section will guide you through the necessary network configuration dialog boxes. When you get to the "FTP Setup" dialog box, come back here.

OK, you're back. You should have entered all the necessary network information, and should now be looking at the "FTP Setup" dialog box. Here's where you point the installation program at the FTP site of your choice (see Figure 4.13). Enter the name or IP address of the FTP site you are installing from, and the name of the directory there which contains the RedHat directory for your architecture. For example, if the FTP site contains the directory /pub/mirrors/redhat/i386/RedHat, enter /pub/mirrors/redhat/i386. If you are not using anonymous FTP, or if you need to use a proxy FTP server (if you're behind a firewall, for example), check the check box, and another dialog box will request the FTP account and proxy information.

Figure 4.13: Installing via FTP

If everything has been specified properly, you should see a message box indicating that base/hdlist is being retrieved.

If you are doing a workstation- or server-class installation, please turn to Chapter 5 on page 63. Otherwise, turn to Section 4.9 on page 58 to continue installing Red Hat Linux.

4.7   For SMB Installations Only...

If you are *not* performing an SMB installation, please skip ahead to Section 4.8 on the next page.

If you *are* performing an SMB installation, please mark this place in the manual, because you'll be returning here later. Turn to Section 3.4.3 on page 36. This section will guide you through the necessary network configuration dialog boxes. When you get to the "SMB Setup" dialog box, come back here...

At this point, you should have entered all the necessary network information, and should now be looking at the "SMB Setup" dialog box. This is where you'll specify which SMB server, share, and account information the installation program should use (See Figure 4.14).

Figure 4.14: Installing via SMB

First, you'll need to enter the SMB server name. It's important to note that the name expected here is the server's Microsoft Networking name, and not a fully qualified domain name.

Next, enter the name of the shared volume. Since different implementations of the SMB protocol handle share names differently, you might find that the case of the share name is important. In most cases (no pun intended) entering the share name in lower case seems to work best.

Next, enter the account name and password. In general, the account name should be guest. A password (which *is* case-sensitive) *must* be present. If the share is made available *without* a password, it will most likely not work.

After entering all the required information, select **Ok**, and press Space . If everything is working properly, there will be a slight delay as the list of available packages is read by the installation program.

If you are doing a workstation- or server-class installation, please turn to Chapter 5 on page 63. Otherwise, turn to Section 4.9 on the next page to continue installing Red Hat Linux.

4.8   For Hard Drive Installations Only...

If you are *not* performing a hard drive installation, please skip ahead to Section 4.9 on the following page. Otherwise, read on.

At this point, a dialog box entitled "Select Partition" is displayed (see Figure 4.15). Enter the device name of the partition holding the RedHat directory tree. There is also a field labelled "Directory". If the RedHat directory is not in the root directory of that partition (for example, /test/new/RedHat), enter the path to the RedHat directory (in our example, /test/new).

Figure 4.15: Selecting Partition for HD Install

If the installation program was unable to find the necessary files on the partition and directory you've specified, you'll be returned to the "Select Partition" dialog box to make the necessary corrections.

If everything has been specified properly, you should see a message box indicating that the packages are being scanned.

If you are doing a workstation- or server-class installation, please turn to Chapter 5 on page 63. Move on to the next section to continue installing Red Hat Linux.

4.9   Formatting Partitions

The next dialog box presents a list of partitions to format (see Figure 4.16). All
newly created partitions should be formatted. In addition, any already-existing
partitions that contain old data you no longer need should be formatted. However,
partitions such as /home or /usr/local must not be formatted if they contain
data you wish to keep. Select each partition to format and press ⌜Space⌝. If you
wish to check for bad blocks while formatting each filesystem, select **Check for
bad blocks during format**. Select **OK**, and press ⌜Space⌝.

Figure 4.16: Formatting Partitions

4.10   Selecting and Installing Packages

After your partitions have been configured and selected for formatting, you are
ready to select packages for installation. You can select *components*, which group
packages together according to function, individual packages, or a combination of
the two.

4.10.1   Selecting Components

Components group packages together according to the functionality they provide. For example, **C Development**, **Networked Workstation**, or **Web Server**.
Select each component you wish to install and press ⌜Space⌝. Selecting **Everything**
(which can be found at the end of the component list) installs all packages included
with Red Hat Linux (see Figure 4.17 on the facing page). Selecting every package
will require over 700 MB of free disk space.

Figure 4.17: Selecting System Components

If you wish to select or deselect individual packages, check the **Select individual packages** check box.

4.10.2 Selecting Individual Packages

After selecting the components you wish to install, you may select or deselect individual packages. The installation program presents a list of the package groups available; select a group to examine and press (Enter). The installation program presents a list of the packages in that group, which you may select or deselect by using the arrow keys to highlight a package, and pressing (Space) (see Figure 4.18 on the next page).

Please Note: Some packages (such as the kernel and certain libraries) are required for every Red Hat Linux system and are not available to select or deselect.

When you are finished selecting individual packages, press **OK** in the **Select Group** dialog box.

Getting Information About A Package

You may view a detailed description of the currently-highlighted package by pressing (F1). A dialog box will appear containing a description of the package. You can use the arrow keys to scroll through the description if there is more than can fit on the screen. When you're done reading the description, press **Ok**, and the box will disappear. You can then continue selecting packages (and viewing their descriptions).

Figure 4.18: Selecting Packages

Please Note: If you'd rather read the package descriptions on paper, please turn to Appendix B on page 215.

4.10.3   Package Dependencies

Many software packages, in order to work correctly, depend on other software packages or libraries that must be installed on your system. For example, many of the graphical Red Hat system administration tools require the python and pythonlib packages. To make sure your system has all the packages it needs in order to be fully functional, Red Hat Linux checks these package *dependencies* each time you install or remove software packages.

After you have finished selecting packages to install, the installation program checks the list of selected packages for dependencies. If any package requires another package which you have not selected to install, the program presents a list of these *unresolved dependencies* and gives you the opportunity to resolve them (see Figure 4.19 on the next page). If you simply press **OK**, the program will resolve them automatically by adding all required packages to the list of selected packages.

4.10.4   Package Installation

After all package dependencies have been resolved, the installation program presents a dialog box telling you that a log file containing a list of all packages installed will be written to /tmp/install.log on your Red Hat Linux system. Select **Ok** and press Space to continue.

At this point, the installation program will format every partition you selected for

Figure 4.19: Unresolved Dependencies

formatting. This can take several minutes (and will take even longer if you directed the installation program to check for bad blocks).

Once all partitions have been formatted, the installation program starts to install packages. A window entitled "Install Status" is displayed with the following information:

Package – The name of the package currently being installed.

Size – The size of the package (in kilobytes).

Summary – A short description of the package.

Package Installation Progress Bar – A bar showing how complete the current package installation is.

Statistics Section – This section has three rows labeled "Total", "Completed", and "Remaining". As you might guess, these rows contain statistics on the total number of packages that will be installed, statistics on the number of packages that have been completely installed, and statistics on the packages that have not yet been installed. The information tracked on these three rows includes:

    Packages – The number of packages.

    Bytes – The size.

    Time – The amount of time.

Overall Progress Bar – This bar changes color showing how close to completion the entire installation is.

If you're doing an FTP installation, a message box will pop up as each package is retrieved from the FTP site.

At this point there's nothing left for you to do until all the packages have been installed. How quickly this happens depends on the number of packages you've selected, and your computer's speed. Once all the packages have been installed, please turn to the next chapter to finish your installation of Red Hat Linux.

5

Finishing the Installation

5.1 Configuring a Mouse

Next, the installation program will probe your system and try to find a mouse. Some mice may be detected automatically; in this case, a dialog box is displayed showing the port on which the mouse was found. You may then be asked to give additional information, such as whether you have a two-button mouse, and would like it to emulate a three-button mouse. Make the appropriate selections, and continue to the next section.

More commonly, you will see a screen similar to the one in Figure 5.1 on the following page.

The installation program's "best guess" as to your system's mouse type will be highlighted. If the mouse type is not accurate, use the ⬆ and ⬇ keys to scroll through the different mouse types. In general, you should use the following approach to selecting your system's mouse type:

- If you find an *exact* match for your mouse in the list, highlight that entry.

- If you find a mouse that you are *certain*[1] is compatible with your mouse, highlight that entry.

- Otherwise, select one of the **Generic** entries, based on your mouse's number of buttons, and its interface. To determine your mouse's interface, follow

---

[1] No guessing allowed!

Figure 5.1: Mouse Configuration

the mouse cable back to where it plugs into your system. If the connector at the end of the mouse cable plugs into a rectangular connector, you have a serial mouse. On the other hand, if the connector is round, you have a PS/2 mouse. If you are installing Red Hat Linux on a laptop computer, in most cases the pointing device will be PS/2 compatible.

The **Emulate 3 Buttons** checkbox allows you to use a two-button mouse as if it had three buttons. In general, it's easiest to use the X Window System if you have a three-button mouse. If you select this checkbox, you can emulate a third, "middle" button by pressing both mouse buttons simultaneously.

If you've selected a mouse with a serial interface, you will then see a screen similar to the one shown in Figure 5.2 on the next page. Simply highlight the appropriate serial port for your mouse, select **Ok**, and press [Space].

If you wish to change your mouse configuration after you have booted your Red Hat Linux system, you may use the /usr/sbin/mouseconfig command.

5.2   Configuring X Windows

After setting up your mouse, if you installed the X Windows packages, you will have the opportunity to configure your X server. If you did not choose to install the X Window System, you may skip to Section 5.3 on page 66.

Figure 5.2: Serial Mouse Port Selection

5.2.1 Configuring an XFree86 Server

If you wish to use XFree86, the installation program launches the Xconfigurator utility.

Xconfigurator first probes your system in an attempt to determine what type of video card you have. Failing that, Xconfigurator will present a list of video cards. Select your video card from the list and press (Enter). If your video card does not appear on the list, XFree86 may not support it. However, if you have technical knowledge about your card, you may choose **Unlisted Card** and attempt to configure it by matching your card's video chipset with one of the available X servers.

Once you have selected your video card, the installation program installs the appropriate XFree86 server, and Xconfigurator presents a list of monitors. If your monitor appears on the list, select it and press (Enter). Otherwise, select **Custom**. If you do select **Custom**, Xconfigurator prompts you to select the horizontal sync range and vertical sync range of your monitor (these values are generally available in the documentation which accompanies your monitor, or from your monitor's vendor or manufacturer).

Caution: It is not recommended to select a monitor "similar" to your monitor unless you are certain that the monitor you are selecting does not exceed the capabilities of your monitor. If you do so, it is possible you may overclock your monitor and damage or destroy it.

Next, Xconfigurator prompts you for the amount of video memory installed on your video card. If you are not sure, please consult the documentation accompanying your video card. It will not damage your video card by choosing more memory than is available, but the XFree86 server may not start correctly if you do.

If the video card you selected might have a video clockchip, Xconfigurator presents a list of clockchips. The recommended choice is **No Clockchip Setting**, since XFree86 can automatically detect the proper clockchip in most cases.

Finally, Xconfigurator prompts you to select the video modes you wish to use; select one or more modes by pressing (Space). Xconfigurator then writes a configuration file containing all of your choices to /etc/X11/XF86Config.

5.3   Configuring Networking

Next, the installation program gives you an opportunity to configure (or reconfigure) networking. If you are installing from CD-ROM or from a local hard disk, the installation program asks if you want to configure networking. If you choose **No**, your Red Hat Linux system will be a standalone workstation. If you choose **Yes**, you may configure networking as described below.

If you are installing Red Hat Linux via NFS, FTP, or SMB, you have already entered temporary networking information that was used during the installation. The install program offers you three choices (see Figure 5.3):

Figure 5.3: Network Configuration Options

- **Keep this setup** – Keeps the network configuration you used during the installation. All the networking information you entered previously becomes part of your system's permanent configuration.

- **Reconfigure network now** – The installation program presents the network configuration dialogs in Section 3.4.3 on page 36. The values you used during installation will be filled in as defaults. Choose this if your system will be installed on a network other than the one you used to install Red Hat Linux.

- **Don't setup networking** – Don't set up networking at all. Your system will not have networking configured. Choose this if you installed your system over a network, but it will be used as a standalone workstation.

5.3.1 Network Configuration Dialogs

If you elected to configure networking at this time, you will be presented with a series of dialog boxes. Please turn to Section 3.4.4 on page 36 for more information.

5.4 Configuring the Clock

Next, the installation program presents a dialog to help you configure your Red Hat Linux system's timezone (see Figure 5.4).

If you wish to set the hardware (CMOS) clock to GMT (Greenwich Mean Time, also known as UTC, or Coordinated Universal Time), select **Hardware clock set to GMT**. Setting your hardware clock to GMT means your Red Hat Linux system will properly handle daylight savings time, if your timezone uses it. Most networks use GMT.

Please Note: If your computer runs another operating system from time to time, setting the clock to GMT may cause the other operating system to display the incorrect time. Also keep in mind that if more than one operating system is allowed to automatically change the time to compensate for daylight savings time, it is likely that the time will be improperly set.

Figure 5.4: Configuring Timezones

Select the timezone your system will be operating in from the list, and press Enter.

If you wish to change your timezone configuration after you have booted your Red
Hat Linux system, you may use the `/usr/sbin/timeconfig` command.

5.5   Selecting Services for Start on Reboot

Please Note: If you're performing a workstation- or server-class installation, this
part of the installation is automatically done for you. Please skip ahead to Section 5.6.

Next you'll see a dialog box entitled "Services" (see Figure 5.5). Displayed in this
box is a list of services with a check box by each. Scroll through this list, and
check every service that you would like automatically started every time your Red
Hat Linux system boots. If you're not sure what a particular service is, move the
highlight to it and press [F1]. You'll then get a brief description of the service.

Figure 5.5: Selecting Services

Note that you can run `/usr/sbin/ntsysv` or `/sbin/chkconfig` after the installation to change which services automatically start on reboot.

5.6   Configuring a Printer

After you have set up networking, the installation program asks whether you
would like to configure a printer. If you choose **Yes**, a dialog box will ask you
to indicate how the printer is connected to your computer (see Figure 5.6 on the
next page).

Here is a brief description of the three types of printer connections available:

Figure 5.6: Selecting Printer Type

Local – This printer is directly connected to your computer.

Remote lpd – This printer is connected to your local area network (either through another computer, or directly), and is capable of communicating via `lpr/lpd`.

LAN Manager – This printer is connected to another computer which shares the printer via LAN Manager (or SMB) networking.

After selecting a printer type, you'll be presented with a dialog box entitled "Standard Printer Options" (see Figure 5.7 on the following page). Enter the name of the queue and the spool directory you'd like to use, or accept the default information.

The dialog box you'll see next depends on the printer connection type you selected. Turn to the section that corresponds to your printer connection type:

Local – Section 5.6.1.

Remote lpd – Section 5.6.2 on page 71.

LAN Manager – Section 5.6.3 on page 71.

5.6.1   Locally Attached Printers

If you selected "Local" as your printer's connection type, you'll see a dialog box similar to the one in Figure 5.8 on the following page.

Enter the printer device name in the field provided. As a convenience, the installation program attempts to determine which printer ports are available on your computer. Select **Next**, and press (Space). Now turn to Section 5.6.4 on page 71 to continue.

Figure 5.7: Standard Printer Options

Figure 5.8: Local Printer Device

5.6.2 Remote lpd Printers

If you selected "Remote lpd" as your printer's connection type, you'll see a dialog box similar to the one in Figure 5.9.

Figure 5.9: Remote lpd Printer Options

Enter the name of the computer to which the printer is directly connected in the "Remote hostname" field. The name of the queue *on the remote computer* that is associated with the remote printer goes in the "remote queue" field. Select **Next**, and press Space. Now turn to Section 5.6.4 to continue.

5.6.3 LAN Manager Printers

If you selected "LAN Manager" as your printer's connection type, you'll see a dialog box similar to the one in Figure 5.10 on the following page.

Enter the necessary information in the fields provided. Select **Next**, and press Space.

5.6.4 Finalizing Printer Setup

Next, you'll see a dialog box entitled "Configure Printer" (see Figure 5.11 on the next page). Select the printer type that most closely matches your printer. Select **Next**, and press Space to continue.

After selecting the printer type, you will see a dialog box similar to the one in Figure 5.12 on page 73. Set the paper size and resolution appropriately. The **Fix**

Figure 5.10: LAN Manager Printer Options

Figure 5.11: Configure Printer

stair-stepping of text check box should be checked if your printer does not auto-matically perform a carriage return after each line.

Figure 5.12: Printer Settings

Finally, you'll see a dialog box that contains all the information pertaining to your printer (see Figure 5.13 on the next page). Verify that the information is correct. If everything looks OK, select **Done**. If you need to make changes, select **Edit**. You can also select **Cancel** if you'd rather not configure a printer at this time.

If you select **Done**, you will be given the option to configure another printer, or you may continue with the installation.

5.7   Setting a Root Password

The installation program will next prompt you to set a *root password* for your sys-tem (see Figure 5.14 on page 75). You'll use the root password to log into your Red Hat Linux system for the first time.

The root password must be at least six characters long; the password you type is not echoed to the screen. You must enter the password twice; if the two passwords do not match, the installation program will ask you to enter them again.

You ought to make the root password something you can remember, but not some-thing that is easy for someone else to guess. Your name, your phone number, `qwerty`, `password`, `root`, `123456`, and `anteater` are all examples of poor pass-words. Good passwords mix numerals with upper and lower case letters and do not contain dictionary words: `Aard387vark` or `420BMttNT`, for example. Re-member that the password is case-sensitive. Write down this password and keep it in a secure place.

Please Note: The *root* user (also known as the *superuser*) has complete access to

Figure 5.13: Verifying Printer Information

the entire system; for this reason, logging in as the root user is best done *only* to perform system maintenance or administration. Please see Chapter 8 on page 107 for instructions on how to add a user account for yourself after you reboot your system. A more basic method of creating a new user account can also be found in Section 6.2.3 on page 85.

5.8   Creating a Boot Diskette

Next, you'll be given the opportunity to create a customized boot diskette for your Red Hat Linux system (see Figure 5.15 on page 76).

A boot diskette can be handy for a number of reasons:

- **Use It Instead of LILO** – You can use a boot diskette instead of LILO. This is handy if you're trying Red Hat Linux for the first time, and you'd feel more comfortable if the boot process for your other operating system is left unchanged. With a boot diskette, going back to your other operating system is as easy as removing the boot diskette and rebooting.

- **Use It In Emergencies** – The boot diskette can also be used in conjunction with a rescue disk, which will give you the tools necessary to get an ailing system back on its feet again[2].

- **Use It When Another Operating System Overwrites LILO** – Other operating systems may not be as flexible as Red Hat Linux when it comes to

---

[2]To do this, you'll need to create a rescue diskette from the rescue.img image contained in the images directory of your Red Hat Linux CD-ROM. Appendix A on page 213 explains how to do this.

Figure 5.14: Root Password

supported boot methods. Quite often, installing or updating another operating system can cause the master boot record (originally containing LILO) to be overwritten, making it impossible to boot your Red Hat Linux installation. The boot diskette can then be used to boot Red Hat Linux so you can reinstall LILO.

Given these reasons to create a boot diskette, you should seriously consider doing so. Select **Yes** and press ⌷Space⌷ to create a boot diskette. Next, you'll see a dialog box directing you to insert a blank diskette in your computer's diskette drive. Select **Ok**, and press ⌷Space⌷ when you've done so.

After a short delay, your boot diskette will be done. After removing it from your diskette drive, label it clearly. Note that if you would like to create a boot diskette after the installation, you'll be able to do so. If you boot your system with the boot diskette (instead of LILO), make sure you create a new boot diskette if you make any changes to your kernel. For more information, please see the `mkbootdisk` man page.

5.9   Installing LILO

Please Note: If you're performing a workstation- or server-class installation, this part of the installation is automatically done for you. Please skip ahead to Section 5.10 on page 79.

In order to be able to boot your Red Hat Linux system, you usually need to install LILO (the LInux LOader). You may install LILO in one of two places:

Figure 5.15: Creating a Boot Diskette

The Master Boot Record (MBR) is the recommended place to install LILO, unless the MBR already starts another operating system loader, such System Commander or OS/2's Boot Manager. The master boot record is a special area on your hard drive that is automatically loaded by your computer's BIOS, and is the earliest point at which LILO can take control of the boot process. If you install LILO in the MBR, when your machine boots, LILO will present a boot: prompt; you can then boot Red Hat Linux or any other operating system you configure LILO to boot (see below).

The first sector of your root partition is recommended if you are already using another boot loader on your system (such as OS/2's Boot Manager). In this case, your other boot loader will take control first. You can then configure that boot loader to start LILO (which will then boot Red Hat Linux).

A dialog box will appear that will let you select the type of LILO installation you desire (see Figure 5.16 on the facing page). Select the location you wish to install LILO and press **OK**. If you do not wish to install LILO, press **Skip**.

Please Note: If you choose **Skip**, you will not be able to boot your Red Hat Linux system directly, and will need to use another boot method (such as a boot diskette). Use this option only if you know you have another way of booting your Red Hat Linux system!

5.9.1   Adding Options to the LILO Boot Command Line

Next, the installation program will ask if you wish to add default options to the LILO boot command (see Figure 5.17 on page 78). Any options you enter will be passed to the Linux kernel every time it boots. When you reviewed your computer's BIOS settings in Section 2.3.1 on page 9, if you found your computer ac-

Figure 5.16: Installing LILO

cesses a hard drive in LBA mode, check **Use linear mode**. Select **OK** and press ⎡Space⎤ when finished.

Finally, the installation program will display a screen similar to the one in Figure 5.18 on page 79. Every partition that may be bootable is listed, including partitions used by other operating systems. The "Boot label" column will be filled in with the word linux on the partition holding your Red Hat Linux system's root filesystem. Other partitions may also have boot labels. If you would like to add boot labels for other partitions (or change an existing boot label), use the arrow keys to highlight the desired partition. Then use the ⎡Tab⎤ key to select the **Edit** button, and press ⎡Space⎤. You'll then see a small dialog box permitting you to enter/modify the partition's boot label. Press **Ok** when done.

Please Note: The contents of the "Boot label" column will be what you will need to enter at LILO's Boot: prompt in order to boot the desired operating system. However, if you forget the boot labels defined on your system, you can always press ⎡?⎤ at LILO's Boot: prompt to display a list of defined boot labels.

There is also a column labeled "Default". Only one partition will contain an asterisk under that column. The partition marked as the default will be the partition LILO will boot if there is no user input during the boot process. Initially the root partition for your Red Hat Linux installation will be selected as the default. If you'd like to change this, use the arrow keys to highlight the partition you'd like to make the default, and press ⎡F2⎤. The asterisk should move to the selected partition. When you've finished, select **Ok**, and press ⎡Space⎤.

Figure 5.17: LILO options

5.9.2   Alternatives to LILO

If you do not wish to use LILO to boot your Red Hat Linux system, there are a few
alternatives:

Boot Diskette   You can use the boot diskette created by the installation program
(if you elected to create one).

LOADLIN   can load Linux from MS-DOS; unfortunately, it requires a copy of the
Linux kernel (and an initial ram disk, if you have a SCSI adapter) to be available on an MS-DOS partition. The only way to accomplish this is to boot
your Red Hat Linux system using some other method (e.g., from LILO on
a diskette) and then copy the kernel to an MS-DOS partition. LOADLIN is
available from
ftp://sunsite.unc.edu/pub/Linux/system/boot/dualboot/
and sunsite's various mirror sites.

SYSLINUX   is an MS-DOS program very similar to LOADLIN; it is also available
from
ftp://sunsite.unc.edu/pub/Linux/system/boot/dualboot/ and
sunsite's
various mirror sites.

Some commercial bootloaders, such as System Commander, are able to boot
Linux (but still require LILO to be installed in your Linux root partition).

Figure 5.18: Selecting Bootable Partitions

5.10   Finishing Up. . .

After you have completed LILO installation, the installation program will prompt you to prepare your system for reboot (see Figure 5.19 on the following page). Don't forget to remove any diskette that might be in the diskette drive (Unless you decided to skip the standard LILO installation, in which case you'll need to use the boot diskette created during the installation).

After your computer's normal power-up sequence has completed, you should see LILO's standard prompt, which is `boot:`. At the `boot:` prompt, you can do any of the following things:

- **Pressing** Enter – Causes LILO's default boot entry (as defined by the dialog box shown in Figure 5.18) to be booted.

- **Entering a Boot Label, followed by** Enter – Causes LILO to boot the operating system corresponding to the entered boot label.

- **Doing Nothing** – After LILO's timeout period, (which, by default, is five seconds) Lilo will automatically boot the default boot entry.

Do whatever is appropriate to boot Red Hat Linux. You should see one or more screens worth of messages scroll by. Eventually, you should see a `login:` prompt.

Congratulations! Your Red Hat Linux installation is complete! If you're not sure what to do next, turn to Chapter 6.

Figure 5.19: Ready for Reboot

6

What Do I Do Now?

Now that your installation of Red Hat Linux is complete, you might be wondering, "What do I do now?" If so, this chapter is for you. We'll start with some basic things you should know in order to properly start and stop your Red Hat Linux system. Then we'll show you how to do some post-installation configuration so you can set things up just the way *you* want it. But before we do any of that, let's talk about documentation. . .

6.1 Getting the Documentation That's Right For You

As we mentioned in Section 2.1 on page 6, it is critical to make sure you have documentation that is appropriate to your level of Linux expertise. There is no more certain way to make your experience using Red Hat Linux a failure than to not have the documentation you need, when you need it.

As the name implies, the *Official Red Hat Linux 5.2 Installation Guide* is just that – a guide to installing Red Hat Linux on your system. While we make every effort to give you the information you need to get your Red Hat Linux system running, the Installation Guide can't do it all. For one, the Guide would balloon to more than a thousand pages. Besides, then we'd have to change the title, because it wouldn't be just an "Installation Guide" anymore!

Instead, let's take those categories we discussed back in Section 2.1 on page 6, and let's try to be more explicit in terms of the documentation you'll need. Let's start by figuring out your experience level. Here are the three basic categories:

New To Linux – Has never used any Linux (or Linux-like) operating system before, or has had only limited exposure to Linux. May or may not have experience using other operating systems (such as Windows). Is this you? If so, please turn to Section 6.1.1.

Some Linux Experience – Has installed and successfully used Linux (but not Red Hat Linux) before. Or, may have equivalent experience with other Linux-like operating systems. Does this describe you? If so, please turn to Section 6.1.2 on the next page.

Old Timer – Has installed and sucessfully used Red Hat Linux before. Are you an old-timer? If so, please turn to Section 6.1.3 on the facing page.

6.1.1   Documentation For First-Time Linux Users

"A journey of a thousand miles begins with a single step." This old saying can be applied to just about any endeavor; we're going to apply it to learning to use your Red Hat Linux system. Learning to use a Linux system effectively can be a long, rewarding journey, where you find that you can easily do things that people with other operating systems can only dream of. But like all journeys, you've got to start somewhere, and take that first step.

And the first step you need to take is to get yourself some documentation! This cannot be stressed enough; without documentation you will only become frustrated at your inability to get your Red Hat Linux system working the way you want.

Here's what you should look for in terms of Linux documentation:

- **An brief history of Linux** – Many aspects of Linux are the way they are because of historical precedent. There is also a Linux culture that, again, is based to a great deal on past history. A bit of knowledge about the history of Linux will serve you well, particularly as you interact with more experienced Linux users on the Internet.

- **An explanation of how Linux works** – While it's not necessary to delve into the most arcane aspects of the Linux kernel, it's a good idea to know something about how Linux is put together. This is particularly important if you've been working with other operating systems; some of the assumptions you hold about how computers work may not transfer from that operating system to Linux. A few paragraphs that discuss how Linux works (and particularly how it differs from the operating system you're used to), can be invaluable in getting off to a good start with your Red Hat Linux system.

- **An introductory command overview (with examples)** – This is probably the most important thing to look for in Linux documentation. The design philosophy behind Linux is that it's better to use many small commands connected together in different ways than it is to have a few large (and complex) commands that do the whole job themselves. Without some examples that illustrate the Linux approach to doing things, you will find yourself intimidated by the sheer number of commands available on your Red Hat Linux system.

As you gain more experience using your Red Hat Linux system, you'll probably find that you'll need more in-depth information. Continue reading the next section to find out more about the kinds of documentation that will help you at that point.

6.1.2 Documentation For More Experienced Linux Users

If you've used other Linux distributions, you probably already have a basic grasp of the most frequently used commands. You may have installed your own Linux system, and maybe you've even downloaded and built software you found on the Internet. What sorts of information will you need?

- **An extensive list of available commands** – While you can find this sort of information on-line in the man pages, you might also want it in book form. While there are several such books on the market, Red Hat sells the *Linux Complete Command Reference*. This book contains the man page entries for hundreds of commands, system calls and file formats, all formatted for easy reading. Best of all, there is a comprehensive index, and a searchable version of the book on CD-ROM. A book like this is invaluable for:
  - Finding the right command for a particular task.
  - Learning how to use that command properly.

- **Task-oriented information** – Many times, you'll find that you'd like to configure your Red Hat Linux system in a certain way, but you're not sure where to begin. In this case, it's often a big help to see what others in similar circumstances have done. This is where the Linux Documentation Project (also known as the LDP) can come in handy. Each of their HOWTOs document a particular aspect of Linux, from low-level kernel esoterica, to using Linux in an amateur radio station.

  If you selected one of the various howto packages when you installed Red Hat Linux, you'll find the HOWTOs on your system in /usr/doc/HOWTO. If, on the other hand, you'd like a printed version of these documents, Red Hat Software sells *Linux Undercover*, which is a compendium of the most popular LDP documents.

6.1.3 Documentation For Linux Gurus

If you're a long-time Red Hat Linux user, you probably already know that the following pretty much says it all when it comes to documentation:

Use the Force – Read the source!

There are times when you'll just have to sit there and look at the sources to understand things. Fortunately, because of the freely available nature of Linux, it's easy to get the sources. Now if it were only that easy to understand them...

Now that we've covered documentation, let's look at some of the most commonly-performed system tasks.

6.2 Basic System Tasks

Remember when everyone upgraded from Windows 3.1 to Windows 95? For a while, people scrambled to figure out how to do the same things under '95 that they had done for a years under 3.x. It's no different here. If you have experience with other operating systems, but not with Linux, you'll need to adjust to different ways of doing things. Some tasks may be similar, some may be entirely different, and some may have no equivalent to anything you've ever done before.

Let's start by going through a few of the more common tasks.

6.2.1 Booting Your Red Hat Linux System

The process required to get your computer running Red Hat Linux may vary a bit from what you're used to. If you have no other operating system installed on your computer, just apply power, and wait. You'll see the computer pause for a moment while it says something about "LILO", but it should continue, displaying all sorts of strange messages.

However, if you are sharing your computer between Red Hat Linux and another operating system, you may have one of the following tasks to perform:

- **Selecting Red Hat Linux at the LILO prompt** – If you elected to install LILO, and you entered boot labels for other partitions containing other operating systems, your computer will be configured to *dual boot*. This means that you can enter the name of the operating system you want to boot at the LILO Boot: prompt. If you press the (Tab) key at the LILO prompt, you'll see a list of the operating systems LILO can boot for you. Select the entry for your Red Hat Linux installation, and you're off and running!

- **Booting from a diskette** – If you created a boot diskette when you installed Red Hat Linux, you can boot from that to get Linux running. Make sure the diskette is inserted in your computer's first diskette drive, and start the boot sequence by applying power, pressing the reset button, or typing the (Ctrl), (Alt), and (Del) keys simultaneously.

6.2.2 Logging In, Logging Out

After Red Hat Linux boots, you'll see something similar to this on your screen:

```
Red Hat Linux release 5.1 (Manhattan)
Kernel 2.0.34 on an i586
login:
```

As you might guess from the last line, it's time to log in. . .

Logging In

The first time you log into your Red Hat Linux system, you'll have to log in as "root". This is the name of the user account that has full access to everything on the system. Normally, the root account is only used when performing system administration tasks, such as creating new user accounts, shutting down the system, etc. That's because root's unrestricted access can wreak havoc if you enter the wrong command. So be careful when logged in as root, and use the root account only when needed!

To log in, enter `root` at the `login:` prompt. Press the (Enter) (or (Return)) key. A `Password:` prompt should appear. Type the same password you entered back in Section 5.7 on page 73, pressing (Enter) when done. You should then see something like this:

```
[root@bigdog /root]#
```

Congratulations! You've successfully logged in! Next, it's time to learn how to log out.

Logging Out

When you're done using your Red Hat Linux system, you should log out. Although many shells have a `logout` command, most people simply type (Ctrl)-(D). This should return you to the login prompt you first saw when you booted your Red Hat Linux system.

Please Note: If you're using the X Window System, your log out procedure will be different, depending on how you've started X. We'll cover this in more detail later.

Now that you know how to log in and out, let's move on...

6.2.3 Accounts and Passwords

As we mentioned earlier, it's a bad idea to use the root account all the time. Inevitably, you'll end up making a mistake, and the access checks that normally protect you won't be there.

Well, if you're not supposed to log in as root, *who* exactly are you supposed to log in as?

Yourself, of course.

But to do that, you'll need to know how to add user accounts to your Red Hat Linux system.

Accounts

As it turns out, there are several different ways of creating new accounts. We'll use the most basic method; the useradd command. Basically, all you need to enter (as root, remember!) is:

```
[root@bigdog /root]# useradd blarg
[root@bigdog /root]#
```

That wasn't very exciting, was it? Well, let's try to login:

```
Red Hat Linux release 5.1 (Manhattan)
Kernel 2.0.34 on an i586
login: blarg
Password:
Login incorrect

login:
```

Not knowing what blarg's password was, we just pressed (Enter). Guess that wasn't the right password. Say, how *do* you specify a password for a new account?

Passwords

The passwd command can be used to:

- Specify passwords for newly-created user accounts.

- Change an already-existing account's password.

- Change the password of the account you're logged into.

The first two scenarios are really one and the same; there's really no difference (as far as passwd is concerned) between an account that's just be created, or one that has existed for the past five years. All you need to remember is that you must be logged in as root, and that you must specify the account name whose password you want to change. Using the account we just created as an example, let's give passwd a try:

```
[root@bigdog /root]# passwd blarg
New UNIX password:
Retype new UNIX password:
passwd: all authentication tokens updated successfully
[root@bigdog /root]#
```

As you might have guessed, the password is not displayed when you enter it. You also have to type the password twice, to make sure you didn't make a mistake while entering it. Let's try logging into the new account again:

```
Red Hat Linux release 5.1 (Manhattan)
Kernel 2.0.34 on an i586
login: blarg
Password:
[blarg@bigdog blarg]$
```

Once you're logged in to an account, you can change that account's password by using the passwd command without the account name. In this case, you will be asked for the account's current password, followed by the new password:

```
[blarg@bigdog blarg]$ passwd
Changing password for blarg
(current) UNIX password:
New UNIX password:
Retype new UNIX password:
passwd: all authentication tokens updated successfully
[blarg@bigdog blarg]$
```

It's as simple as that.

The su Command

There may be times when you'd like to issue a command or two as another user. Normally, system administrators need this capability – they (like all good sysadmins) use their personal, non-privileged account most of the time. But maybe a user's password needs to be changed, or the permissions on a system file need to be modified. Such things only take a minute, so it's a pain logging out, logging in as root, doing whatever it was they needed to do as root, logging out, and – finally – logging back into their personal accounts.

A much simpler approach is to use the su command. With su, your current login session can "become" a root (or other user's) login session. In the following example, user blarg decides they need to do something as root:

```
[blarg@bigdog blarg]$ su
Password:
[root@bigdog blarg]#
```

As you can see, after issuing the su command, the user is prompted for a password – the root password. After it's been entered correctly, the usual shell prompt is displayed. But if you look closely, you'll note that the shell prompt *is* different. For one, it starts with root, indicating that the current user has changed. The other difference is the prompt's ending character, which changed from a dollar sign ($) to a pound sign (#). This is a traditional way of indicating whether a shell is running as root or not.

It's also possible to use su to become another user. To do this, run su, giving only the user's account name. So, to become user blarg, one need only issue the command su blarg. If you ran su from your own account, you'll need to enter the other user's password (in our example, user blarg's password would be required). However, if you were already root, no password is required, as it would be somewhat redundant.

You'll find that su will come in handy, particularly if you, like most Linux users, act as your own system administrator.

6.2.4   Shutting Down Your Red Hat Linux System

When you're done using your Red Hat Linux system, you'll need to shut it down. However, this is a bit more involved than simply pressing the power switch. Here's why:

Even though *you* may not be running any programs when you're ready to shutdown, that doesn't mean there's nothing running on your Red Hat Linux system. To see what we mean, issue this command:

```
ps ax
```

Each one of the lines displayed by ps represents a *process*. You can think of each process as being a "running program". Each process may be working with files, and if you simply turn off your computer, these processes won't have a chance to close those files, and finish running in a clean manner. So when the time comes to shut your system down, you'll need some way of telling all these processes to finish up, and exit cleanly. And the way this is normally done is with the shutdown command.

The shutdown command can only be run by root, so you'll need to either be logged in as root, or you can use the su command to "become" root. The basic syntax for shutdown is:

```
shutdown <options> <time>
```

Please Note: The shutdown program resides in /sbin. If your PATH environment variable does not include /sbin, you will need to include the full path when you enter the command (i.e.,
/sbin/shutdown -h now).

In most cases, you should include one of the following options:

* -h – Halt the system when the shutdown is complete.

- -r – Reboot the system when the shutdown is complete.

If you don't include either option, shutdown will bring your system into "single user" mode. Unless you know why you want to be in single-user mode, you probably don't want to be in single-user mode. Simply enter the shutdown command (this time with -h or -r), and the shutdown will complete normally.

The shutdown command also gives you quite a bit of flexibility in terms of timing. If you want the shutdown to proceed right away, just enter the word "now". If you want to shut the system down five minutes from now, you can enter "+5". Therefore, this command:

```
shutdown -r +15
```

means, "shut the system down starting fifteen minutes from now, and reboot after the shutdown has completed". While shutdown has more options available, we've only described the basics necessary to perform a clean shutdown. If you're interested in learning more, enter man shutdown to learn more about shutdown's capabilities.

6.3   The X Window System

While there are people that will use the character-cell interface present when you first log in, many people prefer a graphically-oriented user interface. For Linux systems, the graphical user interface of choice is the X Window System.

In order to run X, you need to have the necessary packages installed. If you selected the "X Window System" component to be installed when you originally installed Red Hat Linux, everything should be ready to go. In that case, please refer to section 6.3.2 on page 91.

6.3.1   If You Haven't Installed X

If you didn't select the "X Window System" component when you installed Red Hat Linux, your Red Hat Linux system won't have the necessary software installed. While it is possible to manually install the required packages, you'll probably find it easier to re-do the installation, particularly if you're new to Linux.

XFree86 Configuration

There are three methods for configuring XFree86 on your machine:

- Xconfigurator
- xf86config

- by hand

Xconfigurator and xf86config are functional equivalents and should work equally well. If you are unsure of anything in this process, a good source of additional documentation is:

      http://www.xfree86.org

Xconfigurator is a full-screen menu driven program that walks you through setting up your X server. xf86config is a line oriented program distributed with XFree86. It isn't as easy to use as Xconfigurator, but it is included for completeness. If these utilities fail to provide a working XF86Config file, you may have an unsupported card or you may need to write the config file by hand. Usually the former is the case, so check and make sure your card is supported before attempting to write the config file yourself.If your card is not supported by XFree86 you may wish to consider using a commercial X server. If you have questions about whether or not your video card is supported you can check out http://www.xfree86.org for information on XFree86.

The X Server   Provided you selected the proper video card at install time, you should have the proper X server installed. When later running Xconfigurator or xf86config, you need to make sure you select the same video card or the autoprobe will fail.

If you think you installed the wrong X server for your video card, you will have to install the correct one before it can be configured. For instance, if the CD is mounted on /mnt/cdrom, and you need to install the S3 server, enter the following commands:

```
cd /mnt/cdrom/RedHat/RPMS
rpm -ivh XFree86-S3-3.1.2-1.i386.rpm
ln -sf ../../usr/X11R6/bin/XF86_S3 /etc/X11/X
```

This will install the S3 server and make the proper symbolic link.

Xconfigurator   To configure X Windows you must first select your video card. Scroll down the list of supported cards until you locate the card in your machine. Figure 6.1 may help you determine the video server that matches your hardware. If your card is not listed it may not be supported by XFree86.In this case you can try the last card entry on the list (Unlisted Card) or a commercial X Windows server.

The next step is to select your monitor. If your monitor is not listed you can select one of the generic monitor entries or "Custom" and enter your own parameters. Custom monitor configuration is recommended only for those who have a sound understanding of the inner workings of CRT displays. The average user should probably use one of the generic selections from the list. After selecting a monitor you need to tell Xconfigurator how much video memory you have. Move the high-light to the appropriate list entry and then press (Enter) or (F12) to continue. For the next step it is recommended that you select the default (No Clockchip Setting) entry, but experienced users may want to select a specific clockchip.

Selecting your Server If you are unsure what chipset you have, the best way to find out is usually to look at the card. Figure 6.1 lists which chipsets and boards require which servers. Pick the one that best matches your hardware.

Server	Chipset
8514	IBM 8514/A Boards and true clones
AGX	All XGA graphics boards
I128	#9 Imagine 128 (including Series II) boards
Mach32	ATI boards using the Mach32 chipset
Mach64	ATI boards using the Mach64 chipset
Mach8	ATI boards using the Mach8 chipset
Mono	VGA boards in monochrome
P9000	Diamond Viper (but not the 9100) and Others
S3	#9 Boards, most Diamonds, some Orchids, Others
S3V	Boards using the S3 ViRGE (including DX, GX, VX) chipset
SVGA	Tridents, Cirrus Logic, C & T, ET4000, S3 ViRGE, Others
VGA16	All VGA boards (16 color only)
W32	All ET4000/W32 cards, but not standard ET4000's

Figure 6.1: XFree86 X Servers

Finishing Up If later you want to increase your refresh rate for your monitor, you can edit the config file by hand or you can run Xconfigurator again and pick a monitor from our list that more closely matches the specs of your monitor.

The final configuration step consists of selecting the video modes that you want to include in your XF86Config file. Use the arrow keys to move the cursor up and down the list under each color depth (8, 16 and 24 bit). Use the (Spacebar) to select individual resolutions and the (Tab) key to move between color depth fields. When you have selected the video modes you want to use move the cursor to the "OK" button and press (Enter), or use the (F12) shortcut. An information screen will give you the most current information on selecting video modes, starting and stopping the X server.

6.3.2 If You've Already Installed X

If you selected the "X Window System" component when you installed Red Hat Linux, you should be all set. All you'll need to do is to get X running. As it turns out, there are two ways to do this. You can:

- Start X manually after you log in.

- Start X automatically whenever the system boots.

Let's start with the manual procedure.

Starting X Manually

Red Hat Linux, as installed, will not start X automatically for you. Therefore, you'll see the same character-cell login prompt you saw when you first booted your Red Hat Linux system.

In order to get X started, you'll first need to log in. Do so (using your non-root account), and then enter the `startx` command. The screen should go blank, and (after a short delay) you should see a graphical desktop with one or more windows. The appearance of the desktop you'll see will vary, depending on the packages you installed and other variables.

When you're done, and you'd like to leave X, you can click on any part of the desktop (in other words, the part of the screen without any windows) using your mouse's primary button. Select the "Exit Fvwm", "Quit", or "logout" menu entry, and X will shut down, leaving you at your original character-cell shell prompt. You can then logout as usual.

Starting X Automatically

Please Note: Make sure you verify that your X configuration works properly before making X start automatically. Failure to do so can make it difficult to log into your Red Hat Linux system. If you haven't done so already, review the previous section before continuing.

It is possible to configure your Red Hat Linux system such that X will start automatically whenever the system is booted. When configured in this manner, `xdm` will run, which will present a graphically-oriented login screen. After logging in, you will have a regular X session running, just as if you had issued a `startx` command manually. Pretty neat, eh?

Here's a quick overview of how it's done:

- Test `xdm` using `telinit`.

- Edit `/etc/inittab`.

- Reboot.

Let's look at each step in more detail.

Testing xdm **Using** telinit – The telinit command is used to change your Red Hat Linux system's "run level". It is the run level that controls various aspects of system operation, including whether xdm should be started or not. Newly-installed Red Hat Linux systems use run level 3 as their default; this results in the character-cell login prompt you've seen. Since xdm is started at run level 5, you'll need to issue the command:

```
/sbin/telinit 5
```

Please Note: You will need to be logged in as root in order to use telinit. Also note that you should *not* be running anything else on your Red Hat Linux system when you change run levels, as any running programs may be killed by the run level change.

If everything is configured properly, after a short delay you should see an xdm login screen. Log in, verifying that an X desktop appears. Then log out to make sure that xdm reappears. If it does, your system is configured properly to automatically start X. If there are problems, you can go back to run level 3 using telinit (ie, "/sbin/telinit 3"), or by rebooting.

Editing /etc/inittab – The file /etc/inittab is used to, among other things, determine the system's default run level. We need to change the default run level from 3 to 5; therefore, we'll need to edit /etc/inittab. Using the text editor of your choice, change this line in /etc/inittab:

```
id:3:initdefault:
```

When you're done, it should look like this:

```
id:5:initdefault:
```

Please Note: Make sure you change *only* the number 3 to be 5! Do not change anything else, otherwise your Red Hat Linux system may not boot at all! When you've made the change, exit the editor, and use this command to review your handiwork:

```
less /etc/inittab
```

(Press the [Space] key to page through the file; [Q] will exit.) If everything looks OK, it's time to reboot.

Rebooting – Refer to Section 6.2.4 on page 88 to properly reboot your Red Hat Linux system. Congratulations! You're now fully graphical (well, your system is, at least)...

Changing Your Desktop

Thanks to wmconfig, it's easy to change the appearance of your desktop. Simply select the **Preferences** menu entry, and (under **WM Style**) you'll be able to pick from several different desktop (also known as window manager) styles. If you want to learn more about the nuts and bolts behind the scenes, read the wmconfig man page for more information.

Virtual Consoles and X

Note that even if you're running X, you still have access to the regular character-cell user interface. That's because Red Hat Linux uses *virtual consoles* while X is running. To switch to a virtual console, press [Ctrl]-[Alt]-[Fn], where [Fn] is any one of the first six function keys. When switching virtual consoles, you should see a standard login prompt; at this point you can login and use the system normally on any (or all) of the virtual consoles.

When you'd like to go back to your X session, simply press [Ctrl]-[Alt]-[F7].

Please Note: Some people remap keys under X; if you do this, be aware that your X keyboard mappings will only be active when in X. This can be confusing if, for example, you've swapped the [Ctrl] and [Caps Lock] keys under X, as you will have to use two different keystrokes to switch between X and non-X virtual consoles.

Handy X-Based Tools

There are several tools that can make life easier for the new Red Hat Linux user. They perform tasks that either require root access, or can only be done by memorizing arcane commands. They all require X to run, so you'll need to get that set up first. These tools are:

- **User Information Tool** – Makes it easy to update your "gecos", or basic account information. Run /usr/bin/userinfo to start it.

- **User Password Tool** – Changing passwords is simple with this tool. It's started by running /usr/bin/userpasswd

- **Filesystem Mounting Tool** – Makes mounting and unmounting filesystems simple. Every user-mountable filesystem must have the user option present in /etc/fstab (see the mount man page for more information on the user option). Run /usr/bin/usermount to start it.

- **Network Device Tool** – Starting and stopping network interfaces becomes a point-and-click operation with this tool. Run /usr/bin/usernet to start this tool. Requires that every interface to be controlled by usernet is configured to be "user-controllable" This can be done by using netcfg, and selecting the interface's **Allow any user to (de)activate interface** checkbox.

6.4   Configuring Your Red Hat Linux System For Sound

By default, the only sound you'll hear out of your newly-installed Red Hat Linux system is the ordinary, boring, default beep. If your computer system has sound hardware, chances are you can make it work under Red Hat Linux. In some cases (particularly with non-Intel systems) sucessfully getting sound support to work requires a kernel rebuild. However, most of the time it's possible to use the modular sound drivers.

6.4.1   Modular Sound Drivers

Red Hat Linux 5.2 includes modular versions of the standard OSS/Free sound drivers. This makes it possible to load and unload the various sound drivers without recompiling the kernel or rebooting.

For additional information, please consult the README files in the `rhsound` documentation directory (`/usr/doc/rhsound*`). The latest information can always be found at `ftp://ftp.redhat.com/pub/sound/`.

If you have any issues concerning the modular sound drivers, please send mail to `sound-bugs@redhat.com`. There is also a mailing list associated with the modular sound drivers (`sound-list@redhat.com`). To subscribe, send mail to `sound-list-request@redhat.com` with "subscribe" as the subject line.

Recognized Sound Cards

At this point, most sound cards should be recognized by the modular sound drivers; however, drivers for the following sound cards were among the first to be developed, and as such, have received the most testing:

- Sound Blaster 1.0
- Sound Blaster 2.0
- Sound Blaster Pro
- Sound Blaster 16
- Sound Blaster 16 PnP
- Sound Blaster AWE32/AWE64

6.4.2   Sound Card Configuration Tool

Also included in Red Hat Linux 5.2 is `sndconfig`, a screen-oriented utility that can properly configure modular sound card drivers.

There are a few things that you should know about `sndconfig`:

Plug and Play Aware – `sndconfig` is able to detect and automatically configure Plug and Play sound cards such as the Sound Blaster 16 PnP. The configuration information is stored in the `/etc/isapnp.conf` file, along with the configuration information for any other Plug and Play devices. In order to ensure that no configuration will be lost, `sndconfig` saves your original `/etc/isapnp.conf` file as `/etc/isapnp.conf.bak`.

Modifies `/etc/conf.modules` – `sndconfig` modifies the module configuration file
`/etc/conf.modules` by adding information about the module options required for your sound card. Note that `sndconfig` saves your original `/etc/conf.modules` file as
`/etc/conf.modules.bak`.

To set up your sound card, run `/usr/sbin/sndconfig`. Note that you must be root in order to run `sndconfig`. If your system contains a Plug and Play sound card, `sndconfig` will identify it, and configure it appropriately.

If you do not want `sndconfig` to probe for Plug and Play sound cards, run `sndconfig` with the `--noprobe` option. It is also possible to manually specify the settings for your sound card; to do so, run `sndconfig` with the `--noautoconfig` option.

If `sndconfig` cannot automatically identify your system's sound card (or you ran `sndconfig` with the `--noprobe` option), you'll be asked to select the type of sound card you have (See Figure 6.2). Use the ⬆ and ⬇ keys to scroll through the different cards listed, and position the highlight on the entry that matches your system's sound card.

Figure 6.2: Selecting Sound Card Type

If you've run `sndconfig` with the `--noautoconfig` option, you'll see a screen similar to the one in Figure 6.3. Here is where you can specify the settings for your sound card. Using the (Tab) key, select a field. Then use the arrow keys to select the desired setting for that field. When finished, select **Ok**, and press (Space).

Figure 6.3: Configuring Sound Card

After this screen, you may see an informational dialog box saying that `/etc/conf.modules` already exists. select **Ok** and press (Space) to continue.

Finally, `sndconfig` will attempt to play a sound sample to verify proper config-uration of your sound card. If you can hear the sound sample (make sure the speaker volume is turned up), you're done!

6.5   Mouse configuration

To configure your mouse (or reconfigure your mouse after installation) enter the command
`/usr/sbin/mouseconfig`. You will be presented with the same interface used during the Red Hat Linux installation process; please turn to Section 5.1 on page 63 for more details.

6.6   World Wide Web

The World Wide Web is one of the hottest aspects of the Internet today. Red Hat Linux lets you get in on the action in two ways – as a web browser, and as a web server. Let's look at both.

6.6.1   World Wide Web Browsers

A variety of web browsers are available for Linux, including freely distributable browsers such as arena, lynx, and grail. The most popular commercial browsers are those from Netscape Communications Corporation. And now they're available with Red Hat Linux 5.2! If you selected the netscape-communicator or netscape-navigator packages, you're ready to surf. Enjoy!

6.6.2   World Wide Web Server

If you installed the Apache web server (from the apache package), then your Web service is already up and running! Just point your web browser at http://localhos

The default page shown is /home/httpd/html/index.html. You can edit this file (or completely replace it) to your liking. All the CGI programs, icons, and html pages are stored in /home/httpd, but this can be changed in the apache configuration files, all of which are stored in /etc/httpd/conf/. Logs of all httpd activity are kept in /var/log/httpd/. Setting up your web site is as easy as adding your own HTML pages and links to the /home/httpd/html/ directory. For more information on customizing your web server we recommend a reference such as *HTML: The Definitive Guide* by Chuck Musciano & Bill Kennedy, published by O'Reilly & Associates.

7

Finding Documentation

Red Hat Linux includes thousands of pages of online documentation to help you learn how to use the system. The man pages, info documents, and plain text files included provide information on almost every aspect of Linux. If you've installed it, Red Hat Linux also includes documentation produced by the Linux Documentation Project.

7.1 On Line Help

When you are looking for general help on commands and error messages, the best place to start is right on your system. There are several different sources of information at your fingertips:

- **Man Pages** – Authoritative reference material for commands, file formats, and system calls.

- **Package Documentation** – Many packages include additional documentation; RPM can help you find it.

- **HOWTOs and FAQs** – Helpful information from the Linux Documentation Project.

- **The** `locate` **Command** – A command that can help bridge the gap between a command and its documentation.

- `info` **Pages** – Hypertext documentation without the Web.

Let's take a look at each information source.

7.1.1   Man Pages

Almost every command on your system has an associated "man" page. This is documentation that you can get to instantly should you have questions or problems. For example, if you were having trouble with the ls command, you could use man to get more information by entering man ls. This will bring up the man page for ls.

The man page is viewed through the less program (which makes it easy to page forward and backward screen by screen), so all of the options to less will work while in a man page. The more important keystrokes for less are:

- q to quit

- Enter to page down line by line

- Space to page down page by page

- b to page back up by one page

- / followed by a string and Enter to search for a string

- n to find the next occurrence of the previous search

There are times when it's just a lot more convenient to read something from a sheet of paper. Providing you have a working printer, you can print man pages as well. If you don't have Postscript printing capability and just want to print ASCII, you can print man pages with:

```
man COMMAND | lpr
```

If you do have a postscript printer, you will probably want to print with:

```
man -t COMMAND | lpr
```

In both of those commands substitute "COMMAND" for the command you are trying to get help for.

Sometimes you'll find that certain system components have more than one man page. Here is a table showing the sections that are used to divide man pages:

Section	Contents
1	user commands
8	system commands
2	system calls
3	library calls
4	devices
5	file formats
6	games
7	miscellaneous
9	kernel internals
n	Tcl/Tk commands

This is also the order in which the sections are searched. This can be important; here's an example:

Let's say that you want to see the man page for the swapon system call. So, you type man swapon. You will actually get the man page for swapon(8), which is actually the command used to control swapping. Using the chart above, you can see that what you want is a "system call" and is located in section 2. You can then type man 2 swapon. All of this is because man searches the man directories in the order shown above, which means that the swapon(8) man page would be found before the swapon(2) man page.

You can also search the man pages for strings. You do this using man -k string_to_search_for. This won't work, however, unless the make-whatis database has been created. Under Red Hat Linux, this is done by a cron job overnight. If you don't leave your system running overnight the database won't get created. If that is the case, run the following command as the root user:

```
/etc/cron.weekly/makewhatis.cron
```

Once you've done that (note that it might take a while), you could enter man -k swapon. That command would return:

```
# man -k swapon
swapon, swapoff (2) - start/stop swapping to file/device
swapon, swapoff (8) - enable/disable devices and files
                      for paging and swapping
```

So you can see that there are pages in section 2 and 8 both referring to swapon (and swapoff in this case).

How to Read a Man Page

Man pages provide a great deal of information in very little space. Because of this, they can be difficult to read. Here's a quick overview of the major sections in most man pages:

- **Name** – The name of the program or programs documented in the man page. There may be more than one name, if the programs are closely related.

- **Synopsis** – An overview of the program's command syntax, showing all options and arguments.

- **Description** – A short description of the program's function.

- **Options** – A list of all options, with a short description of each (often combined with the previous section).

- **See Also** – If present, lists the names of other programs that are related in some way to this program.

- **Files** – If present, contains a list of files that are used and/or modified by the program.

- **History** – If present, indicates important milestones in the program's development.

- **Authors** – The people that wrote the program.

If you are new to Linux, don't expect to be able to use man pages as tutorials; they are meant as concise reference material. Trying to learn about Linux using the man pages is similar to trying to learn how to speak English from reading a dictionary. But there are other sources of information that may be more useful to those people just starting out with Linux; let's continue our search for documentation…

7.1.2 Package Documentation

Many packages have README files and other documentation as part of the source package. Packages built for Red Hat Linux define a standard place to install those documents so that you don't have to search through the sources to find the documents. Every package containing documentation (other than man pages, and files that need to be in specific locations) places their documentation in a subdirectory of /usr/doc.

The name of the subdirectory depends on the package name and version number. For example, For example, the tin package might be at version 1.22. Therefore, the path to its documentation would be /usr/doc/tin-1.22.

For the most part, the documents in /usr/doc are in ASCII. You can view them with more *filename* or less *filename*.

Having this special documentation area can be handy, but what if you're looking for documentation on a specific command (or file), and you don't know what package that command came from? No problem! Take, for example, the file /usr/bin/rtin. You're not sure what package it's part of, but you'd like to learn a bit more about it. Simply enter:

```
rpm -qdf /usr/bin/rtin
```

This command will return a listing of all the documentation (including man pages) from the package containing the file /usr/bin/rtin. RPM is capable of a lot more than this simple example. For more information on RPM, turn to Chapter 9 on page 161.

Of course, maybe this kind of information is not exactly what you're looking for. Maybe you're more interested in task-oriented documentation. If so, read on...

7.1.3   HOWTOs and FAQs

If you elected to install it, most of the contents of the Linux Documentation Project (LDP) are available in /usr/doc on your system.

The directory /usr/doc/HOWTO contains the ASCII versions of all the available HOWTOs at the time your Red Hat Linux CD-ROM was mastered. They are compressed with gzip to save space, so you'll need to decompress them before reading. One way of reading compressed HOWTOs without cluttering your disk with uncompressed versions is to use zless:

```
zless 3Dfx-HOWTO.gz
```

The zless command uses the same keystrokes as less, so you can easily move back and forth through a HOWTO.

/usr/doc/HOWTO/mini contains the ASCII versions of all the available mini-HOWTOs. They are not compressed and can be viewed with more or less. /usr/doc/HOWTO/other-formats/html contains the HTML versions of all the HOWTOs and the *Linux Installation and Getting Started* guide. To view things here, just use the web browser of your choice.

/usr/doc/FAQ contains ASCII versions (and some HTML versions) of some popular FAQs, including the RedHat-FAQ. They can be viewed using more or less, or (in the case of HTML files) with the web browser of your choice.

7.1.4   The "locate" Command

When you don't know the full name of a command or file, but need to find it, you can usually find it with locate. locate uses a database to find all files on your system. Normally, this database gets built from a cron job every night. This won't happen, however, if your machine isn't booted into Linux all the time. So, if that is the case, you may occasionally want to run the following command:

```
/etc/cron.daily/updatedb.cron
```

You will need to be root on your system when doing that. That will allow locate to work properly.

So, if you know you need to find all the "finger" files, you could run:

```
locate finger
```

It should return something like:

```
/usr/bin/finger
/usr/lib/irc/script/finger
/usr/man/man1/finger.1
/usr/man/man8/in.fingerd.8
/usr/sbin/in.fingerd
```

One thing to note, however, is that `locate` not only returns hits based on file name, but also on path name. So if you have a `/home/djb/finger/` directory on your system, it would get returned along with all files in the directory.

7.1.5 "info" Pages

While man is the most ubiquitous documentation format, `info` is much more powerful. It provides hypertext links to make reading large documents much easier and many features for the documentation writer. There are some very complete `info` documents on various aspects of Red Hat (especially the portions from the GNU project).

To read `info` documentation, use the `info` program without any arguments. It will present you with a list of available documentation. If it can't find something, it's probably because you don't have the package installed that includes that documentation. Install it with RPM and try again.

If you're comfortable using emacs, it has a built in browser for `info` documentation. Use the [Ctrl-h] [i] key sequence to see it.

The `info` system is a hypertext based system. Any highlighted text that appears is a link leading to more information. Use [Tab] to move the cursor to the link, and press [Enter] to follow the link. Pressing [p] returns you to the previous page, [n] moves you to the next page, and [u] goes up one level of documentation. To exit `info`, press [Ctrl-x] [Ctrl-c] (control-x followed by control-c).

The best way to learn how to use `info` is to read the info documentation on it. If you read the first screen that `info` presents you'll be able to get started.

7.2 Help from the Internet Community

7.2.1 Red Hat Mailing Lists

If you can't find help for your problem on line and you have WWW access, you should see
`http://www.redhat.com/support/mailing-lists/`. Here you can search the archives of the redhat-list. Many questions have already been answered there.

The subscription addresses for our lists follow this format:

```
<list-name>-request@redhat.com
```

Simply replace <list-name> with one of the following:

```
applixware-list
axp-list
blinux-list
cde-list
gnome-announce
gtk-list
hurricane-list
linux-alert
linux-security
m68k-list
pam-list
redhat-announce-list
redhat-devel-list
redhat-install-list
redhat-list
redhat-ppp-list
rpm-list
sound-list
sparc-list
```

To subscribe, send mail to the address of the list you want to subscribe to with subscribe in the Subject: line.

To unsubscribe, send mail to the address of the list you want to unsubscribe from with
unsubscribe in the Subject: line.

Then to send mail to the list, you just send it to the address above without the -request in the name.

7.2.2   USENET Newsgroups

Another good source of help is the comp.os.linux hierarchy on USENET. If you are familiar with news, you should check it out.

Red Hat-Specific Newsgroups

Red Hat Software currently hosts a number of newgroups specifically for users of our software. You can either read these groups directly from news.redhat.com, or ask your news admin to add the redhat.* hierarchy to their news server.

8

System Configuration

After installing your Red Hat Linux system, it's easy to think that the decisions you made during the installation are engraved in granite, never to be changed again. Nothing could be further from the truth!

One of the main strengths of Linux is that the operating system can be configured to do just about anything. Here at Red Hat Software, we've worked hard to try to make system configuration as easy and accessible as possible. To that end, we've worked hard on two fronts:

- By developing system configuration tools in-house.

- By working with outside developers of world-class system configuration tools.

Anyone familiar with Red Hat Linux over the years has probably seen what we call our "control panel" system configuration tools. These tools have been developed by Red Hat Software to make system configuration easier. And while these tools *do* make life easier for the Red Hat Linux user, we began a search for a system configuration tool with even more flexibility and power.

Our search ended with the inclusion of linuxconf into Red Hat Linux 5.1 in June of 1998. Now, with this version of Red Hat Linux, we've been able to more fully document the more popular aspects of system configuration using linuxconf.

Note that we said "more popular aspects". One of linuxconf's greatest strengths – the incredible range of configuration options under its control – is actually a liability when it comes time to document them all. Rest assured however, that we will continue to expand linuxconf documentation as new versions of Red Hat Linux are released.

But what about the control panel tools? They're still there. While linuxconf at present can do nearly everything the control panel tools can, there are two areas in which the control panel still holds the upper hand:

- Printer configuration

- Kernel daemon control

To that end, we've left the control panel documentation in this manual as the second half of this chapter.

But now, let's take a look at linuxconf...

8.1   System Configuration With Linuxconf

Linuxconf is a utility that allows you to configure and control various aspects of your system, and is capable of handling a wide range of programs and tasks. Fully documenting linuxconf could be a separate book in its own right and certainly more than we can cover in this chapter. So we'll focus on those areas that address common tasks such as adding new users and getting connected to the network.

More information on linuxconf, including its status, most recent release, and more can be found at the Linuxconf Project homepage (shown in Figure 8.1 on the facing page):

```
http://www.solucorp.qc.ca/linuxconf/
```

This website includes fairly extensive information on linuxconf including description, rationale, history, list of contacts and a lot of other information in addition to the software itself. It is maintained by linuxconf's creator, Jacques Gelinas, so it's the best source of linuxconf information on the Internet.

Notation

Accurately describing the location of specific screens within linuxconf is easy, but lengthy given linuxconf's hierarchical nature. If the structure was a family tree, most of the data entry screens are in the fourth generation. To describe the path to the screen where you would add new users to your system, we could write this out as:

> "select the Config option from the main screen, then the users accounts option off of that; on the users accounts screen that appears, select the normal option and then select the user accounts option."

Rather lengthy and not immediately accessible. Given the structural similarity to a family tree, we could write it as

Figure 8.1: Linuxconf Project Homepage

"main window beget Users accounts tab, beget Normal tab..."

But that's an awful lot of begets. Instead, we'll use the following format:

Config ⇒ Users accounts ⇒ Normal ⇒ User accounts

It's much more concise and clear. It assumes as its base the linuxconf entry screen. The other advantage to this approach is that it's not interface specific, so regardless of which interface you're using, you know exactly where the information is. You're happy, we're happy, and the trees who lobbied against lengthy descriptions are happy. What could be better?

8.1.1 Running Linuxconf

To run linuxconf you must have root access. If you are logged in as something other than root, there are two easy ways to handle this situation. The first is to run Linuxconf by typing `linuxconf`. Linuxconf will then prompt you for root's password (see figure 8.2 on the next page).

The other option is to use the `su` command to become root. In case you aren't familiar with it yet, type `su` at the shell prompt and hit Enter. The password it asks you for is the root account's. Once you've entered that correctly you'll have phenomenal cosmic power! Well, complete control of your system at any rate[1]. Anyway, type `linuxconf` at the shell prompt to begin the program. Linuxconf has the following user interfaces:

---

[1]One could argue that it's pretty much the same thing.

Figure 8.2: root Access Verification Screen

- **Command line** – Linuxconf's command-line mode is handy for manipulating your system's configuration in scripts.

- **Character-Cell** – Using the same user interface style as the Red Hat Linux installation program, the character-cell interface makes it easy to navigate your way through linuxconf, even if you aren't running X.

- **X Window-Based** – Linuxconf can take advantage of X, and give you an easy-to-use "point and click" tree menu interface. This form of navigation is new in Linuxconf! Please see the **Tree Menu Interface** subsection of section 8.1.1 for more information. This is the interface we'll use for illustrations throughout this chapter.

- **Web-Based** – A web-based interface makes remote system administration a breeze. The web interface will even play nice with the Lynx character-cell web browser!

Linuxconf will normally start in either character-cell or X mode, depending on the DISPLAY environment variable. The first time you run linuxconf, an introductory message will be displayed; although it is only displayed once, accessing help from the main screen will give you the same basic information.

Linuxconf has context-specific help available. For information on any specific aspect of linuxconf, please select **Help** from the screen you'd like help with. Note that not all help screens are complete at this time; as help screens are updated, they will be included in subsequent versions of linuxconf.

Tree Menu Interface

The new version of Linuxconf comes complete with a tree menu interface.

Finding the appropriate panel should be simple and fast! You can collapse and expand sections by clicking on the menu item icons. Click the icon once to activate it for that particular sub-menu. A single click will then collapse it; another single click will expand it again.

Selected entries will appear as tabs in the right-hand panel and will remain there until closed. This will greatly reduce the clutter of windows on your desktop that

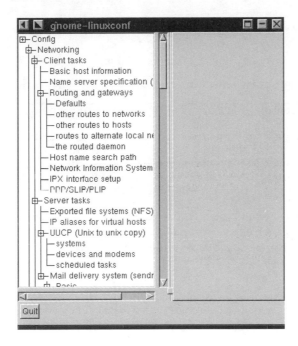

Figure 8.3: Linuxconf Entry Screen

Linuxconf has typically caused. If you end up with more tabs open than you like, just hit **Cancel** on the bottom of each tab to close it without making any changes, or **Accept** to implement them.

Please Note: If you've grown fond of the previous X Windows interface, it's still available. To return to it:

1. Start Linuxconf by typing `linuxconf` at the shell prompt

2. Enter root's password when prompted (if not already root)

3. Open [Control] ⇒ [Control files and systems] ⇒ [Linuxconf modules]

4. De-select the **This module is active** checkbox for the **treemenu** module.

5. Click **Accept**

6. Click **Quit**

7. Restart Linuxconf

Enabling Web-Based Linuxconf Access

For security reasons, web-based access to linuxconf is disabled by default. Before attempting to access linuxconf with a web browser, you'll need to enable access.

Here's how to do it from the text-mode interface:

1. Start Linuxconf by typing `linuxconf` at the shell prompt

2. Enter root's password when prompted (if not already root)

3. Open [Config] ⇒ [Networking] ⇒ [Misc] ⇒ [Linuxconf network access]

4. In the **Linuxconf html access control** dialog box, enter the hostname of any computers that should be allowed access to linuxconf. This would also include your own system, if you wish to use the web-based interface locally. Web accesses related to linuxconf may be logged to your system's `htmlaccess.log` file by selecting the check box shown.

5. Select the **Accept** button and press [Space]. Then select the **Quit** buttons on each dialog box to back out of the menu hierarchy. When you come to a dialog box labelled **Status of the system**, press [Enter] to take the default action, which is to apply the changes you've made.

At this point, web-based access has been enabled. To test it out, go to one of the systems that you added to the access control list. Launch your web browser, and enter the following URL:

```
http://<host>:98/
```

(Replacing `<host>` with your system's hostname, of course.) You should see the main linuxconf page. Note that you will need to enter your system's root password to gain access beyond the first page.

Adding a User Account – Quick Reference

1. Start Linuxconf by typing `linuxconf` at the shell prompt

2. Enter root's password when prompted (if not already root)

3. Open [Config] ⇒ [Users accounts] ⇒ [Normal] ⇒ [User accounts]

4. Select **Add**

5. Enter the account's login and full names

6. Enter information in other fields only as necessary

7. Select **Accept**

8. Enter the initial password for the account

9. Reenter the initial password for the account in the **Confirmation** field

10. Select **Accept**

Adding a User Account – General Overview

Adding a user is one of the most basic tasks you will encounter in administering your system. To add a user:

- Start Linuxconf by typing `linuxconf` at the shell prompt

- Enter root's password when prompted (if not already root)

- Open [Config] ⇒ [Users accounts] ⇒ [Normal] ⇒ [User accounts] This will open the **Users accounts** tab (see figure 8.5 on the next page).

- If you have more than 15 accounts on the system, Linuxconf will provide you with a filter screen (see figure 8.4). You can use this to select a smaller range of accounts than the full list. To get the full list, select **Accept** without changing any of the parameters. For detailed information on the various filters, select the **Help** button on the **Filter control** screen.

- Select **Add**. This will open the **User account creation** tab (see figure 8.6 on page 115).

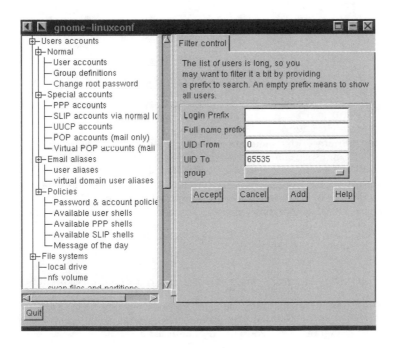

Figure 8.4: Filter Control Screen

The **User account creation** tab is where you enter all the information on the new account. There are a number of fields you should be aware of, some required, some optional.

Figure 8.5: Users Accounts Screen

Required Fields:

- **Login name** – the name of the account. Usually all lowercase letters. First or last names, initials or some combination thereof are fairly common login names. For a user named John T. Smith, "smith", "john", "jts", or "jsmith" would be common user names. Of course "spike" or something else works just fine, too. You can also use numbers so "jts2" would be fine if you had a second person with the same initials. There is no default for this field.

Optional Fields:

- **Full name** – this is the name of the user or the account. For an individual, it would be their name, "John T. Smith" for example. If the account represents a position rather than a person, the full name might be the title. So an account called "webmaster" might have a full name of "Red Hat Webmaster" or just "Webmaster". There is no default for this field.

- **group** – here you can specify the group associated with the account. The default is a group that's the same as the login name. So "jsmith" would have the group "jsmith".

- **Supplementary groups** – here is where you can specify any additional groups. We suggest that if you want to add a user to a group or groups, you

Figure 8.6: User account creation

do so here, rather than changing the **group** field. Group names should be separated by spaces. The default for this field is blank, meaning no supplementary groups.

- **Home directory** – specifies the home or login directory for the account. The default is /home/*login*, where *login* is replaced by the login name. A home directory is your starting point in the directory structure when you log in, or if in X, for each xterm window opened. This is also where account specific preference files are stored.

- **Command interpreter** – specifies the location of the command interpreter. Command interpreters are usually referred to as shells. The default is displayed in the drop down box.

- **User ID** – the number associated with each user account. This is automatically generated by the system when the account is created.

The **User account creation** screen has a number of fields; only the login name is required, though filling in the **Full name** field is strongly recommended. Once you have entered the login name and any other desired information select the **Accept** button at the bottom of the screen. If you decide against creating a new user, hit **Cancel** instead.

Upon hitting **Accept** linuxconf will prompt you to enter the password. There is also a field called **Confirmation** where you will need to type the password again.

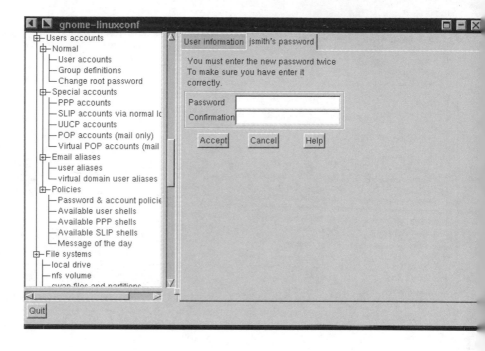

Figure 8.7: Change Password Screen

This is to prevent you from mistyping the password. Passwords must be at least 6 characters in length. They may contain numbers as well as a mix of lowercase and uppercase letters. Hit **Accept** when finished.

Modifying a User Account – Quick Reference

1. Start Linuxconf by typing `linuxconf` at the shell prompt

2. Enter root's password when prompted (if not already root)

3. Open (Config) ⇒ (Users accounts) ⇒ (Normal) ⇒ (User accounts)

4. Select the user account

5. Modify entries as desired

6. Select **Accept**

Modifying a User Account – General Overview

- Start Linuxconf by typing `linuxconf` at the shell prompt

- Enter root's password when prompted (if not already root)

- Open [Config] ⇒ [Users accounts] ⇒ [Normal] ⇒ [User accounts] This will open the **Users accounts** tab (see figure 8.5 on page 114).

- If you have more than 15 accounts on the system, Linuxconf will provide you with a filter screen (see figure 8.4 on page 113). You can use this to select a smaller range of accounts than the full list. To get the full list, select **Accept** without changing any of the parameters. For detailed information on the various filters, select the **Help** button on the **Filter control** screen.

- Select the account you wish to modify. This will open the **User information** tab.

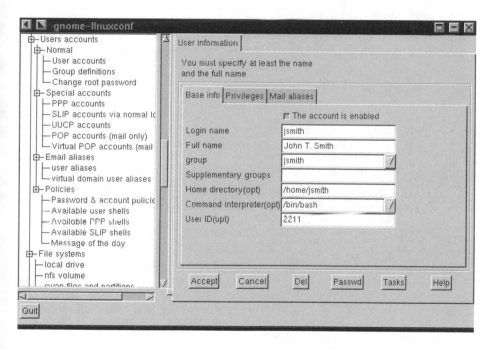

Figure 8.8: User Information Screen

On the **User information** screen, the information can be changed as desired. To implement the changes select **Accept**. If you decide against making any changes select **Cancel**. This guarantees that no changes are made.

Changing a User's Password – Quick Reference

1. Start Linuxconf by typing `linuxconf` at the shell prompt

2. Enter root's password when prompted (if not already root)

3. Open [Config] ⇒ [Users accounts] ⇒ [Normal] ⇒ [User accounts]

4. Select the user account

5. Select **Passwd**

6. Enter the user's new password

7. Reenter the user's new password in the **Confirmation** field

8. Select **Accept**

Changing a User's Password – General Overview

- Start Linuxconf by typing linuxconf at the shell prompt

- Enter root's password when prompted (if not already root)

- Open [Config] ⇒ [Users accounts] ⇒ [Normal] ⇒ [User accounts] This will open the **Users accounts** tab (see figure 8.5 on page 114).

- If you have more than 15 accounts on the system, Linuxconf will provide you with a filter screen (see figure 8.4 on page 113). You can use this to select a smaller range of accounts than the full list. To get the full list, select **Accept** without changing any of the parameters. For detailed information on the various filters, select the **Help** button on the **Filter control** screen.

- Select the account whose password you wish to change. This will open the **User information** tab (see figure 8.8 on the preceding page).

- Select **Passwd** from the options at the bottom of the screen.

Linuxconf will then prompt you to enter the new password. There is also a field called **Confirmation** where you will need to type the password again. This is to prevent you from mistyping the password. Passwords must be at least 6 characters in length. They may contain numbers as well as a mix of lowercase and uppercase letters. If you decide against changing the password, just hit **Cancel**. Once you have entered the new password select **Accept**.

Changing the root Password – Quick Reference

1. Start Linuxconf by typing linuxconf at the shell prompt

2. Enter root's password when prompted (if not already root)

3. Open [Config] ⇒ [Users accounts] ⇒ [Normal] ⇒ [Change root password]

4. Enter the current root password

5. Select **Accept**

6. Enter the new root password

7. Reenter the new root password in the **Confirmation** field

8. Select **Accept**

Changing the root Password – General Overview

Changing the roots password isn't handled in the same manner as changing a user's password. Because of both the importance and security considerations surrounding root access, linuxconf requires you to verify that you currently have access to the root account.

- Start Linuxconf by typing `linuxconf` at the shell prompt

- Enter root's password when prompted (if not already root)

- Open Config ⇒ Users accounts ⇒ Normal ⇒ Change root password

Figure 8.9: Root Password Verification Screen

The screen is a little confusing because neither the title, nor the description really explains the screen's purpose. Linuxconf seems to be asking for the new password, which isn't actually the case. Instead linuxconf wants the current root password to verify access to the root account. Linuxconf does require root access to run, but once running there's nothing to keep anyone from sitting down at the computer if the person using linuxconf steps out for a minute. The potential pitfalls are extensive! If the person who was originally using linuxconf, logs out of root, they won't be able to get back into it. A lack of validation would also give free reign over the computer to whoever had changed root's password.

Once you have entered root's current password, it will prompt you for a new password. There is also a field called **Confirmation** where you will need to type the password again (see figure 8.7 on page 116). This is to prevent you from mistyping the password. Passwords must be at least 6 characters in length. They may contain numbers as well as a mix of lowercase and uppercase letters. If you decide against changing the root password, just hit **Cancel**. Once you have entered the new password select **Accept**. The change takes place immediately and is effective not only for logging in as root, but also for becoming root using the su command.

Disabling a User Account – Quick Reference

1. Start Linuxconf by typing linuxconf at the shell prompt

2. Enter root's password when prompted (if not already root)

3. Open [Config] ⇒ [Users accounts] ⇒ [Normal] ⇒ [User accounts]

4. Select the account

5. De-select **the account is enabled** checkbox

6. Select **Accept**

Disabling a User Account – General Overview

Why disable an account? Good question! There's no single answer, but we can provide some reasons why this option is available. The biggest reason is security. For example, you may have created a special account to be used by clients, coworkers, or friends to access specific files on your system. This account gets used from time to time, but should only be used when you know there's a need. Leaving an unused account around is a target for people who'd want to break into your system. Deleting it requires you to recreate it every time you want to use it. Disabling an account solves both problems by allowing you to simply select or de-select a check-box.

To disable an account:

- Start Linuxconf by typing linuxconf at the shell prompt

- Enter root's password when prompted (if not already root)

- Open [Config] ⇒ [Users accounts] ⇒ [Normal] ⇒ [User accounts]

- De-select the check-box that states that **The account is enabled**. Select the choiceAccept button at the bottom of the window and you're all set.

The account is disabled and can be enabled later using a similar method.

Enabling a User Account

By default, all newly-created user accounts are enabled. If you need to enable an account, you can use Linuxconf to do it.

- Start Linuxconf by typing linuxconf at the shell prompt

- Enter root's password when prompted (if not already root)

- Open Config ⇒ Users accounts ⇒ Normal ⇒ User accounts

- Select the account you want to enable.

- Select the **The account is enabled** check-box and then select **Accept** at the bottom of the screen.

Deleting a User Account – Quick Reference

1. Start Linuxconf by typing linuxconf at the shell prompt

2. Enter root's password when prompted (if not already root)

3. Open Config ⇒ Users accounts → User accounts

4. Select the account you wish to delete

5. On the **User information** screen select **Del**

6. On the **Deleting account...** screen, choose the appropriate option for the account's data

7. Select **Accept**

Deleting a User Account – General Overview

Please Note: While there are a couple options that let you retain files associated with an account, any information or files deleted are gone and effectively unrecoverable. Take care when using this option!

To delete an account:

- Start Linuxconf by typing linuxconf at the shell prompt

- Enter root's password when prompted (if not already root)

- Open [Config] ⇒ [Users accounts] ⇒ [User accounts]

- On the **User accounts** screen (see figure 8.5 on page 114) select the account you wish to delete

- At the bottom of the **User information** screen (see figure 8.8 on page 117) select **Del** to delete the account.

Linuxconf will then prompt you with a list of options.

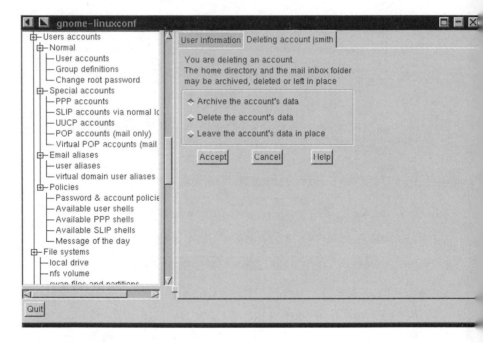

Figure 8.10: Deleting Account Screen

The default option is to archive the account's data. The archive options has the following effects:

1. Removes the user from the user accounts list

2. Takes everything contained in the user's home directory and archives it (using tar and gzip compression), storing the resulting file in a directory called oldaccounts. For an account named useraccount the file name would be:

useraccount-1998-10-10-497.tar.gz

The date indicates when the account was deleted, and the number following it is the process ID of the process that actually performed the deletion. The `oldaccounts` directory is created in the same place as all of your user directories, and is created automatically the first time you remove a user account using this option.

3. Files not contained in the user's home directory, but owned by that user remain. The file is owned by the deleted account's user ID (UID). If you create a new account and specifically assign it the UID of a deleted account, it will then become the owner of any remaining files.

Selecting **Delete the account's data** on the **Deleting account** <*accountname*> screen (see figure 8.10 on the facing page) will:

1. Remove the user from the user accounts list

2. Remove the user's home directory and all its contents

Please Note: Files not contained in the user's home directory, but owned by that user will remain on the system. The file will still be owned by the deleted account's user ID (Uid). If you create a new account and specifically assign it the Uid of a deleted account, it will then become the owner of any such "orphaned" files.

Selecting **Leave the account's data in place** on the **Deleting account** <*accountname*> screen (see figure 8.10 on the preceding page) will:

1. Remove the user from the user accounts list

2. Leave the user's home directory (with all its files) in place.

Please Note: Files and directories owned by the deleted account's user ID (Uid) will remain on the system. If you create a new account and specifically assign it the Uid of a deleted account, it will then become the owner of these "orphaned" files.

8.1.2 Groups

All users belong to one or more groups. Just as each file has a specific owner, each file belongs to a particular group as well. The group might be specific to the owner of the file, or may be a group shared by all users. The ability to read, write or execute a file can be assigned to a group; this is separate from the owner's rights. For example, the owner of a file will be able to write to a document, while other group members may only be able to read it.

Creating a Group – Quick Reference

1. Start Linuxconf by typing `linuxconf` at the shell prompt

2. Enter root's password when prompted (if not already root)

3. Open [Config] ⇒ [Users accounts] ⇒ [Normal] ⇒ [Group definition]

4. Select **Add**

5. Enter the Group name, and optionally alternate members

6. Select **Accept**

Creating a Group – General Overview

To create a new group:

- Start Linuxconf by typing `linuxconf` at the shell prompt

- Enter root's password when prompted (if not already root)

- Open [Config] ⇒ [Users accounts] ⇒ [Normal] ⇒ [Group definition]

If you have more than 15 groups, you will be given the option to select the groups by providing a prefix.

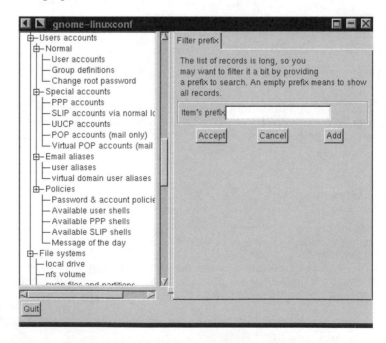

Figure 8.11: Group Filter Screen

You may add a group directly from this screen, or move on to the **User groups** screen. To move on select choiceAccept with or without a prefix, to add a new group, hit choiceAdd.

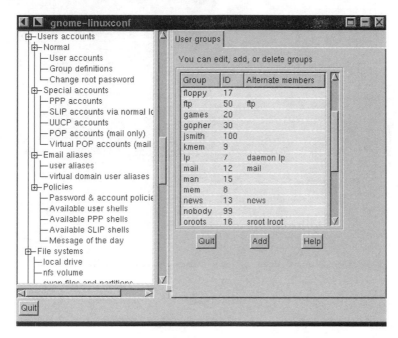

Figure 8.12: User groups screen

Select **Add** at the bottom of the **User groups** screen.

Enter a group name. You may also wish to specify members of the group and can do so in the **Alternate members** field. The list of users should be space delimited, meaning that each username must have a space between it and the next one. When you're finished, select **Accept** and the group will be created.

Deleting a Group – Quick Reference

1. Start Linuxconf by typing `linuxconf` at the shell prompt

2. Enter root's password when prompted (if not already root)

3. Open Config ⇒ Users accounts ⇒ Normal ⇒ Group definitions

4. Select the group you wish to delete

5. Select **Del**

6. Confirm deletion

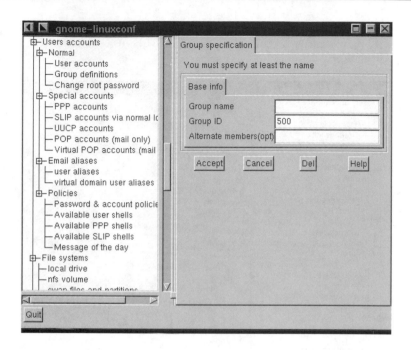

Figure 8.13: Group specification screen

Deleting a Group – General Overview

To delete a group:

- Start Linuxconf by typing `linuxconf` at the shell prompt

- Enter root's password when prompted (if not already root)

- Open (Config) ⇒ (Users accounts) ⇒ (Normal) ⇒ (Group definitions)

If you have more than 15 groups, you will be given a filter screen (see figure 8.11 on page 124) to narrow your choice of groups by specifying a prefix.

- With or without a prefix select **Accept** at the bottom of the screen.

- On the **User groups** screen (see figure 8.12 on the page before) select the group you wish to delete.

- You'll be presented with the **Group specification** screen (see figure 8.13)

- Select **Del** to delete the group. Linuxconf will then prompt you to confirm the deletion. Choose **yes** to delete the group.

The group's files will still remain and their respective owners will still have sole control over them. The group name will be replaced with the deleted group's ID. The files may be assigned to a new group by using the chgrp command. More information on chgrp can be found by typing the command info chgrp or man chgrp at the shell prompt. If a new group is created and the deleted group's ID is specified then the new group will have access to the deleted group's files. Don't worry, linuxconf doesn't recycle old group numbers any more than it does old user IDs, so it won't happen by accident.

Modifying Group Membership

There are two ways to modify the list of users that belong to a group. You can either update each user account itself, or you can update the group definitions. In general, the fastest way is to update each of the group definitions. If you're planning on changing more information for each user than just the group information, then updating each user account may prove easier.

Modifying Group Membership – Quick Reference

- Under Groups

1. Start Linuxconf by typing linuxconf at the shell prompt

2. Enter root's password when prompted (if not already root)

3. Open Config ⇒ Users accounts ⇒ Normal ⇒ Group definitions

4. Select the group to which you wish to add or remove users

5. Add or remove new users to the **Alternate members(opt)** field; make sure all user names are separated with a space " " character

   5. Select **Accept**

Modifying Group Membership – Quick Reference

- Under Users

1. Start Linuxconf by typing linuxconf at the shell prompt

2. Enter root's password when prompted (if not already root)

3. Open Config ⇒ Users accounts ⇒ Normal ⇒ User accounts

4. Select a user to which you wish to add or remove groups

   Adjust the **Supplementary groups** field accordingly; make sure all the group names are separated with a space " " character

5. Select **Accept**

6. Repeat steps 3 through 5 for each additional user to be added

Modifying Group Membership – General Overview

We'll start by detailing the group definitions method.

- Start Linuxconf by typing `linuxconf` at the shell prompt

- Enter root's password when prompted (if not already root)

- Open (Config) ⇒ (Users accounts) ⇒ (Normal) ⇒ (Group definitions)

If you have more than 15 groups, you will be given a filter screen (see figure 8.11 on page 124) to narrow your choice of groups by specifying a prefix.

- With or without a prefix, select **Accept** at the bottom of the screen.

- Select the group you wish to modify. This will open the **Group specification** screen (see figure 8.13 on page 126).

- Add or remove each user from the **Alternate members** field. Make sure that all of the user names are separated by a space " " character.

- Once you've done this select **Accept** which can be found at the bottom of the screen.

This will automatically update each user account with the group showing up in the **Supplementary groups** field if added or absent if removed.

Adding and removing groups can also be done by modifying each individual user account.

- Start Linuxconf by typing `linuxconf` at the shell prompt

- Enter root's password when prompted (if not already root)

- Open (Config) ⇒ (Users accounts) ⇒ (Normal) ⇒ (User accounts)

If you have more than 15 accounts on the system, Linuxconf will provide you with a filter screen (see figure 8.4 on page 113).

- On the **User accounts** screen (see figure 8.5 on page 114), select a user that you wish to update. You will be presented with the **User information** screen (see figure 8.8 on page 117).

- Add or remove the desired groups from the, choiceSupplementary groups field. Each group should be separated by a space " " character.

- Once you've made all the changes you'd like, select choiceAccept at the bottom of the screen.

This will automatically update the group definitions. Repeat the process for each user.

8.1.3   CD-ROMs, Diskettes, Hard Drives and Filesystems – the Inside Track

A filesystem is composed of files and directories, all starting from a single root directory. The root directory may contain any number of files and other directories, with each directory in turn following suit. The average filesystem often looks like an inverted tree with the directories as branches and the files as leaves. Filesystems reside on mass storage devices such as diskette drives, hard drives, and CD-ROMs.

For example, a diskette drive on DOS and Windows machines is typically referenced by `A:\`. This describes both the device (`A:`), and the root directory on that device (`\`). The primary hard drive on the same systems is typically referred to as the "C" drive because the device specification for the first hard drive is `C:`. To specify the root directory on the C drive, you would use `C:\`.

Under this arrangement, there are two filesystems – the one on `A:`, and the one on `C:`. In order to specify *any* file on a DOS/Windows filesystem, you must either explicitly specify the device on which the file resides, or it must be on the system's default drive (which is where DOS' infamous C prompt comes from – that's the default drive in a system with a single hard drive).

Under Linux, it is possible to link the filesystems on several mass storage devices together into a single, larger, filesystem. This is done by placing one device's filesystem "under" a directory on another device's filesystem. So while the root directory of a diskette drive on a DOS machine may be referred to as `A:\`, the same drive on a Linux system may be accessible as `/mnt/floppy`.

The process of merging filesystems in this way is known as *mounting*. When a device is mounted, it is then accessible to the system's users. The directory "under" which a mounted device's filesystem becomes accessible is known as the *mount point*. In the previous paragraph's example, `/mnt/floppy` was the diskette drive's mount point. Note that there are no restrictions (other than common conventions) as to the naming of mount points. We could just as easily mounted the floppy to
`/long/path/to/the/floppy/drive`.

One thing to keep in mind is that all of a device's files and directories are relative to its mount point. Consider the following example:

- **A Linux System**

    - `/` – system root directory
    - `/foo` – mount point for the CD-ROM

- **A CD-ROM**

    - / – CD-ROM's root directory
    - /images – a directory of images on the CD-ROM
    - /images/old – a directory of old images

So, if the above describes the individual filesystems, and you mount the CD-ROM at /foo, the new operating system directory structure would be:

- **A Linux System (with the CD-ROM mounted)**

    - / – system root directory
    - /foo – CD-ROM root directory
    - /foo/images – a directory of images on the CD-ROM
    - /foo/images/old – a directory of old images

To mount a filesystem make sure to be logged in as root, or become root using the su command. For the latter, type su at the shell prompt and then enter the root password. Once you are root, type mount followed by the device and then the mount point. For example, to mount the first diskette drive on /mnt/floppy, you would type the command mount /dev/fd0 /mnt/floppy.

At installation, Red Hat Linux will create /etc/fstab. This file contains information on devices and associated mount points. The advantage to this file is that it allows you to shorten your mount commands[2]. Using the information in /etc/fstab, you can type mount and then either the mount point or the device. The mount command will look for the rest of the information in /etc/fstab. It's possible to modify this file by hand, or by using linuxconf. To use linuxconf, please see Sections 8.1.3 and 8.1.3 on page 133.

Reviewing Your Current Filesystem – Quick Reference

1. Start Linuxconf by typing linuxconf at the shell prompt

2. Enter root's password when prompted (if not already root)

3. Open [Config] ⇒ [File systems] ⇒ [Access local drive] or to look at your network environment: Open [Config] ⇒ [File systems] ⇒ [Access nfs volume]

Reviewing Your Current Filesystem – General Overview

We'll start by looking at your current directory structure.

- Start Linuxconf by typing linuxconf at the shell prompt

---

[2]It also controls which filesystems are automatically mounted when the system is booted.

- Enter root's password when prompted (if not already root)

- Open [Config] ⇒ [File systems] ⇒ [Access local drive]

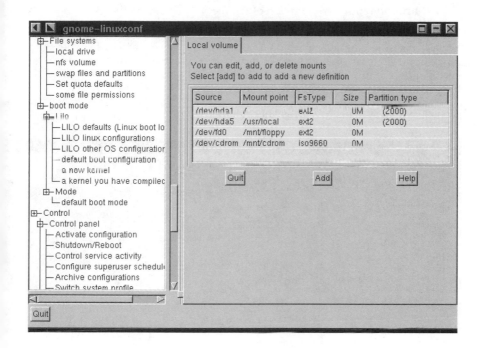

Figure 8.14: Local volume screen

The fields are:

- **Source** – The physical hardware; hd indicates an IDE hard drive, fd indicates a diskette drive, and cdrom typically indicates a CD-ROM drive. If your system has a SCSI drive, you will see an sd instead. More than one drive of a type are listed by letters, so hda represents the first IDE drive, while hdb would be the second. In some cases, you'll see numbers following these letters; on hard drives, the numbers represent the partitions on that drive, while for diskette drives, this number refers to the actual unit.

- **Mount point** – This is where in the system the drive is to be mapped when mounted.

- **FsType** – This is where the type of filesystem is indicated. A standard Linux partition uses the ext2 filesystem type. A filesystem type of vfat indicates a DOS filesystem with long filename support, while a fat filesystem type is for DOS filesystems supporting traditional 8.3 filenames. The iso9660 filesystem type indicates a CD-ROM drive, as seen in figure 8.14.

  Please Note: Red Hat Linux 5.2 can access FAT32 filesystems using the **vfat** filesystem type.

- **Size** – Size indicates the size of the filesystem in megabytes (M). For removable media devices such as diskette and CD-ROM drives the stated size is listed as zero.

- **Partition type** – A description of the filesystem used on that partition.

Filesystems from other machines on a network may also be available. These can range from single small directories or entire volumes. No information on Size or Partition type is available for these partitions, either. Additional information on these filesystems (should you have any available) will be contained under:

[Config] ⇒ [File systems] ⇒ [Access nfs volume]

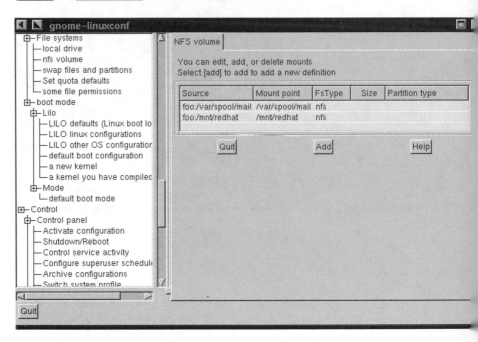

Figure 8.15: NFS Volume Screen

The screen is similar to the **Local volume** screen (see figure 8.14 on the page before), with some notable differences in the information provided for each entry:

- **Source** – This will be the name of the machine serving the filesystem, followed by the remote directory. For example: `foo:/var/spool/mail` where `foo` is the machine serving the directory, and `/var/spool/mail` is the directory being served.

- **FsType** – This will always be "nfs".

Adding NFS Mounts – Quick Reference

1. Start Linuxconf by typing `linuxconf` at the shell prompt

2. Enter root's password when prompted (if not already root)

3. Open ⌐Config⌐ ⇒ ⌐File systems⌐ ⇒ ⌐Access nfs volume⌐

4. Select **Add**

5. Enter the host name where the filesystem resides

6. Enter the path to the remote filesystem in the **Volume** field. For example, `/var/spool/mail`

7. Specify the mount point on your system. For example, `/mnt/foo`
   Select **Accept**

Adding NFS Mounts – General Overview

NFS stands for Network FileSystem. It is a way for computers to share sections of their local filesystem across a network. These sections may be as small as a single directory, or include thousands of files in a vast hierarchy of directories. For example, many companies will have a single mail server with individuals' mail files served as an NFS mount to each users' local systems.

To add an NFS mount:

- Start Linuxconf by typing `linuxconf` at the shell prompt

- Enter root's password when prompted (if not already root)

- Open ⌐Config⌐ ⇒ ⌐File systems⌐ ⇒ ⌐Access nfs volume⌐

- On the **NFS volume** screen (see figure 8.15 on the facing page), select **Add**

The three fields on the **Base** tab are what you'll need to concern yourself with.

- **Server** – The host name of the machine the desired filesystem resides on. For example, `foo.bar.com`.

- **Volume** – The filesystem you wish to add. For example, `/var/spool/mail`.

- **Mount point** – Where in your system you want the remote file system accessible from. For example, `/mnt/mail`.

This is all you need to get the mount created. Linuxconf will update your `/etc/fstab` file accordingly. If you are aware of additional requirements, please read the help file on the **Volume specification** screen and see the `mount` man page for more information.

Once you have entered the information, select **Accept**.

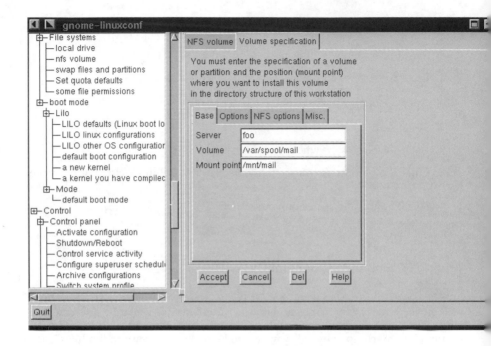

Figure 8.16: Volume Specification Screen

8.1.4   Getting Connected (Network Configuration)

The first thing to determine when getting hooked up, is whether you're connecting
to a local area network, such as a group of computers in an office, or a wide area
network, such as the Internet. Before continuing, it's important to know what
hardware you have and how you intend to connect. If you're going to dial into
another computer, then make sure your modem is installed and that the cables
are arranged properly. If you're using a network card, make sure it is installed
properly and that the cables are correctly connected. Regardless of what network
configuration you specify, if every phone line or cable is not in place, you'll never
get connected. We'll start with modem connections and then move on to using
network cards.

Adding Modem/PPP/SLIP connections – Quick Reference

1. Start Linuxconf by typing `linuxconf` at the shell prompt

2. Enter root's password when prompted (if not already root)

3. Open (Config) ⇒ (Networking) ⇒ (PPP/SLIP/PLIP)

4. Select **Add**

5. Select the type of connection

6. Enter the Phone number, login name and password.

7. Select **Use PAP authentication** only if necessary (only available for PPP accounts)

8. Select **Accept**

Adding Modem/PPP/SLIP connections – General Overview

There are several pieces of information you will need to get from your ISP (Internet Service Provider) or systems administrator before getting your PPP or SLIP account working. In the case of some providers, you may have to sort through directions on how to set up a PPP connection on a Linux system. Some ISPs are ill-equipped to handle individuals using Linux. Don't worry, you can still get connected; you just need some additional information from your ISP. The following is what you need for a connection with Red Hat Linux. The ISP representatives may tell you you don't need this information, or may tell you you need more than this. Red Hat has streamlined the information needed using intelligent defaults and tools such as linuxconf to simplify this process for you. Unless they have a document specifically for Red Hat Linux, just request the information below and go from there. Specifically, you'll need:

- the IP address for a domain nameserver (DNS)

- the telephone number to dial

- your login and password

- an IP address for your machine if the network you are connecting to isn't going to provide you a dynamic one

- whether or not your ISP uses an authentication method such as PAP, CHAP or MS-CHAP. If so, you will need a secret to enable authentication. The secret will be a word or sequence of characters. CHAP and MS-CHAP are not currently supported using linuxconf, and are rarely used.

Additional information which may be helpful, but isn't necessary includes a secondary nameserver address, and a search domain. Once you have all this information, you're ready to get connected.

- Start Linuxconf by typing `linuxconf` at the shell prompt

- Enter root's password when prompted (if not already root)

- Open (Config) ⇒ (Networking) ⇒ (PPP/SLIP/PLIP)

- Select **Add**

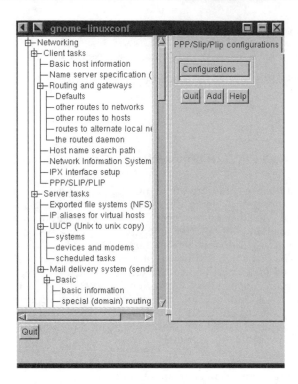

Figure 8.17: PPP/SLIP/PLIP Configurations Screen

Initially there won't be any configurations specified. When you select **Add** you will be given a choice between PPP, SLIP and PLIP.

PPP is the most commonly used interface and is the default. To set up a PPP connection select **PPP** and hit **Accept**.

You'll see the following fields:

- Phone number - number used to access to remote system
- Modem port - indicates where your modem is. Should already be set.
- Use PAP authentication (checkbox) - check if you know that the system you are dialing into requires this
- Login name - your login name for the PPP account
- Password - your password for the PPP account

Notice that the title bar is **PPP interface ppp0**. ppp0 is the first PPP interface, ppp1 would be the second and so on. It's important to keep track of which interface

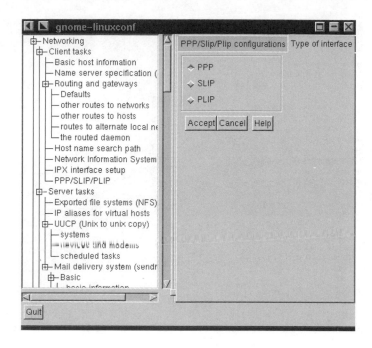

Figure 8.18: Type of Interface Screen

you're using if you have more than one. SLIP connections use sl instead of ppp for their interface prefix. With the exception of a PAP authentication option, the entry screens for adding a PPP or a SLIP account are identical.

Enter the complete phone number for the remote machine, and make sure to include any numbers required to access outside lines. For example, if you need to dial "9" and then the number, and the computer you're connecting to has a telephone number of "555 0111", then you'd enter "95550111". The next thing it asks you for is the modem port. This is a drop down box of available ports. If you're using a dual-boot Linux/Windows system and you know the COM port your modem is on, the following map may be of use:

Map to Windows COM ports are as follows:

- cua0 – COM1: under MS-DOS
- cua1 – COM2: under MS-DOS
- cua2 – COM3: under MS-DOS
- cua3 – COM4: under MS-DOS

The login name is the one for the PPP account. The password you enter will be shown in plain text, so be careful who you have around when you enter it! If you

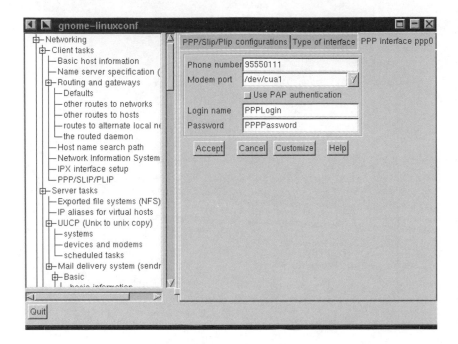

Figure 8.19: PPP Interface Screen

will be using PAP authentication, check the box; when you've entered the other required information, select the **Customize** button at the bottom of the screen. All the other information is provided on the various tabs and can be set within the **Customize** screen, but it's easier to find the information all in one place on the primary screen.

Select the **PAP** tab and enter your username and then the secret the ISP has provided you in the **Secret** field. The other defaults should be sufficient, but if you need to, you can edit the initial settings using the **Customize** option.

Modifying a PPP or SLIP Configuration – Quick Reference

1. Start Linuxconf by typing linuxconf at the shell prompt

2. Enter root's password when prompted (if not already root)

3. Open Config ⇒ Networking ⇒ PPP/SLIP/PLIP

4. Select the configuration to modify

5. Change the desired settings; most are on the **Communications** tab

6. Select **Accept**

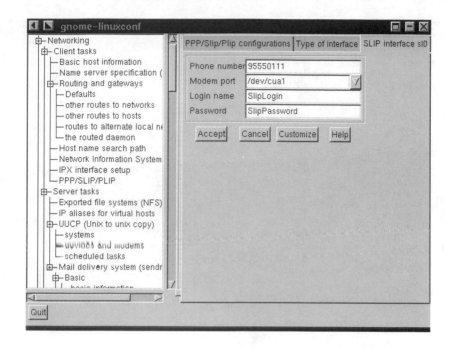

Figure 8.20: SLIP Interface Screen

Modifying a PPP or SLIP Configuration – General Overview

You can edit an existing configuration as well as delete it by selecting it from the list on the
PPP/SLIP/PLIP configurations screen.

- Start Linuxconf by typing `linuxconf` at the shell prompt

- Enter root's password when prompted (if not already root)

- Open (Config) ⇒ (Networking) ⇒ (PPP/SLIP/PLIP)

- You will then be presented with the choicePPP/SLIP/PLIP configurations screen (see figure 8.17 on page 136). Select the configuration you would like to modify or delete.

This will open the appropriate interface screen for your configuration. If you wish to delete the configuration, the handy **Del** button is there at the bottom of the screen. The Modem port is on the **Hardware** tab and, again, is a drop down menu. If you want to change the other settings you entered when you originally created the configuration, you'll want to select the **Communication** tab. The first **Send** field contains your login, and the next **Send** field contains your password. The

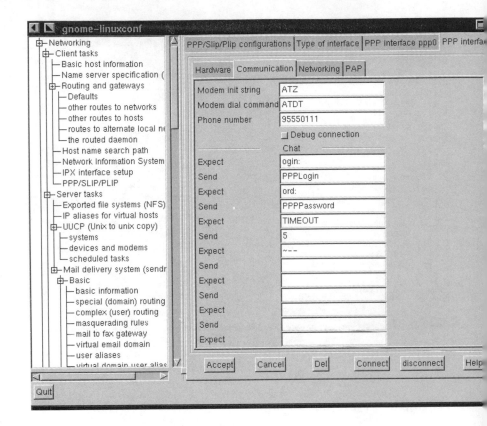

Figure 8.21: PPP Interface Customization Screen

Expect fields correspond to the `login:` and `password:` prompts, which explains the `ogin:` and `ord:` entries.

Once you have made your changes, you can test to see if your configuration is working. Select **Connect** from the bottom of the screen. This will attempt to connect you to the remote system using the information you've entered. Once you've finished configuring and testing your setup, we recommend using the `usernet` utility to control your dial-up networking connection on a daily basis. See the `usernet` man page for more information.

Other Network Connections – Quick Reference

Due to the number of possible choices and sub-choices, no quick reference is available for this section.

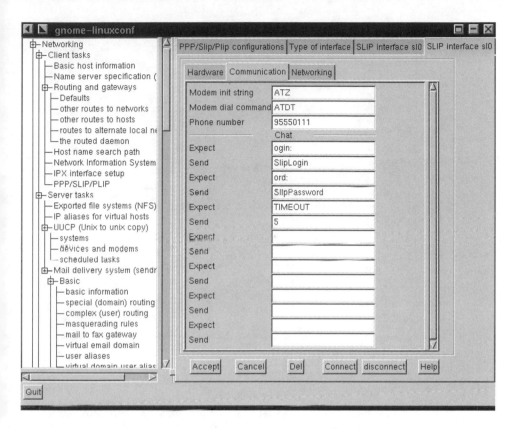

Figure 8.22: SLIP Interface Customization Screen

Other Network Connections – General Overview

Setting up a network connection over ethernet requires an entirely different type of setup. Network connections to token ring or arcnet networks follow a similar procedure, but will not be discussed here.

- First you will need to have an Ethernet card installed.

- then start Linuxconf by typing linuxconf at the shell prompt

- Enter root's password when prompted (if not already root)

- Open Config ⇒ Networking ⇒ Client tasks ⇒ Basic host information. The **Host name** tab will request a host name, which should be specified as localhost.localdomain. Skip this tab. Select the tab for **Adaptor 1**.

The first item on this screen is a checkbox to indicate whether this adaptor is enabled or not. It should be checked if this is the one you intend to use. Below that

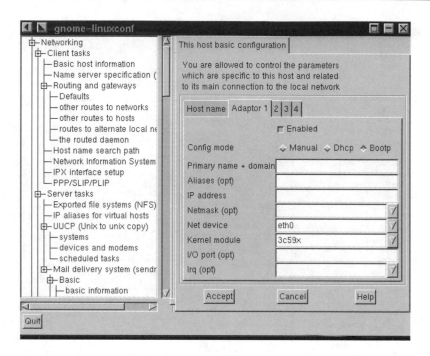

Figure 8.23: Adaptor 1

is a choice of Config modes. **Manual** means that you will be providing all the information and entering it yourself. **DHCP** and **bootp** retrieve their information from a remote server of the corresponding kind. If you're not sure what option to choose, talk to your systems administrator. If you're the systems administrator and you're not sure, select Manual, and consider a career in the food-services industry. . .

DHCP and bootp Required fields:

- Net device - The type of network card you are using; for example, eth0 would be the appropriate entry to use the first Ethernet card.

- Kernel module - The correct module based on your network card; for further information see the list below.

For DHCP and bootp configurations you only need to specify the **Net device** and the **Kernel module**. For the **Net device**, you will choose from a list where the eth prefix represents ethernet cards, the arc specifies an arcnet card and the tr specifies token ring cards. A complete list of network cards and their respective modules can be found in Section C.4 on page 294. For the most recent up to date list, please see our website at:

        http://www.redhat.com

The netmask information will be set by default, though depending on what kind of network you are setting up, or becoming a part of, you may need to specify this. If you are connecting to an ISP, ask them for the information. Most likely it will be 255.255.255.0 (the default).

Required fields for **Manual Configuration**:

- Primary name + domain – the primary name is the name of your computer, while the domain is how your network is specified. For example, foo.bar.com; foo is the primary name and bar.com is the domain.

- IP address – this is the address of the machine and will follow the pattern of x.x.x.x. For example, 192.168.0.13

- Net device – type of network card you are using; eth0 would be the appropriate entry to use the first ethernet card

- Kernel module – the correct module based on your network card

Information on net devices and kernel modules is described above. The appropriate primary name + domain and IP address will depend on whether you are adding the computer to an existing network or creating a new network. For connecting to an existing network, contact your systems administrator for the information. Getting a network connected to the Internet is beyond the scope of this book, and we recommend the following starting point:

TCP/IP Network Administration, 2nd Edition, by Craig Hunt (O'Reilly and Associates)

If you're setting up a private network that won't *ever* be connected to the Internet, then you can choose any primary name + domain name you would like and have several choices for IP addresses (See Figure 8.24).

Addresses available	Examples
10.0.0.0 - 10.255.255.255	10.5.12.14
172.16.0.0 - 172.31.255.255	172.16.9.1, 172.28.2.5
192.168.0.0 - 192.168.255.255	192.168.0.13

Figure 8.24: Private Address Ranges

The three sets of numbers above, correspond to class a, b, and c networks respectively. The classes are used to describe the number of IP addresses available as well as the range of numbers used to described each. The numbers above have been set aside for private networks.

Please Note: You cannot use these IP addresses if you connect to the Internet. If you want your network to be connected to the Internet, or think you might want to at some point in the future, do yourself a favor, and get yourself non-private addresses now.

Nameserver Specification

A nameserver and default domain are also needed to establish a network connection. The nameserver is used to translate host names such as private.network.com to their corresponding IP address such as 192.168.7.3. The default domain tells the computer where to look if a fully qualified hostname isn't specified. Fully qualified means that the full address is given, so foo.redhat.com is the fully qualified hostname, while the hostname is simply foo. If you specified your default domain as redhat.com, then you could use just the hostname to connect successfully. For example ftp foo would be sufficient if your search domain is redhat.com, while ftp foo.redhat.com would be required if it wasn't.

To specify the nameserver, open Config ⇒ Networking ⇒ Name server specification (DNS).

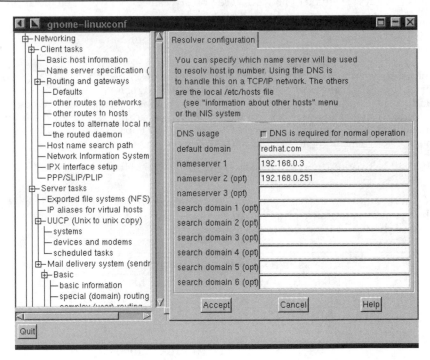

Figure 8.25: Resolver Configuration Screen

Nameservers are ranked according to the order in which they are accessed, so it's not unusual to see nameservers referred to as primary, secondary, tertiary and so on down the list if more than one is specified. Each of these must be an IP address and not a name. The computer has no way to resolve the name until it connects to a nameserver. Screamingly obvious when stated, but occasionally overlooked when people are simply asked to supply an address for a computer.

In addition to a default domain, you can also specify search domains. Search domains work differently; they progress from one to six in a similar manner to the nameserver. However, they all take precedence over the default domain! Keep this in mind when specifying search domains. Search domains are not commonly used.

The one item not yet covered is the checkbox for DNS usage. If you are running a small private network with no Internet connection, then using /etc/hosts files and keeping them all synchronized will work. As you add more and more machines, the complexity increases until it is easier to have a single machine run a DNS than to continue to sync /etc/hosts files.

There is another reason for not using DNS, and that is if your network is going to use NIS instead. Note that NIS can be used in conjunction with DNS. So to sum it all up, unless you know why using /etc/hosts or NIS would be best for your situation, DNS is probably going to be your best choice.

You can add, modify, or delete entries from the /etc/hosts file using linuxconf. Open Config ⇒ Networking ⇒ Misc ⇒ Information about other hosts.

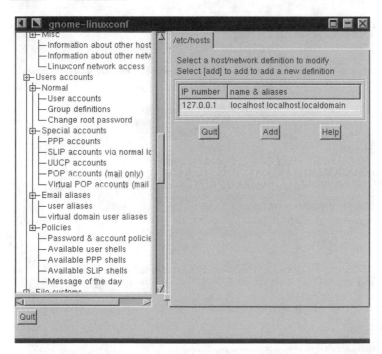

Figure 8.26: /etc/hosts Screen

To modify or delete an entry select it. To delete the entry, select **Del** at the bottom of the **host/network definition** screen.

To modify it, change the information as necessary. To add a new entry, select **Add** at the bottom of the /etc/hosts screen. This will also open the **host/network**

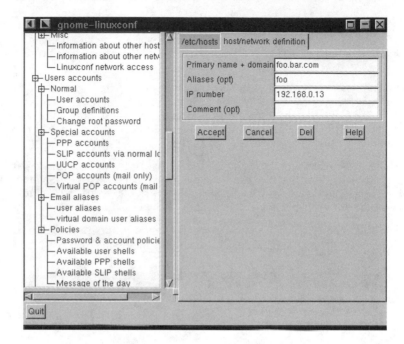

Figure 8.27: Host/Network Definition Screen

definition screen.

Required Fields:

- **Primary name + domain** – the primary name is the name of the computer, while the domain is how the network it is attached to is specified. For example, given foo.bar.com, foo is the primary name and bar.com is the domain.

- **IP number** – also referred to as IP address; this is the address of the machine and will follow the pattern of *x.x.x.x*. For example, 192.168.0.13

Optional Fields:

- **Alias** – A shorthand for the fully qualified domain name. This is often the same as the primary name. So, for example, if the fully qualified domain name is foo.bar.com, you could select foo as the alias.

- **Comment** – a comment on the machine. For example, "The remote name-server".

You will need to specify both the primary name + domain and the IP number. The other fields are optional. Once finished, select **Accept**.

Date and Time

To get to the **date & time** control panel:

- Start Linuxconf by typing `linuxconf` at the shell prompt

- Enter root's password when prompted (if not already root)

- Open (Control) ⇒ (Date & Time)

Figure 8.28: Workstation Date & Time

The **zone** field is a pull-down list that is long and extensive. It is often designated by a large region and then a city or zone within it. Examples include `Europe/Vienna` and `US/Eastern`. There is a checkbox to **Store date in CMOS in GMT format**. Hours are specified from 0 (midnight) to 23 (11 PM). Months are specified by number as well. For the year, please specify all four digits. All other fields should be self explanatory.

8.2   System Configuration With the Control Panel

Please Note: The inclusion of linuxconf with Red Hat Linux 5.2 gives our customers a more comprehensive system configuration utility. Most of what can be done with the control panel applications can also be done using linuxconf. In addition, linuxconf supports both character-cell *and* graphical user interfaces. Please refer to Section 8.1 on page 108 for an introduction to linuxconf.

The control panel is a launching pad for a number of different system administration tools (See Figure 8.29). These tools make your life easier by letting you configure things without remembering configuration file formats and awkward command line options.

Figure 8.29: The Control Panel

To start the control-panel, start the X Window System as root with `startx` and type
`control-panel` in an xterm. You will need to be root to run the control-panel tools successfully. You can do this as well if you already have X running as a normal user. Just type `su -c control-panel` and then type the root password when prompted. If you plan to do other tasks as root, you could type `su` followed by the root password when prompted.

Please Note: If you are not running X as root, you may need to give root access to your system's X server. To do this, enter the following command on a *non-root* terminal window:

```
xhost +localhost
```

After starting the control panel, simply clicking on an icon starts up a tool. Please note that you are not prevented from starting two instances of any tool, but doing so is a very bad idea because you may try to edit the same files in two places and end up overwriting your own changes. If you do accidentally start a second copy of a tool, you should quit it immediately. Also, do not manually edit any files managed by the control-panel tools while the tools are running. Similarly, do not run any other programs (such as linuxconf) that may change those files while the tools are running.

8.2.1 Printer Configuration

The printer configuration tool (printtool) maintains the /etc/printcap file, print spool directories, and print filters. The filters allow you to print many different types of files, including:

- plain text (ASCII) files

- PostScript files

- TEX .dvi files

- GIF, JPEG, TIFF, and other graphics formats

- RPMs

In other words, simply printing a GIF or RPM file using the lpr command will result in the printer doing "the right thing".

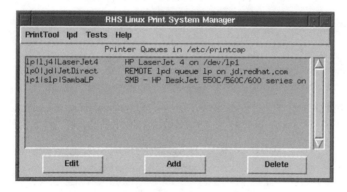

Figure 8.30: Print Tool

In order to create a new *print queue*, choose **Add**. Then, select what type of printer is being added. There are four types of print queues which can be configured with printtool:

- **Local** print queues are for printers attached to a printer or serial port on your Red Hat Linux system.

- **Remote** print queues are attached to a different system which you can access over a TCP/IP network.

- **SMB** print queues are attached to a different system which uses LAN-Manager-type (SMB) networking.

- **NCP** print queues are attached to a different system which uses Novell's NetWare network technology.

Figure 8.31: Selecting a Printer Type

After choosing the printer type, a dialog box requests further information about the print queue (See Figure 8.32 on the facing page). All types of print queues require the following information:

- **Queue Name**: What the queue will be called. Multiple names can be specifed with the | (pipe) character separating entries.

- **Spool Directory**: This is the directory on the local machine where files are stored before printing occurs. Be careful to not have more than one printer queue use a given spool directory.

- **File Limit**: Maximum size print job accepted, in kilobytes (1 kb = 1024 bytes). A size of 0 indicates no limit should be imposed.

- **Input Filter**: Filters convert printed files into a format the printer can handle. Press **Select** to choose the filter which best matches your printer (See Figure 8.33 on page 152).

  In addition to configuring print queues able to print graphical and PostScript output, you can configure a *text-only* printer, which will only print plain ASCII text. Most printer drivers are also able to print ASCII text without converting it to PostScript first; simply choose **Fast text printing** when you configure the filter. **Please Note:** This only works for non-PostScript printers.

- **Suppress Headers**: Check this if you don't want a header page printed at the beginning of each print job.

For *local* printers, the following information is also required:

- **Printer Device**: Usually /dev/lp1; the name of the port which the printer is attached to. Serial printers are usually on /dev/ttyS? ports. Note that you will need to manually configure serial parameters.

For *remote* printers, the dialog box contains additionsl fields; fill in the following information:

- **Remote Host**: Hostname of the remote machine hosting the printer.

Figure 8.32: Adding a Local Printer

- **Remote Queue**: Name of the queue to print to on the remote machine.

The remote machine must be configured to allow the local machine to print on the desired queue. Typically /etc/hosts.lpd controls this.

For SMB and NCP printers, fill in the following information:

- **Hostname of Printer Server**: Name of the machine to which the printer you want to use is attached.

- **IP number of Server**: The IP address of the machine to which the printer you want to use is attached; this is optional.

- **Printer Name**: Name of the printer on which you want to print.

- **User**: Name of user you must login as to access the printer (typically guest for Windows servers, or nobody for samba servers).

- **Password**: Password (if required) to use the printer (typically blank). Someone should be able to tell you this if you do not already know it.

Please Note: If you need to use a username and password for an SMB (LAN Manager) or NCP (NetWare) print queue, they are stored unencrypted in a local script. Thus, it is possible for another person to learn the username and password. It is therefore recommended that the username and password for use of the printer not to be the same as that for a user account on the local Red Hat Linux system, so that the only possible security compromise would be unauthorized use of the printer. If there are file shares from the SMB server, it is recommended that they also use a different password than the one for the print queue.

After you have added your print queue, you may need to restart the printer daemon (lpd). To do so, choose **Restart lpd** from the **lpd** menu.

You may print a *test page* for any print queue you have configured. Select the type of test page you would like to print from the **Tests** menu.

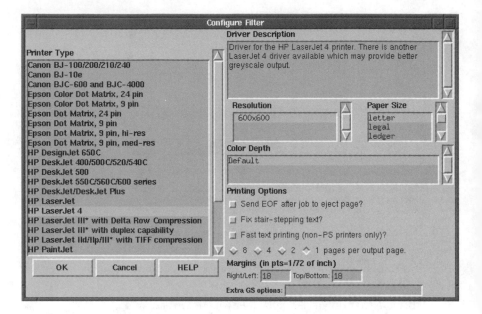

Figure 8.33: Configuring a Print Filter

8.2.2 Kernel Daemon Configuration

Red Hat Linux includes kerneld, the Kernel Daemon, which automatically loads some software and hardware support into memory as it is needed, and unloads it when it is no longer being used.

The tool shown in Figure 8.36 on page 154 manages the configuration file for kerneld. While kerneld can load some things, such as filesystems, without explicit configuration, it needs to be told what hardware support to load when it is presented with a generic hardware request.

For instance, when the kernel wants to load support for ethernet, kerneld needs to know which ethernet card you have, and if your ethernet card requires special configuration, it needs to know about that, too.

Changing Module Options

To change the options being given to a module when it is loaded, click on the line to select it, then click the **Edit** button. kernelcfg will bring up a window which looks like Figure 8.37 on page 154. The options kernelcfg knows about (normally all available options) will each have their own field. Normally, you will want to ignore the **Other arguments** field. Some modules normally take no arguments; just in case, they have an **Arguments** field which allows you to enter configuration information.

Figure 8.34: Adding a Remote Printer

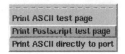

Figure 8.35: Printing a Test Page

Changing Modules

To change which module gets invoked to provide a generic service, such as an ethernet card or SCSI host adapter module, you need to delete the old one and add a new one. To delete a module, select it by clicking on it, then click on **Remove** Then click on **Add** to add the new module, as explained in the following section.

If you have changed your SCSI controller (scsi_hostadapter), remember to make a new initial ramdisk with the /sbin/mkinitrd command as documented in section 11.6.2 on page 196.

Adding Modules

To add a module of any type, click on the **Add** button. You will be presented with a dialog box (Figure 8.38 on the next page) asking you to choose a module type. Ethernet is eth, Token Ring is tr, SCSI controllers are scsi_hostadapter, and so on. Click **OK** to continue to

the next dialog box. If there is more than one module which can be used for the module type you have chosen, you will be presented with a dialog box (Figure 8.39 on page 155) which asks which module you want to use, and may also ask for specifics about the type of module; for ethernet, for example, you need to choose from eth0, eth1, etc. When you are done, click **OK** again to continue to specify any module options in the next dialog box (Figure 8.39 on page 155), which is the same as the dialog for editing a module.

Figure 8.36: Kernel Module Management

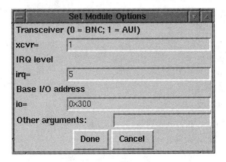

Figure 8.37: Editing Module Options

Figure 8.38: Adding a module

Figure 8.39: Selecting from available modules

now "/etc/modules.conf"

Restarting Kerneld

The changes that you make with the Kernel Daemon Configuration tool will be
made in the
`/etc/conf.modules` file, which kerneld reads whenever it is started. Once you
have made changes, you can restart kerneld by clicking on the **Restart kerneld**
button. This will **not** cause any modules which are currently in use to be reloaded,
it will only notify kerneld to use the configuration when it loads more modules in
the future.

8.2.3   Network Configuration

Please Note: Documentation on network configuration using linuxconf can be
found in Section 8.1.4 on page 134.

The network configuration tool (netcfg) shown in Figure 8.40 on the next page
is designed to allow easy manipulation of parameters such as IP address, gateway
address, and network address, as well as name servers and `/etc/hosts`.

Network devices can be added, removed, configured, activated, deactivated and
aliased. Ethernet, arcnet, token ring, pocket (ATP), PPP, SLIP, PLIP and loopback
devices are supported. PPP/SLIP/PLIP support works well on most hardware,
but some hardware setups may exhibit unpredictable behavior. When using the
Network Configuration Tool click **Save** to write your changes to disk, to quit without making any changes select **Quit**.

Managing Names

The **Names** panel of the Network Configuration tool serves two primary purposes:
setting the hostname and domain of the computer, and determining which name
server will be used to look up other hosts on the network. The Network tool is not
capable of configuring a machine as a nameserver. To edit a field or add information to a field simply click on the field with the left mouse button and type the new
information.

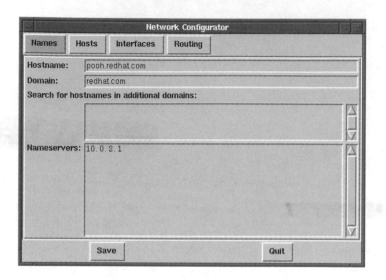

Figure 8.40: Network Configuration Panel

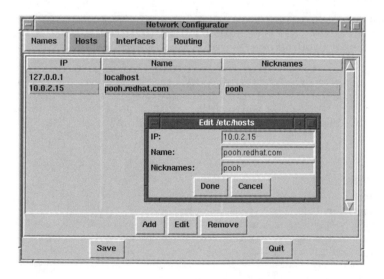

Figure 8.41: Adding/Editing Hosts

Managing Hosts

In the **Hosts** management panel you have the ability to add, edit, or remove hosts from the /etc/hosts file. Adding or editing an entry involves identical actions. An edit dialog box will appear, simply type the new information and click **Done** when you are finished. See Figure 8.41 on the facing page for an example.

Adding a Networking Interface

If you have added a networking interface to your machine since installing Red Hat Linux, or you didn't configure your ethernet card at install time, you can configure it with a few clicks of a mouse.

Please Note: You may need to configure kerneld to load a driver for the network interface you are adding (e.g., eth0); see Section 8.2.2 on page 152 for more information.

Begin adding an interface by clicking on **Interfaces** in the main panel. This will bring up a window of configured devices with a row of available options, see figure 8.42.

Figure 8.42: Configured Interfaces

To add a device, first click the **Add** button then select the type of interface you want to configure from the box that appears (See Figure 8.43 on the next page).

Please Note: There is now a **clone** button available in netcfg. This button can be used to create a "clone" of an already-existing interface. By using clone interfaces, it is possible for a laptop to have one Ethernet interface defined for a work LAN, and a clone Ethernet device defined for a home LAN.

Figure 8.43: Choose Interface Type

PPP Interface   Adding a PPP interface can be as simple as supplying the phone number, login name and password in the **Create PPP Interface** dialog shown in Figure 8.44. If you need to use PAP authentication for your PPP connection, choose **Use PAP authentication**. In many cases some degree of customization will be needed to establish a PPP connection. Choosing the **Customize** button will allow you to make changes to the hardware, communication, and networking settings for the PPP interface.

Figure 8.44: Create PPP Interface

SLIP Interface   In order to configure a SLIP interface you must first supply a phone number, login name, and password. This will supply the initial parameters for the chat script needed to establish a SLIP connection. When you choose **Done**, a dialog titled **Edit SLIP Interface** appears that enables you to further customize the hardware, communication and networking parameters for your SLIP interface.

PLIP Interface   To add a PLIP interface to your system you only have to supply the IP address, the remote IP address, and the Netmask. You can also select if you want to activate the interface at boot time.

Ethernet, Arcnet, Token Ring and Pocket Adaptor Interfaces If you are adding an ethernet, arcnet, token ring or pocket adapter to your computer you will need to supply the following information:

- **Device**: This is determined by netconfig based on the devices already configured.

- **IP Address**: Enter an IP address for your network device.

- **Netmask**: Enter the network mask for your network device.

    The network and broadcast addresses are calculated automatically based on the IP address and netmask you enter.

- **Activate interface at boot time**: If you want the device to be configured automatically when your machine boots select this by clicking on the box.

- **Allow any user to (de)activate interface**: Check this if you want any user to be able to activate or deactivate the interface.

- **Interface configuration protocol**: If you have a BOOTP or DHCP server on your network and would like to use it to configure the interface, choose the appropriate option; otherwise, choose **none**.

After providing the configuration information for your new device, click **Done**. The device should appear in your **Interfaces** list as an inactive device. (The active column should have a label of **no**). To activate the new device, first select it with a mouse click and then choose on the **Activate** button. If it does not come up properly, you may need to reconfigure it by choosing on **Edit**.

Managing Routes

In the Routes management screen you have the ability to add, edit, or remove static networking routes. Adding or editing an entry involves identical actions, just like the Hosts panel. An edit dialog box will appear, simply type the new information and click **Done** when you are finished. See figure 8.45 on the next page for an example.

8.2.4   Time and Date

Please Note: Documentation on setting your system's time and date using linux-conf can be found in Section 8.1.4 on page 147.

The time machine allows you to change the time and date by clicking on the appropriate part of the time and date display and clicking on the arrows to change the value.

The system clock is not changed until you click on the **Set System Clock** button.

Click on **Reset Time** to set the time machine time back to that of the system.

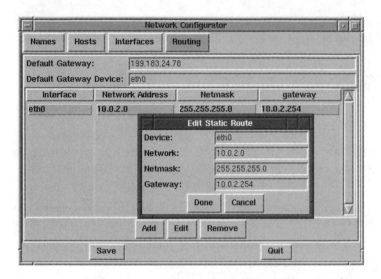

Figure 8.45: Adding/Editing Routes

Please Note: Changing the time can seriously confuse programs that depend on the normal progression of time, and could possibly cause problems. Try to quit as many applications and processes as possible before changing the time or date.

9

Package Management with RPM

The Red Hat Package Manager (RPM), is an open packaging system available for anyone to use, and works on both Red Hat Linux as well as other Linux and UNIX systems. Red Hat Software encourages other vendors to take the time to look at RPM and use it for their own products. RPM is distributable under the terms of the GPL.

For the end user, RPM provides many features that make maintaining a system far easier than it has ever been. Installing, uninstalling, and upgrading RPM packages are all one line commands, and all the messy details are taken care of for you. RPM maintains a database of installed packages and their files, which allows you to perform powerful queries and verification of your system. During upgrades RPM handles configuration files specially, so that you never lose your customizations – a feature that is impossible with straight .tar.gz files.

For the developer, RPM allows you to take source code for software and package it into source and binary packages for end users. This process is quite simple and is driven from a single file and optional patches that you create. This clear delineation of "pristine" sources and your patches and build instructions eases the maintenance of the package as new versions of the software are released.

9.1   RPM Design Goals

Before trying to understand how to use RPM, it helps to have an idea of what the
design goals are.

Upgradability With RPM you can upgrade individual components of your system without completely reinstalling. When you get a new release of an operating system based on RPM (such as Red Hat Linux), you don't need to
reinstall your machine (as you do with operating systems based on other
packaging systems). RPM allows intelligent, fully-automated, in-place upgrades of your system. Configuration files in packages are preserved across
upgrades, so you won't lose your customizations.

Powerful Querying RPM is also designed to have powerful querying options.
You can do searches through your entire database for packages or just certain files. You can also easily find out what package a file belongs to and
where it came from. The files an RPM package contains are in a compressed
archive, with a custom binary header containing useful information about
the package and its contents, allowing you to query individual packages
quickly and easily.

System Verification Another powerful feature is the ability to verify packages. If
you are worried that you deleted an important file for some package, simply
verify the package. You will be notified of any anomalies. At that point,
you can reinstall the package if necessary. Any configuration files that you
modified are preserved during reinstallation.

Pristine Sources A crucial design goal was to allow the use of "pristine" software sources, as distributed by the original authors of the software. With
RPM, you have the pristine sources along with any patches that were used,
plus complete build instructions. This is a big advantage for several reasons.
For instance, if a new version of a program comes out, you don't necessarily have to start from scratch to get it to compile. You can look at the patch
to see what you *might* need to do. All the compiled-in defaults, and all of
the changes that were made to get the software to build properly are easily
visible this way.

This goal may only seem important for developers, but it results in higher
quality software for end users too. We would like to thank the folks from
the BOGUS distribution for originating the pristine source concept.

9.2   Using RPM

RPM has five basic modes of operation (not counting package building): installing,
uninstalling, upgrading, querying, and verifying. This section contains an overview
of each mode. For complete details and options try `rpm --help`, or turn to Section 9.4 on page 169 for more information on RPM.

9.2.1   Installing

RPM packages typically have file names like `foo-1.0-1.i386.rpm`, which includes the package name (`foo`), version (`1.0`), release (`1`), and architecture (`i386`). Installing a package is as simple as:

```
# rpm -ivh foo-1.0-1.i386.rpm
foo                          ###################################
#
```

As you can see, RPM prints out the name of the package (which is not necessarily the same as the file name, which could have been `1.rpm`), and then prints a succession of hash marks as the package is installed, as a sort of progress meter.

Installing packages is designed to be simple, but you can get a few errors:

Package Already Installed

If the package is already installed, you will see:

```
# rpm -ivh foo-1.0-1.i386.rpm
foo                         package foo-1.0-1 is already installed
error: foo-1.0-1.i386.rpm cannot be installed
#
```

If you really want to install the package anyway, you can use `--replacepkgs` on the command line, which tells RPM to ignore the error:

```
# rpm -ivh --replacepkgs foo-1.0-1.i386.rpm
foo                          ###################################
#
```

Conflicting Files

If you attempt to install a package that contains a file that has already been installed by another packages, you'll see:

```
# rpm -ivh foo-1.0-1.i386.rpm
foo             /usr/bin/foo conflicts with file from bar-1.0-1
error: foo-1.0-1.i386.rpm cannot be installed
#
```

To cause RPM to ignore that error, use `--replacefiles` on the command line:

```
# rpm -ivh --replacefiles foo-1.0-1.i386.rpm
foo                    ################################
#
```

Unresolved Dependency

RPM packages can "depend" on other packages, which means that they require other packages to be installed in order to run properly. If you try to install a package for which there is such an unresolved dependency, you'll see:

```
# rpm -ivh bar-1.0-1.i386.rpm
failed dependencies:
        foo is needed by bar-1.0-1
#
```

To handle this error you should install the requested packages. If you want to force the installation anyway (a bad idea since the package probably will not run correctly), use --nodeps on the command line.

9.2.2   Uninstalling

Uninstalling a package is just as simple as installing:

```
# rpm -e foo
#
```

Notice that we used the package *name* "foo", not the name of the original package *file* "foo-1.0-1.i386.rpm".

You can encounter a dependency error when uninstalling a package if some other installed package depends on the one you are trying to remove. For example:

```
# rpm -e foo
removing these packages would break dependencies:
        foo is needed by bar-1.0-1
#
```

To cause RPM to ignore that error and uninstall the package anyway (which is a bad idea since the package that depend on it will probably fail to work properly), use --nodeps on the command line.

9.2.3 Upgrading

Upgrading a package is almost just like installing.

```
# rpm -Uvh foo-2.0-1.i386.rpm
foo                        ###################################
#
```

What you don't see above is the fact that RPM automatically uninstalled any old versions of the foo package. In fact you may want to always use -U to install packages, since it works fine even when there are no previous versions of the package installed.

Since RPM performs intelligent upgrading of packages with configuration files, you may see a message like:

```
saving /etc/foo.conf as /etc/foo.conf.rpmsave
```

This means that your changes to the configuration file may not be "forward compatible" with the new configuration file in the package, so RPM saved your original file, and installed a new one. You should investigate and resolve the differences between the two files as soon as possible to ensure that your system continues to function properly.

Since upgrading is really a combination of uninstalling and installing, you can encounter any errors from those modes, plus one more: If RPM thinks you are trying to upgrade to a package with an *older* version number, you will see:

```
# rpm -Uvh foo-1.0-1.i386.rpm
foo    package foo-2.0-1 (which is newer) is already installed
error: foo-1.0-1.i386.rpm cannot be installed
#
```

To cause RPM to "upgrade" anyway, use --oldpackage on the command line:

```
# rpm -Uvh --oldpackage foo-1.0-1.i386.rpm
foo                        ###################################
#
```

9.2.4 Querying

Querying the database of installed packages is accomplished with rpm -q. A simple use is rpm -q foo which will print the package name, version, and release number of the installed package foo:

```
# rpm -q foo
foo-2.0-1
#
```

Instead of specifying the package name, you can use the following options with -q to specify what package(s) you want to query. These are called *Package Specification Options*.

- -a queries all currently installed packages.

- -f <file> will query the package owning <file>.

- -p <packagefile> queries the package <packagefile>.

There are a number of ways to specify what information to display about queried packages. The following options are used to select the information you are interested in. These are called *Information Selection Options*.

- -i displays package information such as name, description, release, size, build date, install date, vendor, and other miscellaneous information.

- -l displays the list of files that the package "owns".

- -s displays the state of all the files in the package.

- -d displays a list of files marked as documentation (man pages, info pages, README's, etc).

- -c displays a list of files marked as configuration files. These are the files you change after installation to adapt the package to your system (send-mail.cf, passwd, inittab, etc).

For those options that display file lists, you can add -v to your command line to get the lists in a familiar ls -l format.

9.2.5   Verifying

Verifying a package compares information about files installed from a package with the same information from the original package. Among other things, verifying compares the size, MD5 sum, permissions, type, owner and group of each file.

rpm -V verifies a package. You can use any of the *Package Selection Options* listed for querying to specify the packages you wish to verify. A simple use is rpm -V foo which verifies that all the files in the foo package are as they were when they were originally installed. For example:

- To verify a package containing particular file:

```
rpm -Vf /bin/vi
```

- To verify ALL installed packages:

```
rpm -Va
```

- To verify an installed package against an RPM package file:

```
rpm -Vp foo-1.0-1.i386.rpm
```

This can be useful if you suspect that your RPM databases are corrupt.

If everything verified properly there will be no output. If there are any discrepancies they will be displayed. The format of the output is a string of 8 characters, a possible "c" denoting a configuration file, and then the file name. Each of the 8 characters denotes the result of a comparison of one attribute of the file to the value of that attribute recorded in the RPM database. A single "." (period) means the test passed. The following characters denote failure of certain tests:

5 MD5 checksum

S File size

L Symbolic link

T File modification time

D Device

U User

G Group

M Mode (includes permissions and file type)

If you see any output, use your best judgment to determine if you should remove or reinstall the package, or somehow fix the problem.

9.3   Impressing Your Friends with RPM

RPM is a very useful tool for both managing your system and diagnosing and fixing problems. The best way to make sense of all the options is to look at some examples.

- Let's say you delete some files by accident, but you aren't sure what you deleted. If you want to verify your entire system and see what might be missing, you would enter:

```
rpm -Va
```

If some files are missing, or appear to have been corrupted, you should probably either re-install the package or uninstall, then re-install the package.

- Let's say you run across a file that you don't recognize. To find out which package owns it, you would enter:

```
rpm -qf /usr/X11R6/bin/xjewel
```

The output would look like:

```
xjewel-1.6-1
```

- We can combine the above two examples in the following scenario. Say you are having problems with /usr/bin/paste. You would like to verify the package that owns that program but you don't know which package that is. Simply enter:

```
rpm -Vf /usr/bin/paste
```

and the appropriate package will be verified.

- If you are using a program and want to find out more information about it, you can enter the following to find out what documentation came with the package that "owns" that program (in this case ispell):

```
rpm -qdf /usr/bin/ispell
```

The output would be:

```
/usr/man/man4/ispell.4
/usr/man/man4/english.4
/usr/man/man1/unsq.1
/usr/man/man1/tryaffix.1
/usr/man/man1/sq.1
/usr/man/man1/munchlist.1
/usr/man/man1/ispell.1
/usr/man/man1/findaffix.1
/usr/man/man1/buildhash.1
/usr/info/ispell.info.gz
/usr/doc/ispell-3.1.18-1/README
```

- You find a new koules RPM, but you don't know what it is. To find out some information on it, enter:

```
rpm -qip koules-1.2-2.i386.rpm
```

The output would be:

```
Name          : koules    Distribution: Red Hat Linux Colgate
Version       : 1.2               Vendor: Red Hat Software
Release       : 2            Build Date: Mon Sep 02 11:59:12 1996
Install date: (none)       Build Host: porky.redhat.com
Group         : Games      Source RPM: koules-1.2-2.src.rpm
Size          : 614939
Summary       : SVGAlib action game; multiplayer, network
Description :
This arcade-style game is novel in conception and
excellent in execution.  No shooting, no blood, no guts,
no gore.  The play is simple, but you still must develop
skill to play.  This version uses SVGAlib to run on a
graphics console.
```

- Now you want to see what files the koules RPM installs. You would enter:

  ```
  rpm -qlp koules-1.2-2.i386.rpm
  ```

The output is:

```
/usr/man/man6/koules.6
/usr/lib/games/kouleslib/start.raw
/usr/lib/games/kouleslib/end.raw
/usr/lib/games/kouleslib/destroy2.raw
/usr/lib/games/kouleslib/destroy1.raw
/usr/lib/games/kouleslib/creator2.raw
/usr/lib/games/kouleslib/creator1.raw
/usr/lib/games/kouleslib/colize.raw
/usr/lib/games/kouleslib
/usr/games/koules
```

These are just several examples. As you use the system you will find many more uses for rpm.

9.4   Other RPM Resources

For more information on RPM, check out the man page, the help screen (rpm --help), and the RPM documents available at

```
http://www.rpm.org/
```

There is also an RPM book available. It's called Maximum RPM , and is available from Red Hat Software and your local bookstore. It contains a wealth of information about RPM for both the end-user and the package builder. An on-line version of the book is available at http://www.rpm.org/.

There is also a mailing list for discussion of RPM related issues, called
`rpm-list@redhat.com`. The list is archived on
`http://www.redhat.com/support/mailing-lists/`. To subscribe, send
mail to `rpm-list-request@redhat.com` with the word `subscribe` in the subject line.

10

Glint

Red Hat provides a graphical tool to aid in package installation and removal. It's called glint (Graphical Linux INstallation Tool) and runs under the X Window System. It allows easy installation, uninstallation, upgrading, querying, and verification of packages. The interface is similar to the one found in many popular file managers and is simple to use.

Operations are performed in glint by selecting the packages to operate on and then selecting the operation to perform via pushbuttons. Installing a package places all of the components of that package on your system. Uninstalling one removes all traces of the package except for configuration files you have modified. Upgrading a package installs the newly available version and uninstalls all other versions that were previously installed. This allows quick upgrading to the latest releases of packages.

The query operation lets you examine the details of both installed or available packages. You can view the description of the package, where and when it was built, the files in the package, and other attributes. All of the configuration and documentation components of each package are clearly marked as such to reduce the time you spend looking for them.

Using glint to perform all of these operations is the same as using rpm to do them from the command line. However, the graphical nature of glint often makes these operations easier to perform.

The normal way to handle glint is to display the available packages and files, select the ones you want to operate on, and then press a button or choose a menu item that performs the operation. For instance, you can install several packages with a few button clicks.

10.1 Starting glint

To start glint, simply run `glint` & from any X terminal window. That will bring up a window that looks like the one in figure 10.1. Any user can use glint to query and verify packages, but if you need to install, uninstall, or upgrade packages be sure to run glint as root.

There are two main parts to the glint interface. The first, on the left, allows you to browse and select the packages installed on your system. The right side contains buttons that manipulate the selected packages.

Figure 10.1: Main Glint Window

10.2 The Package Display

Each folder icon in glint represents a group of packages. Each group can contain other groups, which allows for flexible locations of packages. Groups are used to place packages that perform similar functions in similar locations. For example, Red Hat includes many application programs such as editors and spreadsheets. All of the text based ones appear in the "Applications" group. Inside of that group, there is another grouping for all of the editors that are shipped.

By convention, groups are written in the same way as UNIX paths. The top most group is written first, and subsequent groups follow with a slash separating the group names. This means that an X-based drawing program appears in the X11/Applications/Graphics group.

To view the packages and subgroups within a group, double click the left mouse button on a group's folder icon. The window then changes to show what that package contains. The top line of the package display shows which group you're currently looking in, as well as the groups leading to the current one. To return to the previous group you were looking at, double click on the "Back" folder, which is always in the upper left hand corner of the folder area (though it often gets scrolled away).

If you'd like to examine a subgroup in a new window, double click the middle mouse button on its folder. If your mouse has only two buttons, click both. This will create a new window with that group in it.

10.2.1 Context Sensitive Menus

Pressing the right mouse button on any icon in the package window brings up a small, *context sensitive* menu. The exact items it contains depends on exactly where you press it. They all contain options to select or deselect the item, and many let you install, uninstall, query, upgrade, or verify the item you clicked on. There's more information on how to do these things later.

To choose an item from a context sensitive menu, press and hold the right mouse button on a icon. While still holding the right button down, move the mouse pointer over the item you'd like to select (which will then become highlighted). Release the right mouse button to select that item and make the menu disappear.

10.2.2 Selecting Packages

To select a single package, click the left mouse button on it. You'll notice a thin border appear around the package's icon (as shown in figure 10.2) which shows that it's currently selected. To unselect it, click the left mouse button on it and the border will disappear. The number of packages currently selected is always displayed at the bottom of the window. A group's folder icon displays the number of packages within that group that have been selected, or All if all have been selected.

Figure 10.2: Selecting Packages in Glint

The context sensitive menu for a package also allows easy selection and unselection. Using the select and unselect options on a package's icon selects or

unselects that package, while those options on a group's folder icon select and unselect all of the packages in that group. Using these menu options makes selecting
groups of packages much quicker than selecting each package individually.

10.2.3   Viewing Available Packages

Figure 10.3: Available Window

To see what packages are available for you to install, choose the Available pushbutton from any glint window. After a few moments, a new window, like the one
shown in figure 10.3, will appear. The differences in the title and buttons indicate
that this window is listing packages you may install. Navigating through these
packages and selecting them is the same as in the other glint windows.

If you get an error message from glint saying that it can't find any RPMs, see the
section below on Configuration.

10.3   Configuration

The only configuration information glint needs is the path to new RPMs. When
you're using your Red Hat Linux CD-ROM, this will probably be
/mnt/cdrom/RedHat/RPMS, which is the default path for glint. If you download
new RPMs from the Internet or want to install RPMs via a NFS mounted CD-ROM
this path will probably be different for you.

To change this path, first be sure to close all of the windows listing available packages you may have open. Then choose the Configuration option from one of
the remaining windows. This will open a dialog box like the one shown in figure
10.4. Here you can type the full path to the RPMs you'd like to look at. Choosing
the Save button will save this path, making it the default for future glint sessions.
The Default button restores the path to the one that glint used when it started.

Figure 10.4: Configuration Window

After changing this path and closing the dialog box, you can use the Available button to view the packages available in the new location.

10.4 Package Manipulation

10.4.1 Querying Packages

The easiest way to query a single package or group is to use the query option from the icon's context sensitive menu. If you want to query a more diverse set of packages, select them all and use the Query button in one of the windows.

Using either of these methods creates a window like the one shown in figure 10.5. If you choose only one package, it will look a bit different however, so some of this won't apply.

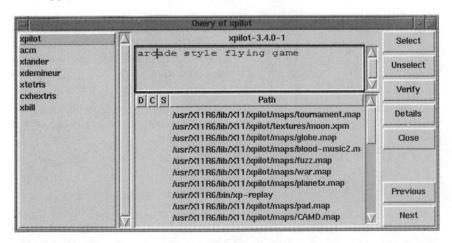

Figure 10.5: Query Window

On the very left of the window is a list of the packages that have been queried.

Selecting one of them will change the information in the rest of the window. You may step through them in order by using the Next and Previous buttons on the right side of the window.

The name, version, and release of the current package are in the top middle of the query window. Immediately below this is the description of the package, which can be quite large. A scroll bar is there to let you read the whole thing.

Below the description is a list of the files contained in the package. Along with the full path to the file, the file list tells you a couple of other things. If a D appears to the left of the path, that file is a documentation file and would be a good thing to read. If a C appears there, then the file is a configuration file. A * means that the correct version of that file is not installed on your system. This can occur because a more recent version of a package was installed or because two packages contain different versions of the same file.

Figure 10.6: Query Details

More information on a package can be seen by clicking on the Details pushbutton. A window like the one in figure 10.6 will then appear. This lists more information about the package being displayed in the main query window. When you select a new package in the query window, the information in the details window will change to reflect your new choice.

You may also select, unselect, or verify a package while querying it by using the buttons provided. Click on the Close button when you are finished looking at the packages.

10.4.2   Verifying Packages

Verifying a package checks all of the files in the package to insure they match the ones present on your system. The checksum, file size, permissions, and owner attributes are all checked against the database. This check can be used when you suspect that one of programs files has become corrupted due to the installation of new programs.

Choosing the packages to verify is the same as choosing the packages to query.

Select the packages and use the `Verify` button or choose the `Verify` entry from a context sensitive menu. A window opens like the one in figure 10.7.

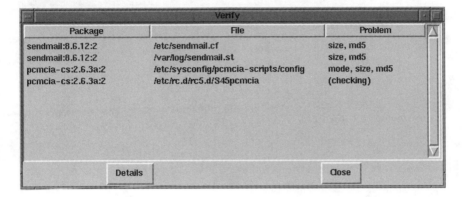

Figure 10.7: Verify Window

The three columns in this window describe the package with a problem in it, the file that has the problem, and a brief description of the discrepancies that were found. While the check is running, the current file being checked appears as the last element in the list, and the problem is listed as (checking). A full list of the problems that can be found through verification appears in figure 10.8.

Problem	Description
missing	The file is no longer on your system
mode	permission bits have changed
size	file's size has changed
uid	owner's uid has changed
gid	owner's gid has changed
md5	the md5 checksum has changed
link	the file is a symlink to the wrong place

Figure 10.8: Possible Problems found by Verification

To get more information on the problems found with a file, double click on the file's path. A window like the one shown in figure 10.9 lists the expected and current values of the attributes that are amiss.

10.4.3   Installing New Packages

Installing new packages from glint is very simple. First look at the packages available for installation (see the section 10.2.3 for how to do this). You may select any number of these (and query them if you're not sure what they are) for installation

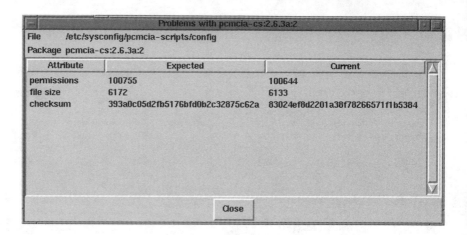

Figure 10.9: Verification Details

(in the same manner you select packages for verification.) If you want to install a single package or group, the context sensitive menus provide a shortcut for doing so. Figure 10.10 shows a window with some packages selected for installation.

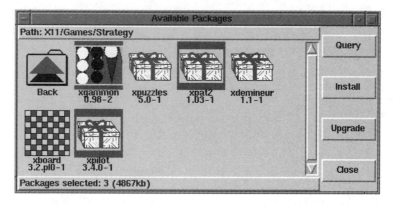

Figure 10.10: Packages Selected for Installation

After you've begun the installation, a window appears like the one in figure 10.11. It tracks the progress of the installation so you'll know something is happening. The top bar shows how much of the current package (whose name is listed inside of it) has been installed while the bottom graph shows how much of the total installation has been finished. The number of packages, package sizes, and time estimates are continually updated.

If a problem occurs during the installation, a window will appear listing any errors that occurred. If this happens, you should correct the problems and then try again.

Figure 10.11: Installation Progress

After the installation has completed, the package and groups that have been installed are moved from the available window to the main glint window to show you that they have been successfully installed.

Upgrading Packages

When a new version of a package has been released, it is easy to install it on your system. Select the packages from the window of available packages in the same way you select packages for installation. Both the Upgrade button and the context sensitive menus will begin the upgrade.

During the upgrade, you'll see a progress indicator like the one for installing packages. When it's finished, the installed packages will appear in the the main glint windows and any old versions of the packages will be removed.

It is much better to use the upgrade option than to uninstall the old versions of a package and then install the new one. Using upgrade ensures that any changes you made to package configuration files get preserved properly, while doing it manually could cause those changes to be lost.

If you run out of disk space during an installation, the install will fail. However, the package which was being installed when the error occurred may leave some files around. To clean this up, reinstall the package after you've made more disk space available.

10.4.4 Uninstalling Packages

Uninstalling a package is not the same as upgrading one. When a package is uninstalled, any files it uses that are not needed by other packages on your system are removed. Changed configuration files are copied to <filename>.rpmsave so you can reuse them later.

Like verifying and querying packages, you can remove a package through the buttons on the right of the glint window or through a context sensitive menu. Remember that when you make a choice from a group's menu, the operation is performed on all of the packages in that group, so be careful!

Figure 10.12: Uninstall Window

Once you've begun the uninstall, glint asks for confirmation, showing a window like the one in figure 10.12. All of the packages that are about to be uninstalled are listed. You should look at them all to ensure you're not about to remove something you want to keep. Clicking the Yes button will start the uninstallation process. After it completes, the packages and groups that have been removed will disappear from any windows they were in.

11

System Administration

This chapter is an overview of the Red Hat Linux system. It will illustrate things that you may not know about the system and things that are somewhat different from other UNIX systems.

11.1 Filesystem Structure

Red Hat Software is committed to the Linux File System Standard, a collaborative document that defines the names and locations of many files and directories. We will continue to track the standard to keep Red Hat compliant.

While compliance with the standard means many things, the two most important are compatibility with other compliant systems, and the ability to mount the /usr partition read-only. The /usr partition contains common executables and is not meant to be changed by users. Because of this, the /usr partition can be mounted from the CD-ROM or from another machine via read-only NFS. The current Linux Filesystem Standard (FSSTND) document is the authoritative reference to any FSSTND compliant filesystem, but the standard leaves many areas undefined or extensible. In this section we provide an overview of the standard and a description of the parts of the filesystem not covered by the standard.

The complete standard can be viewed at:

    http://www.pathname.com/fhs/

11.1.1   Overview of the FSSTND

The directories and files noted here are a small subset of those specified by the FSSTND document. Check the latest FSSTND document for the most up to date and complete information.

The /etc Directory

The /etc directory is reserved for configuration files that are local to your machine. No binaries are to put in /etc. Binaries that were in the past put in /etc should now go into /sbin or possibly /bin.

The X11 and skel directories should be subdirectories of /etc:

```
/etc
  |- X11
  +- skel
```

The X11 directory is for X11 configuration files such as XF86Config. The skel directory is for "skeleton" user files, which are files used to populate a home directory when a user is first created.

The /lib Directory

The /lib directory should contain only those libraries that are need to execute the binaries in /bin and /sbin.

The /sbin Directory

The /sbin directory is for executables used only by the root user, and only those executables needed to boot and mount /usr and perform system recovery operations. The FSSTND says:

> "/sbin typically contains files essential for booting the system in addition to the binaries in /bin. Anything executed after /usr is known to be mounted (when there are no problems) should be placed in /usr/sbin. Local-only system administration binaries should be placed into
> /usr/local/sbin."

At a minimum, the following programs should be in /sbin:

```
clock, getty, init, update, mkswap, swapon,
swapoff, halt, reboot, shutdown, fdisk, fsck.*,
mkfs.*, lilo, arp, ifconfig, route
```

The /usr **Directory**

The /usr directory is for files that are shareable across a whole site. The /usr directory usually has its own partition, and it should be mountable read only. The following directories should be subdirectories of /usr:

```
/usr
   |- X11R6
   |- bin
   |- dict
   |- doc
   |- etc
   |- games
   |- include
   |- info
   |- lib
   |- local
   |- man
   |- sbin
   |- share
   +- src
```

The X11R6 directory is for the X Window System (XFree86 on Red Hat Linux), bin is for executables, doc is for random non-man-page documentation, etc is for site-wide configuration files, include is for C header files, info is for GNU info files, lib is for libraries, man is for man pages, sbin is for system administration binaries (those that do not belong in /sbin), and src is for source code.

The /usr/local **Directory**

The FSSTND says:

> "The /usr/local hierarchy is for use by the system administrator when installing software locally. It needs to be safe from being overwritten when the system software is updated. It may be used for programs and data that are shareable amongst a group of machines, but not found in /usr."

The /usr/local directory is similar in structure to the /usr directory. It has the following subdirectories, which are similar in purpose to those in the /usr directory:

```
/usr/local
       |- bin
       |- doc
```

```
|- etc
|- games
|- include
|- info
|- lib
|- man
|- sbin
+- src
```

The /var **directory**

Since the FSSTND requires that you be able to mount /usr read-only, any programs that write log files or need spool or lock directories probably should write
them to the /var directory. The FSSTND says /var is for

> "... variable data files. This includes spool directories and files, ad-
> ministrative and logging data, and transient and temporary files."

The following directories should be subdirectories of /var:

```
/var
    |- log
    |- catman
    |- lib
    |- local
    |- named
    |- nis
    |- preserve
    |- run
    |- lock
    |- tmp
    +- spool
        |- at
        |- cron
        |- lpd
        |- mail
        |- mqueue
        |- rwho
        |- smail
        |- uucp
        +- news
```

System log files such as wtmp and lastlog go in /var/log. The /var/lib
directory also contains the RPM system databases. Formatted man pages go in
/var/catman, and lock files go in /var/lock. The /var/spool directory has
subdirectories for various systems that need to store data files.

11.1.2 /usr/local **in Red Hat Linux**

In Red Hat Linux, the intended use for /usr/local is slightly different from that specified by the FSSTND. The FSSTND says that /usr/local should be where you store software that is to remain safe from system software upgrades. Since system upgrades from Red Hat Software are done safely with the RPM system and Glint, you don't need to protect files by putting them in /usr/local. Instead, we recommend you use /usr/local for software that is local to your machine.

For instance, let's say you have mounted /usr via read-only NFS from *beavis*. If there is a package or program you would like to install, but you are not allowed to write to *beavis*, you should install it under /usr/local. Later perhaps, if you've managed to convince the system administrator of *beavis* to install the program on /usr, you can uninstall it from /usr/local.

11.2   Special Red Hat File Locations

In addition to the files pertaining to the RPM system that reside in /var/lib/rpm (see chapter 9), there are two other special locations that are reserved for Red Hat Linux configuration and operation.

The control-panel and related tools put lots of stuff in /usr/lib/rhs. There is probably nothing here that you would want to edit. It is mostly small scripts, bitmaps and text files.

The other location, /etc/sysconfig, stores configuration information. The major users of the files in this directory are the scripts that run at boot time. It is possible to edit these by hand, but it would be better to use the proper control-panel tool.

11.3   Users, Groups and User-Private Groups

Managing users and groups has traditionally been tedious. Red Hat Linux has a few tools and conventions that make user and groups easier to manage, and more useful.

The easiest way to manage users and groups is through linuxconf (see Chapter 8. However, you can also use adduser to create a new user from the command line.

11.3.1 Standard Users

Table 11.3.1 lists the standard users set up by the installation process (this is essentially the
/etc/passwd file). The group id (GID) in this table is the *primary group* for the user. See section 11.3.3 for details on how groups are used.

User	UID	GID	Home Directory	Shell
root	0	0	/root	/bin/bash
bin	1	1	/bin	
daemon	2	2	/sbin	
adm	3	4	/var/adm	
lp	4	7	/var/spool/lpd	
sync	5	0	/sbin	/bin/sync
shutdown	6	0	/sbin	/sbin/shutdown
halt	7	0	/sbin	/sbin/halt
mail	8	12	/var/spool/mail	
news	9	13	/var/spool/news	
uucp	10	14	/var/spool/uucp	
operator	11	0	/root	
games	12	100	/usr/games	
gopher	13	30	/usr/lib/gopher-data	
ftp	14	50	/home/ftp	
nobody	99	99	/	

Figure 11.1: Standard Users

11.3.2 Standard Groups

Table 11.3.2 lists the standard groups as set up by the installation process (this is essentially the /etc/group file).

11.3.3 User Private Groups

Red Hat Linux uses a user private group (UPG) scheme, which makes UNIX groups much easier to use. The UPG scheme does not add or change anything in the standard UNIX way of handling groups. It simply offers a new convention for handling groups. Whenever you create a new user, by default, he or she has a unique group. The scheme works as follows:

User Private Group Each user has its own primary group, of which only it is a member.

umask = 002 The traditional UNIX umask is 022, which prevents other users *and other members of a user's primary group* from modifying a user's files. Since every user has their own private group in the UPG scheme, this "group protection" is not needed. A umask of 002 will prevent users from modifying other users' private files. The umask is set in /etc/profile.

setgid bit on Directories If you set the setgid bit on a directory (with chmod g+s *directory*), files created in that directory will have their group set to the directory's group.

Group	GID	Members
root	0	root
bin	1	root,bin,daemon
daemon	2	root,bin,daemon
sys	3	root,bin,adm
adm	4	root,adm,daemon
tty	5	
disk	6	root
lp	7	daemon,lp
mem	8	
kmem	9	
wheel	10	root
mail	12	mail
news	13	news
uucp	14	uucp
man	15	
games	20	
gopher	30	
dip	40	
ftp	50	
nobody	99	
users	100	
floppy	19	

Figure 11.2: Standard Groups

Most computing sites like to create a group for each major project and assign people to the groups they need to be in. Managing files traditionally has been difficult,
though, because when someone creates a file it is owned by the primary group he
or she belongs to. When a single person works on multiple projects, it becomes
hard to make the files owned by the group that is associated with that project. In
the UPG scheme, groups are automatically assigned to files on a project-by-project
basis, which makes managing group projects very simple.

Let's say you have a big project called *devel*, with many people editing the devel
files in a devel directory. Make a group called devel, chgrp the devel directory
to devel, and add the all the devel users to the devel group. Now, all the devel
users will be able to edit the devel files and create new files in the devel directory,
and these files will always retain their devel group. Thus, they will always be
edit-able by other devel users.

If you have multiple projects like *devel*, and users who are working on multiple
projects, these users will never have to change their umask or group when they
move from project to project. The setgid bit on each project's main directory "selects" the proper group.

Since each user's HOME directory is owned by the user and their private group, it
is safe to set the setgid bit on the HOME directory. However, by default, files are
created with the primary group of the user, so the setgid bit would be redundant.

User Private Group Rationale

Since the UPG scheme is new, many people have questions about it, and they wonder why it is necessary. The following is the rationale for the scheme.

- You'd like to have a group of people work on a set of files in say, the
  /usr/lib/emacs/site-lisp directory. You trust a few people to mess
  around in there, but certainly not everyone.
- So you enter:

      chown -R root.emacs /usr/lib/emacs/site-lisp

  and you add the proper users to the group.
- To allow the users to actually create files in the directory you enter:

      chmod 775 /usr/lib/emacs/site-lisp

- But when a user creates a new file it is assigned the group of the users default
  group (usually users). To prevent this you enter

      chmod 2775 /usr/lib/emacs/site-lisp

  which causes everything in the directory to be created with the "emacs"
  group.

- But the new file needs to be mode 664 for another user in the emacs group to be able to edit it. To do this you make the default umask 002.

- Well, this all works fine, except that if your default group is "users", every file you create in your home directory will be writable by everybody in "users" (usually everyone).

- To fix this, you make each user have a "private group" as their default group.

At this point, by making the default umask 002 and giving everyone a private default group, you can easily set up groups that users can take advantage of without doing any magic. Just create the group, add the users, and do the above chown and chmod on the group's directories.

11.4   User Authentication with PAM

Programs which give users access to privileges of any sort need to be able to authenticate the users. When you log into a system, you provide your name and password, and the login process uses those to authenticate the login – to verify that you are who you say you are. Other forms of authentication than passwords are possible, and it is possible for the passwords to be stored in different ways.

PAM, which stands for "Pluggable Authentication Modules", is a way of allowing the system administrator to set authentication policy without having to recompile programs which do authentication. With PAM, you control how the modules are plugged into the programs by editing a configuration file.

Most Red Hat Linux users will never need to touch this configuration file. When you use RPM to install programs that need to do authentication, they automatically make the changes that are needed to do normal password authentication. However, you may want to customize your configuration, in which case you need to understand the configuration file.

11.4.1   PAM Modules

There are four types of modules defined by the PAM standard. auth modules provide the actual authentication, perhaps asking for and checking a password, and set "credentials" such as group membership or kerberos "tickets". account modules check to make sure that the authentication is allowed (the account has not expired, the user is allowed to log in at this time of day, etc.). password modules are used to set passwords. session modules are used once a user has been authenticated to make it possible for them to use their account, perhaps mounting the user's home directory or making their mailbox available.

These modules may be *stacked*, so that multiple modules are used. For instance, rlogin normally makes use of at least two authentication methods: if "rhosts" authentication succeeds, it is sufficient to allow the connection; if it fails, then standard password authentication is done.

New modules can be added at any time, and PAM-aware applications can then be made to use them. For instance, if you have a one-time-password calculator system, and you can write a module to support it (documentation on writing modules is included with the system), PAM-aware programs can use the new module and work with the new one-time-password calculators without being recompiled or otherwise modified in any way.

11.4.2   Services

Each program which uses PAM defines its own "service" name. The login program defines the service type `login`, ftpd defines the service type `ftp`, etc. In general, the service type is the name of the program used to **access** the service, not (if there is a difference) the program used to **provide** the service.

11.4.3   The Configuration Files

The directory `/etc/pam.d` is used to configure all PAM applications. (This used to be
`/etc/pam.conf` in earlier PAM versions; while the `pam.conf` file is still read if no
`/etc/pam.d/` entry is found, its use is deprecated.) Each application (really, each **service**) has its own file. A file looks like this:

```
#%PAM-1.0
auth       required    /lib/security/pam_securetty.so
auth       required    /lib/security/pam_pwdb.so shadow nullo
auth       required    /lib/security/pam_nologin.so
account    required    /lib/security/pam_pwdb.so
password   required    /lib/security/pam_cracklib.so
password   required    /lib/security/pam_pwdb.so shadow ↵
                                             nullok use_authto
session    required    /lib/security/pam_pwdb.so
```

The first line is a comment. Any line that starts with a # character is a comment. Lines two through four stack up three modules to use for login authorization. Line two makes sure that *if* the user is trying to log in as root, the tty on which they are logging in is listed in the `/etc/securetty` file *if* that file exists. Line three causes the user to be asked for a password and the password checked. Line four checks to see if the file `/etc/nologin` exists, and if it does, displays the contents of the file, and if the user is not root, does not let him or her log in.

Note that all three modules are checked, *even if the first module fails*. This is a security decision—it is designed to not let the user know why their authentication was disallowed, because knowing why it was disallowed might allow them to break the authentication more easily. You can change this behavior by changing `required` to `requisite`; if any `requisite` module returns failure, PAM fails immediately without calling any other modules.

The fifth line causes any necessary accounting to be done. For example, if shadow passwords have been enabled, the pam_pwdb.so module will check to see if the account has expired, or if the user has not changed his or her password and the grace period for changing the password has expired.

The sixth line subjects a newly-changed password to a series of tests to ensure that it cannot, for example, be easily determined by a dictionary-based password cracking program.

The seventh line (which we've had to wrap) specifies that if the login program changes the user's password, it should use the pam_pwdb.so module to do so. (It will do so only if an auth module has determined that the password needs to be changed—for example, if a shadow password has expired.)

The eighth and final line specifies that the pam_pwdb.so module should be used to manage the session. Currently, that module doesn't do anything; it could be replaced (or supplemented by stacking) by any necessary module.

Note that the order of the lines within each file matters. While it doesn't really matter much in which order required modules are called, there are other *control flags* available. While optional is rarely used, and never used by default on a Red Hat Linux system, sufficient and requisite cause order to become important.

Let's look at the auth configuration for rlogin:

```
auth    required    /lib/security/pam_securetty.so
auth    sufficient  /lib/security/pam_rhosts_auth.so
auth    required    /lib/security/pam_pwdb.so shadow nullok
auth    required    /lib/security/pam_nologin.so
```

That looks *almost* like the login entry, but there's an extra line specifying an extra module, and the modules are specified in a different order.

First, pam_securetty.so keeps root logins from happening on insecure terminals. This effectively disallows all root rlogin attempts. If you wish to allow them (in which case we recommend that you either not be internet-connected or be behind a good firewall), you can simply remove that line.

Second, pam_nologin.so checks /etc/nologin, as specified above.

Third, if pam_rhosts_auth.so authenticates the user, PAM immediately returns success to rlogin without any password checking being done. If pam_rhosts_auth.so fails to authenticate the user, that failed authentication is ignored.

Finally (if pam_rhosts_auth.so has failed to authenticate the user), the pam_pwdb.so module performs normal password authentication.

Note that if you do not want to prompt for a password if the securetty check fails, you can change the pam_securetty.so module from required to requisite

11.4.4   Shadow Passwords

The pam_pwdb.so module will automatically detect that you are using shadow passwords and make all necessary adjustments. Please refer to Section 11.5 for more information on the utilities that support shadow passwords.

11.4.5   More Information

This is just an introduction to PAM. More information is included in the /usr/doc/pam directory, including a *System Administrators' Guide*, a *Module Writers' Manual*, an *Application Developers' Manual*, and the PAM standard, DCE-RFC 86.0. In addition, documentation is available from the Red Hat web site, at http://www.redhat.com/linux-info/pam/.

11.5   Shadow Utilities

Support for shadow passwords has been enhanced significantly for Red Hat Linux 5.2. Shadow passwords are a method of improving system security by moving the encrypted passwords (normally found in /etc/passwd) to another file with more restrictive file access permissions. The shadow-utils package contains a number of utilities that support:

- Conversion from normal to shadowed passwords and back (pwconv, pwunconv)
- Verification of the password, group, and associated shadow files (pwck, grpck).
- Industry-standard methods of adding, deleting and modifying user accounts (useradd, usermod, and userdel).
- Industry-standard methods of adding, deleting, and modifying user groups (groupadd, groupmod, and groupdel).
- Industry-standard method of administering the /etc/group file (gpasswd).

Please Note: There are a few additional points of interest concerning these utilities:

- The utilities will work properly whether shadowing is enabled or not.
- The utilities have been slightly modified to support Red Hat Software's user private group scheme. For a description of the modifications, please see the useradd man page. For more information on user private groups, please turn to Section 11.3.3 on page 186.
- The adduser script has been replaced with a symlink to /usr/sbin/useradd.

11.6   Building a Custom Kernel

With the introduction of modularization in the Linux 2.0.*x* kernel there have been some significant changes in building customized kernels. In the past you were required to compile support into your kernel if you wanted to access a particular hardware or filesystem component. For some hardware configurations the size of the kernel could quickly reach a critical level. To require ready support for items that were only occasionally used was an inefficient use of system resources. With the capabilities of the 2.0.*x* kernel, if there are certain hardware components or filesystems that are used infrequently, driver modules for them can be loaded on demand. For information on handling kernel modules see Chapter 8.2, Section 8.2.2.

Many people new to Linux often ask, "why should I build my own kernel". Given the advances that have been made in the use of kernel modules, the most accurate response to that question is, "unless you know why you need to build your own kernel, you probably don't". So unless you have a specific reason to build a customized kernel (or you're just the curious sort), you may skip ahead to Section 11.7 on page 196.

11.6.1   Building a modularized kernel

These instructions provide you with the knowledge required to take advantage of the power and flexibility available through kernel modularization. If you do not wish to take advantage of modularization, please see Section 11.6.3 for an explanation of the different aspects of building and installing a monolithic kernel. It is assumed that you have already installed the `kernel-headers` and `kernel-source` packages and that you issue all commands from the `/usr/src/linux` directory.

It is important to begin a kernel build with the source tree in a known condition. Therefore, it is recommended that you begin with the command `make mrproper`. This will remove any configuration files along with the remains of any previous builds that may be scattered around the source tree. Now you must create a configuration file that will determine which components to include in your new kernel. Depending upon your hardware and personal preferences there are three methods available to configure the kernel.

- `make config` An interactive text program. Components are presented and you answer with Y (yes), N (no), or M (module).

- `make menuconfig` A graphic, menu driven program. Components are presented in a menu of categories, you select the desired components in the same manner used in the Red Hat Linux installation program. Toggle the tag corresponding to the item you want included; **Y** (yes), **N** (no), or **M** (module).

- `make xconfig` An X Windows program. Components are listed in different levels of menus, components are selected using a mouse. Again, select **Y** (yes), **N** (no), or **M** (module).

Please Note: In order to use `kerneld` (see Section 8.2.2 for details) and kernel modules you must answer **Yes** to **kerneld support** and **module version (CONFIG_MODVERSIONS) support** in the configuration.

Please Note: If you are building a Linux/Intel kernel on (or for) a machine that uses a "clone" processor (for example, one made by Cyrix or AMD), it is recommended to choose a **Processor type** of **386**.

If you wish to build a kernel with a configuration file (`/usr/src/linux/.config`) that you have already created with one of the above methods, you can omit the `make mrproper` and `make config` commands and use the command `make dep` followed by `make clean` to prepare the source tree for the build.

The next step consists of the actual compilation of the source code components into a working program that your machine can use to boot. The method described here is the easiest to recover from in the event of a mishap. If you are interested in other possibilities details can be found in the Kernel-HOWTO or in the `Makefile` in `/usr/src/linux` on your Linux system.

- Build the kernel with `make boot`.

- Build any modules you configured with `make modules`.

- Move the old set of modules out of the way with:

      rm -rf /lib/modules/2.0.29-old
      mv /lib/modules/2.0.29 /lib/modules/2.0.29-old

  Of course, if you have upgraded your kernel, replace `2.0.29` with the version you are using.

- Install the new modules (even if you didn't build any) with `make modules_install`.

If you have a SCSI adapter and made your SCSI driver modular, build a new `initrd` image (see Section 11.6.2; note that there are few practical reasons to make the SCSI driver modular in a custom kernel).

In order to provide a redundant boot source to protect from a possible error in a new kernel you should keep the original kernel available. Adding a kernel to the LILO menu is as simple as renaming the original kernel in `/boot`, copying the new kernel to `/boot`, adding a few lines in `/etc/lilo.conf` and running `/sbin/lilo`. Here is an example of the default `/etc/lilo.conf` file shipped with Red Hat Linux:

      boot=/dev/hda
      map=/boot/map
      install=/boot/boot.b
      prompt
      timeout=100
      image=/boot/vmlinuz
              label=linux

```
root=/dev/hda1
read-only
```

Now you must update /etc/lilo.conf. If you built a new initrd image you must tell LILO to use it. In this example of /etc/lilo.conf we have added four lines at the bottom of the file to indicate another kernel to boot from. We have re-named /boot/vmlinuz to /boot/vmlinuz.old and changed its label to old. We have also added an initrd line for the new kernel:

```
boot=/dev/hda
map=/boot/map
install=/boot/boot.b
prompt
timeout=100
image=/boot/vmlinuz
        label=linux
        initrd=/boot/initrd
        root=/dev/hda1
        read-only
image=/boot/vmlinuz.old
        label=old
        root=/dev/hda1
        read-only
```

Now when the system boots and you press (Tab) at the LILO boot: prompt two choices will be shown;

```
LILO boot:
linux      old
```

To boot the new kernel (linux) simply press (Enter), or wait for LILO to time out. If you want to boot the old kernel (old), simply enter old and press (Enter).

Here is a summary of the steps;

- mv /boot/vmlinuz /boot/vmlinuz.old
- cp /usr/src/linux/arch/i386/boot/zImage /boot/vmlinuz
- edit /etc/lilo.conf
- run /sbin/lilo

You can begin testing your new kernel by rebooting your computer and watching the messages to ensure your hardware is detected properly.

11.6.2   Making an initrd image

An initrd image is needed for loading your SCSI module at boot time. The shell script
/sbin/mkinitrd can build a proper initrd image for your machine if the following conditions are met:

- The loopback block device is available.

- The /etc/conf.modules file has a line for your SCSI adapter; for example:

    ```
    alias scsi_hostadapter BusLogic
    ```

To build the new initrd image, run /sbin/mkinitrd with parameters such as this:

```
/sbin/mkinitrd /boot/newinitrd-image 2.0.12
```

where /boot/newinitrd-image is the file to use for your new image, and 2.0.12 is the kernel whose modules (from /lib/modules) should be used in the initrd image (not necessarily the same as the version number of the currently running kernel).

11.6.3   Building a monolithic kernel

To build a monolithic kernel you follow the same steps as building a modularized kernel with a few exceptions.

- When configuring the kernel only answer **Yes** and **No** to the questions (don't make anything modular).

- Omit the steps:

    ```
    make modules
    make modules_install
    ```

- Edit the file /etc/rc.d/rc.sysinit and comment out the line depmod -a by inserting a "#" at the beginning of the line.

11.7   Sendmail

A default sendmail.cf file will be installed in /etc. The default configuration should work for most SMTP-only sites. It will *not* work for UUCP sites; you will need to generate a new sendmail.cf if you need to use UUCP mail transfers.

To generate a new `sendmail.cf`, you will need to install `m4` and the `sendmail` source package. Read the README file in the sendmail sources for more details on creating `sendmail` configuration files. Also, O'Reilly & Associates publishes a good sendmail reference entitled *sendmail* by Bryan Costales.

One common sendmail configuration is to have a single machine act as a mail gateway for all the machines on your network. For instance, at Red Hat Software we have a machine `mail.redhat.com` that does all our mail. On that machine we simply need to add the names of machines for which `mail.redhat.com` will handle mail to `/etc/sendmail.cw`. Here is an example:

```
# sendmail.cw - include all aliases for your machine
# here.
torgo.redhat.com
poodle.redhat.com
devel.redhat.com
```

Then on the other machines, `torgo`, `poodle`, and `devel`, we need to edit `/etc/sendmail.cf` to "masquerade" as `mail.redhat.com` when sending mail, and to forward any local mail processing to `redhat.com`. Find the DH and DM lines in `/etc/sendmail.cf` and edit them thusly:

```
# who I send unqualified names to
# (null means deliver locally)
DRmail.redhat.com

# who gets all local mail traffic
DHmail.redhat.com

# who I masquerade as (null for no masquerading)
DMredhat.com
```

With this type of configuration, all mail sent will appear as if it were sent from `redhat.com`, and any mail sent to `torgo.redhat.com` or the other hosts will be delivered to `mail.redhat.com`.

Please be aware that if you configure your system to masquerade as another any email sent from your system to your system will be sent to the machine you are masquerading as. For example, in the above illustration, log files that are periodically sent to `root@poodle.redhat.com` by the `cron` daemon would be sent to `root@mail.redhat.com`.

11.8   Controlling Access to Services

As a security measure, most network services are managed by a protective program called a *TCP wrapper*. The protected services are those listed in

/etc/inetd.conf that specify /usr/sbin/tcpd. tcpd can allow or deny access to a service based on the origin of the request, and the configuration in /etc/hosts.allow and /etc/hosts.deny. By default Red Hat Linux allows all service requests. To disable or limit services you can edit /etc/hosts.allow. Here is an example
/etc/hosts.allow file:

```
ALL: redhat.com .redhat.com
in.talkd: ALL
in.ntalkd: ALL
in.fingerd: ALL
in.ftpd: ALL
```

This configuration allows all connections from redhat.com and *.redhat.com machines. It also allows talk, finger, and ftp requests from all machines.

tcpd allows much more sophisticated access control, using a combination of /etc/hosts.allow and /etc/hosts.deny. Read the tcpd(8) and hosts_access(5) man pages for complete details.

11.9   Anonymous FTP

Setting up anonymous FTP is simple. All you need to do is install the anon-ftp rpm package (which you may have already done at install time). Once it is installed, anonymous FTP will be up and running.

There are a few files you might wish to edit to configure your FTP server.

/etc/ftpaccess This file defines most of the access control for your ftp server. Some of the things that you can do are: set up logical "groups" to control access from different sites, limit the number of simultaneous FTP connections, configure transfer logging, and much more. Read the ftpaccess man page for complete details.

/etc/ftphosts The ftphosts file is used to allow or deny access to certain accounts from various hosts. Read the ftphosts man page for details.

/etc/ftpusers This file lists all the users that are *not* allowed to ftp into your machine. For example, root is listed in /etc/ftpusers by default. That means that you can not ftp to your machine and log in as root. This is a good security measure, but some administrators prefer to remove root from this file.

11.10   NFS Configuration

NFS stands for Network File System, and is a way to share files between machines as if they were on your local hard drive. Linux can be both an NFS server and an

NFS client, which means that it can *export* filesystems to other systems, and *mount* filesystems exported from other machines.

11.10.1   Mounting NFS Filesystems

Use the `mount` command to mount a NFS filesystem from another machine:

```
mkdir /mnt/local # Only required if /mnt/local doesn't exist
mount bigdog:/mnt/export /mnt/local
```

In this command, `bigdog` is the hostname of the NFS fileserver, `/mnt/export` is the filesystem that bigdog is exporting, and `/mnt/local` is a directory on my local machine where we want to mount the filesystem. After the `mount` command runs (and if we have the proper permissions from `bigdog`) we can enter `ls /mnt/local` and get a listing of the files in `/mnt/export` on `bigdog`.

11.10.2   Exporting NFS Filesystems

The file that controls what filesystems you wish to export is `/etc/exports`. Its format is:

```
directory        hostname(options)
```

the `(options)` are optional. For example:

```
/mnt/export       speedy.redhat.com
```

would allow `speedy.redhat.com` to mount `/mnt/export`, but:

```
/mnt/export       speedy.redhat.com(ro)
```

would just allow `speedy` to mount `/mnt/export` read-only.

Each time you change `/etc/exports`, you need to tell the NFS daemons to examine it for new information. One simple way to accomplish this is to just stop and start the daemons:

```
/etc/rc.d/init.d/nfs stop
/etc/rc.d/init.d/nfs start
```

The following will also work:

```
killall -HUP rpc.nfsd rpc.mountd
```

See the following man pages for more details: nfsd(8), mountd(8), and exports(5). Another good reference is *Managing NFS and NIS Services* by Hal Stern, published by O'Reilly & Associates.

11.11   The Boot Process, Init, and Shutdown

This section contains information on what happens when a Red Hat Linux system is booted and shut down. Let's start with information on the files in /etc/sysconfig

11.11.1   Sysconfig Information

The following information outlines the various files in /etc/sysconfig, their function, and their contents.

Files in /etc/sysconfig

The following files are normally found in /etc/sysconfig:

- /etc/sysconfig/clock
- /etc/sysconfig/keyboard
- /etc/sysconfig/mouse
- /etc/sysconfig/network
- /etc/sysconfig/pcmcia
- /etc/sysconfig/amd
- /etc/sysconfig/tape

Let's take a look at each one.

/etc/sysconfig/clock – The /etc/sysconfig/clock file controls the interpretation of values read from the system clock. Earlier releases of Red Hat Linux used the following values (which is deprecated):

- **CLOCKMODE=*mode***, where *mode* is one of the following:
  - **GMT** – indicates that the clock is set to UTC.
  - **ARC** – on alpha only indicates the ARC console's 42-year time offset is in effect.

Currently, the correct values are:

- **UTC=*boolean***, where **boolean** is one of the following:

  - **true** – indicates that the clock is set to UTC. Any other value indicates that it is set to local time.

- **ARC=*boolean***, where **boolean** is one of the following:

  - **true** – (for Alpha-based systems only) Indicates the ARC console's 42-year time offset is in effect; Any other value indicates that the normal Unix epoch is assumed.

/etc/sysconfig/keyboard – The `/etc/sysconfig/keyboard` files controls the behavior of the keyboard. The following values may be used:

- **KEYTABLE=*file***, where **file** is the name of a keytable file. For example: `KEYTABLE="/usr/lib/kbd/keytables/us.map"`

/etc/sysconfig/mouse – The `/etc/sysconfig/mouse` file is used to specify information about the available mouse. The following values may be used:

- **MOUSETYPE=*type***, where `type` is one of the following:

  - **microsoft** – A Microsoft mouse.
  - **mouseman** – A MouseMan mouse.
  - **mousesystems** – A Mouse Systems mouse.
  - **ps/2** – A PS/2 mouse.
  - **msbm** – A Microsoft bus mouse.
  - **logibm** – A Logitech bus mouse.
  - **atibm** – An ATI bus mouse.
  - **logitech** – A Logitech mouse.
  - **mmseries** – A older MouseMan mouse.
  - **mmhittab** – A mmhittab mouse.

- **XEMU3=*emulation***, where **emulation** is one of the following:

  - **yes** – Three mouse buttons should be emulated.
  - **no** – The mouse already has three buttons.

In addition, `/dev/mouse` is a symlink that points to the actual mouse device.

/etc/sysconfig/network – The /etc/sysconfig/network file is used to specify information about the desired network configuration. The following values may be used:

- **NETWORKING=*answer***, where **answer** is one of the following:

  - **yes** – Networking should be configured.
  - **no** – Networking should not be configured.

- **HOSTNAME=*hostname***, where **hostname** should be the FQDN (Fully Qualified Domain Name), but can be whatever hostname you want.

  Please Note: For compatibility with older software that people might install (such as trn), the /etc/HOSTNAME file should contain the same value as here.

- **FORWARD_IPV4=*answer***, where **answer** is one of the following:

  - **yes** – Perform IP forwarding.
  - **no** – Do not perform IP forwarding.

  (The current Red Hat Linux installation sets this to "no" by default (for RFC compliance), but if FORWARD_IPV4 is not set at all, forwarding is *enabled* for compatibility with the configuration files used on Red Hat Linux versions 4.2 and earlier.)

- **GATEWAY=*gw-ip***, where **gw-ip** is the IP address of the network's gateway.

- **GATEWAYDEV=*gw-dev***, where **gw-dev** is the gateway device (e.g. eth0).

- **NISDOMAIN=*dom-name***, where **dom-name** is the NIS domain name.

/etc/sysconfig/pcmcia – The /etc/sysconfig/pcmcia file is used to specify PCMCIA configuration information. The following values may be used:

- **PCMCIA=*answer***, where **answer** is one of the following:

  - **yes** – PCMCIA support should be enabled.
  - **no** – PCMCIA support should not be enabled.

- **PCIC=*pcic-type***, where **pcic-type** is one of the following:

  - **i82365** – The computer has an i82365-style PCMCIA socket chipset.
  - **tcic** – The computer has a tcic-style PCMCIA socket chipset.

- **PCIC_OPTS=*option***, where **option** is the socket driver (i82365 or tcic) timing parameters.

- **CORE_OPTS=*option***, where **option** is the list of pcmcia_core options.

- **CARDMGR_OPTS=*option***, where **option** is the list of options for the PCMCIA cardmgr.

/etc/sysconfig/amd – The `/etc/sysconfig/amd` file is used to specify operational parameters for amd. The following values may be used:

- **ADIR=*path*,** where *path* is the amd directory. It should be "`/.automount`", and is normally never changed.

- **MOUNTPTS=*mountpts*,** where *mountpts* is, for example, "`/net /etc/amd.conf`"

- **AMDOPTS=*options*,** where *options* are any extra options for AMD.

/etc/sysconfig/tape – The `/etc/sysconfig/tape` file is used to specify tape-related configuration information. The following values may be used:

- **DEV=*devnam*,** where *devnam* is the tape device (for example, "`/dev/nst0`"). Use the non-rewinding device for these scripts.

  For SCSI tapes this is "`/dev/nst#`", where "#" is the number of the tape drive you want to use. If you only have one, then use "`/dev/nst0`".

  For IDE tapes you use "`/dev/ht#`", where "#" is the number of the tape drive you want to use. If you only have one, then use "`/dev/ht0`".

  For floppy tape drives use "`/dev/ftape`".

- **ADMIN=*account*,** where *account* is the user account to send mail to if the backup fails for any reason. Normally set to "`root`".

- **SLEEP=*time*,** where *time* is the time to sleep between tape operations. Some drives need a bit more than others, but "5" seems to work for 8mm, 4mm, and DLT.

- **BLOCKSIZE=*size*,** where *size* is the tape drive's optimal block size. A value of "`32768`" worked fine for 8mm, then 4mm, and now DLT. An optimal setting is probably however much data your drive writes at one time.

- **SHORTDATE=*date*,** where *date* is a string that evaluates to a short date string, to be used in backup log filenames. The default setting is: "`$(date +%y:%m:%d:%H:%M)`"

- **DAY=*date*,** where *date* is a string that evaluates to a date string, to be used for log file directory. The default setting is: "`$(date +log-%y:%m:%d)`"

- **DATE=*date*,** whre *date* is a string that evaluates to a reguarl date string, to be used in log files. The default setting is: "`$(date)`"

- **LOGROOT=*path*,** where *path* is the root of the logging directory.

- **LIST=*file*,** where *file* is the file name the incremental backup will use to store the incremental list. It will be followed by a sequence number.

- **DOTCOUNT=*count*,** where *count* is the name of a file used for counting as you go, to know which incremental list to use.

- **COUNTER=*count-file*,** where *count-file* is used for rewinding when done (might not use).

- **BACKUPTAB=*file*,** where *file* is the name of the file in which we keep our list of backup(s) we want to make.

Files in /etc/sysconfig/network-scripts/

The following files are normally found in /etc/sysconfig/network-scripts:

- /etc/sysconfig/network-scripts/ifup
- /etc/sysconfig/network-scripts/ifdown
- /etc/sysconfig/network-scripts/network-functions
- /etc/sysconfig/network-scripts/ifcfg-<*interface-name*>
- /etc/sysconfig/network-scripts/ifcfg-<*interface-name*>- ↩ <*clone-name*>
- /etc/sysconfig/network-scripts/chat-<*interface-name*>
- /etc/sysconfig/network-scripts/dip-<*interface-name*>
- /etc/sysconfig/network-scripts/ifup-post
- /etc/sysconfig/network-scripts/ifdhcpc-done

Let's take a look at each one.

/etc/sysconfig/network-scripts/ifup, /etc/sysconfig/network-scripts/ifdo
– Symlinks to /sbin/ifup and /sbin/ifdown, respectively. These are the only two scripts in this directory that should be called directly; these two scripts call all the other scripts as needed. These symlinks are here for legacy purposes only – they will probably be removed in future versions, so only /sbin/ifup and /sbin/ifdown should currently be used.

These scripts take one argument normally: the name of the device (e.g. "eth0"). They are called with a second argument of "boot" during the boot sequence so that devices that are not meant to be brought up on boot (ONBOOT=no, see below) can be ignored at that time.

/etc/sysconfig/network-scripts/network-functions – Not really a public file. Contains functions which the scripts use for bringing interfaces up and down. In particular, it contains most of the code for handling alternative interface configurations and interface change notification through netreport.

/etc/sysconfig/network-scripts/ifcfg-<*interface-name*>,
/etc/sysconfig/network-scripts/ifcfg-<*interface-name*>-<*clone-name*> –
The first
file defines an interface, while the second file contains only the parts of the definition that are different in a "clone" (or alternative) interface. For example, the
network numbers might be different, but everything else might be the same, so
only the network numbers would be in the clone file, while all the device information would be in the base ifcfg file.

The items that can be defined in an ifcfg file depend on the interface type.

The following values are common to all base files:

- **DEVICE=*name***, where **name** is the name of the physical device (except
  dynamically-allocated PPP devices where it is the "logical name").

- **IPADDR=*addr***, where **addr** is the IP address.

- **NETMASK=*mask***, where **mask** is the netmask value.

- **NETWORK=*addr***, where **addr** is the network address.

- **BROADCAST=*addr***, where **addr** is the broadcast address.

- **GATEWAY=*addr***, where **addr** is the gateway address.

- **ONBOOT=*answer***, where **answer** is one of the following:

  - **yes** – This device should be activated at boot-time.
  - **no** – This device should not be activated at boot-time.

- **USERCTL=*answer***, where **answer** is one of the following:

  - **yes** – Non-root users are allowed to control this device.
  - **no** – Non-root users are not allowed to control this device.

- **BOOTPROTO=*proto***, where **proto** is one of the following:

  - **none** – No boot-time protocol should be used.
  - **bootp** – The bootp protocol should be used.
  - **dhcp** – The dhcp protocol should be used.

The following values are common to all PPP and SLIP files:

- **PERSIST=*answer***, where **answer** is one of the following:

  - **yes** – This device should be kept active at all times, even if deactivated
    after a modem hangup.
  - **no** – This device should not be kept active at all times.

- **MODEMPORT=*port***, where ***port*** is the modem port's device name (for exmaple, "/dev/modem").

- **LINESPEED=*baud***, where ***baud*** is the modem's linespeed (for example, "115200").

- **DEFABORT=*answer***, where ***answer*** is one of the following:

    - **yes** – Insert default abort strings when creating/editing the script for this interface.
    - **no** – Do not insert default abort strings when creating/editing the script for this interface.

The following values are common to all PPP files:

- **DEFROUTE=*answer***, where ***answer*** is one of the following:

    - **yes** – Set this interface as the default route.
    - **no** – Do not set this interface as the default route.

- **ESCAPECHARS=*answer***, where ***answer*** is one of the following:

    - **yes** – Use the pre-defined asyncmap.
    - **no** – Do not use the pre-defined asyncmap.

    (This represents a simplified interface; it doesn't let people specify which characters to escape. However, almost everyone can use an asyncmap of 00000000 anyway, and it's possible to set PPPOPTIONS to use an arbitrary asyncmap if so desired.)

- **HARDFLOWCTL=*answer***, where ***answer*** is one of the following:

    - **yes** – Use hardware flow control.
    - **no** – Do not use hardware flow control.

- **PPPOPTIONS=*options***, where ***options*** is an arbitrary option string. It is placed last on the command line so it can override other options (such as asyncmap) that were specified previously.

- **PAPNAME=*name***, where ***name*** is used as part of "name $PAPNAME" on the pppd command line.

    note that the "remotename" option is always specified as the logical ppp device name, like "ppp0" (which might perhaps be the physical device ppp1 if some other ppp device was brought up earlier...), which makes it easy to manage pap/chap files – name/password pairs are associated with the logical ppp device name so that they can be managed together.

    In principle, there shouldn't anything that would keep the logical PPP device names from being "worldnet" or "myISP" instead of "ppp0" – "pppN".

- **REMIP=*addr***, where ***addr*** is the remote ip address (which is normally unspecified).

- **MTU=*value***, where ***value*** is the value to be used as MTU.

- **MRU=*value***, where ***value*** is the value to be used as MRU.

- **DISCONNECTTIMEOUT=*value***, where ***value*** represents the number of seconds to wait before re-establishing the connection after a successfully-connected session terminated.

- **RETRYTIMEOUT=*value***, where ***value*** represents the number of seconds to wait before re-attempting to establish a connection after a previous attempt has failed.

/etc/sysconfig/network-scripts/chat-<*interface-name*> – This file is a chat script for PPP or SLIP connections, and is intended to establish the connection. For SLIP devices, a DIP script is written from the chat script; for PPP devices, the chat script is used directly.

/etc/sysconfig/network-scripts/dip-<*interface-name*> – This write-only script is created from the chat script by netcfg. Do not modify this file. In the future, this file may disappear and instead will be created on-the-fly from the chat script.

/etc/sysconfig/network-scripts/ifup-post – This file is called when any network device (except a SLIP device) comes up. Calls `/etc/sysconfig/network-scripts/ifup-routes` to bring up static routes that depend on that device. Brings up aliases for that device. Sets the hostname if it is not already set and a hostname can be found for the IP for that device. Sends SIGIO to any programs that have requested notification of network events.

Could be extended to fix up nameservice configuration, call arbitrary scripts, etc, as needed.

/etc/sysconfig/network-scripts/ifdhcpc-done – This file is called by dhcpcd once dhcp configuration is complete; sets up `/etc/resolv.conf` from the version dhcpcd dropped in
`/etc/dhcpc/resolv.conf`.

11.11.2 System V Init

This section is a brief description of the internals of the boot process. It basically covers in detail how the machine boots using SysV init, as well as the differences between the init used in older Linux releases, and SysV init.

Init is the program that gets run by the kernel at boot time. It is in charge of starting all the normal processes that need to run at boot time. These include the getty processes that allow you to log in, NFS daemons, FTP daemons, and anything else you want to run when your machine boots.

SysV init is fast becoming the standard in the Linux world to control the startup of software at boot time. This is because it is easier to use and more powerful and flexible than the traditional BSD init.

SysV init also differs from BSD init in that the config files are in a subdirectory of /etc instead of residing directly in /etc. This directory is called rc.d. In there you will find rc.sysinit and the following directories:

```
init.d
rc0.d
rc1.d
rc2.d
rc3.d
rc4.d
rc5.d
rc6.d
```

init.d contains a bunch of scripts. Basically, you need one script for each service you may need to start at boot time or when entering another runlevel. Services include things like networking, nfs, sendmail, httpd, etc. Services do not include things like setserial that must only be run once and then exited. Things like that should go in rc.local or rc.serial.

If you want rc.local, it should be in /etc/rc.d. Most systems include one even though it doesn't do much. You can also include an rc.serial in /etc/rc.d if you need to do serial port specific things at boot time.

The chain of events is as follows:

- The kernel looks in several places for init and runs the first one it finds
- init runs /etc/rc.d/rc.sysinit
- rc.sysinit does a bunch of necessary things and then runs rc.serial (if it exists)
- init runs all the scripts for the default runlevel.
- init runs rc.local

The default runlevel is decided in /etc/inittab. You should have a line close to the top like:

```
id:3:initdefault:
```

From this, you'd look in the second column and see that the default runlevel is 3, as should be the case for most systems. If you want to change it, you can edit /etc/inittab by hand and change the 3. Be very careful when you are messing with the inittab. If you do mess up, you can fix it by rebooting and doing:

```
LILO boot:   linux single
```

This *should* allow you to boot into single user mode so you can fix inittab.

Now, how does it run all the right scripts? If you enter `ls -l` on `rc3.d`, you might see something like:

```
lrwxrwxrwx 1 root root 17 3:11 S10network -> ../init.d/network
lrwxrwxrwx 1 root root 16 3:11 S30syslog -> ../init.d/syslog
lrwxrwxrwx 1 root root 14 3:32 S40cron -> ../init.d/cron
lrwxrwxrwx 1 root root 14 3:11 S50inet -> ../init.d/inet
lrwxrwxrwx 1 root root 13 3:11 S60nfs -> ../init.d/nfs
lrwxrwxrwx 1 root root 15 3:11 S70nfsfs -> ../init.d/nfsfs
lrwxrwxrwx 1 root root 18 3:11 S90lpd -> ../init.d/lpd.init
lrwxrwxrwx 1 root root 11 3:11 S99local -> ../rc.local
```

What you'll notice is that there are no real "files" in the directory. Everything there is a link to one of the scripts in the init.d directory. The links also have an "S" and a number at the beginning. The "S" means to start this particular script and a "K" would mean to stop it. The number is there just for ordering purposes. Init will start all the services based on the order they appear. You can duplicate numbers, but it will only confuse you somewhat. You just need to use a two digit number only, along with an upper case "S" or "K" to start or stop the services you need to.

How does init start and stop services? Simple. Each of the scripts is written to accept an argument which can be "start" and "stop". You can execute those scripts by hand in fact with a command like:

```
/etc/rc.d/init.d/httpd.init stop
```

to stop the httpd server. Init just reads the name and if it has a "K", it calls the script with the "stop" argument. If it has an "S" it calls the script with a "start" argument. Why all these runlevels? Some people want an easy way to set up machines to be multi-purpose. I could have a "server" runlevel that just runs httpd, sendmail, networking, etc. Then I could have a "user" runlevel that runs xdm, networking, etc.

11.11.3 Init Runlevels

Generally, Red Hat Linux runs in run level 3—full multiuser mode. The following runlevels are defined in Red Hat Linux:

0 Halt

1 Single user mode

2 Multiuser mode, without NFS

3 Full multiuser mode

    4 Not used

    5 Full multiuser mode (with an X-based login screen)

    6 Reboot

If your machine gets into a state where it will not boot due to a bad `/etc/inittab`, or will not let you log in because you have a corrupted `/etc/passwd` or have simply forgotten your password, boot into single user mode by typing `linux 1` at the LILO boot prompt. A very bare system will come up and you will be given a shell from which you can fix things.

11.11.4 Initscript Utilities

The `chkconfig` utility provides a simple command-line tool for maintaining the `/etc/rc.d` directory hierarchy. It relieves system administrators from having to directly manipulate the numerous symlinks in `/etc/rc.d`.

In addition, there is the `ntsysv` utility, that provides a screen-oriented interface, versus
`chkconfig`'s command-line interface.

Please see the `chkconfig` and `ntsysv` man pages for more information.

11.11.5 Running Programs at Boot Time

The file `/etc/rc.d/rc.local` is executed at boot time, after all other initialization is complete, and whenever you change runlevels. You can add additional initialization commands here. For instance, you may want to start up additional daemons, or initialize a printer. In addition, if you require serial port setup, you can edit `/etc/rc.d/rc.serial`, and it will be executed automatically at boot time.

The default `/etc/rc.d/rc.local` simply creates a nice login banner with your kernel version and machine type.

11.11.6 Shutting Down

To shut down Red Hat Linux, issue the `shutdown` command. You can read the shutdown man page for complete details, but the two most common usages are:

```
shutdown -h now
shutdown -r now
```

Each will cleanly shutdown the system. After shutting everything down, the first will halt the machine, and the second will reboot.

Although the `reboot` and `halt` commands are now "smart" enough to invoke `shutdown` if run while the system is in runlevels 1-5, it is a bad habit to get into, as not all Linux-like operating systems have this feature.

11.12 Rescue Modes

When things go wrong, there are several ways to work on fixing them. However, they require that you understand the system well. This manual can't teach you what to do, but we will present the ways that you can use our products to get into rescue modes where you can use your own knowledge to rescue the system.

11.12.1 Through LILO

If your system boots, but does not allow you to log in when it has completed booting, you can use the `single` or `emergency` boot option. At the `LILO boot:` prompt, type `linux single` in order to boot in single-user mode. In single-user mode, your local filesystems will be mounted, but your network will not be activated. In emergency mode, almost nothing will be set up. Only the root filesystem will be mounted, and it will be mounted read-only.

11.12.2 Emergency Boot Diskettes

The boot diskette created during installation of Red Hat Linux 5.2 may be used as part of a rescue diskette set. For more information, please read the file `rescue.txt` in the `/doc` on your Red Hat Linux 5.2 CD-ROM.

A Handy Trick

Have you ever rebuilt a kernel and, eager to try out your new handiwork, rebooted before running LILO? And you didn't have an entry for an older kernel in `lilo.conf`? Read on...

Here's a handy trick. In many cases, it's possible to boot your Red Hat Linux/-Intel from the Red Hat Linux boot diskette with your root filesystem mounted and ready to go. Here's how:

Enter the following command at the boot diskette's `boot:` prompt:

```
linux single root=/dev/hdXX initrd=
```

(Replace the XX in `/dev/hdXX` with the appropriate letter and number for your root partition.)

What does this do? First, it starts the boot in single-user mode, with the root partition set to your root partition. The empty `initrd` specification bypasses the installation-related image on the boot diskette, which will cause you to enter single-user mode immediately.

Is there a downside to this trick? Unfortunately, yes. Because the kernel on the Red Hat Linux boot diskette only has support for IDE built-in, those of you with SCSI-based systems won't be able to use this trick. In that case, you'll have to use the boot/rescue diskette combination mentioned above.

Making Installation Diskettes

It is sometimes necessary to create a diskette from an *image file* (for example, you might need to use updated diskette images obtained from the Red Hat Linux Errata).

As the name implies, an image file is a file that contains an exact copy (or image) of a diskette's contents. Since a diskette contains filesystem information in addition to the data contained in files, the image file is not usable until it has been written to a diskette.

To start, you'll need a blank, formatted, high-density (1.44 MB), 3.5-inch diskette. You'll need access to a computer with a 3.5-inch diskette drive, and capable of running a DOS program, or the dd utility program found on most Linux-like operating systems.

The image files are found in the following directories on your Red Hat Linux CD:

- `images` – Contains the boot and supplemental images for Red Hat Linux/- Intel.

Once you've selected the proper image, it's time to transfer the image file onto a diskette. As mentioned previously, this can be done on a DOS-capable system, or on a system running a Linux-like operating system.

A.1   Making a Diskette Under MS-DOS

To make a diskette under MS-DOS, use the `rawrite` utility included on the Red
Hat Linux CD in the `dosutils` directory. First, label a blank, formatted 3.5-inch
diskette appropriately (eg. "Boot Diskette", "Supplemental Diskette", etc). Insert
it into the diskette drive. Then, use the following commands (assuming your CD
is drive `d:`):

```
C:\> d:
D:\> cd \dosutils
D:\dosutils> rawrite
Enter disk image source file name: ..\images\boot.img
Enter target diskette drive: a:
Please insert a formatted diskette into drive A: and
press --ENTER-- : [Enter]
D:\dosutils>
```

`rawrite` first asks you for the filename of a diskette image; enter the directory
and name of the image you wish to write (for example, `..\images\boot.img`).
Then `rawrite` asks for a diskette drive to write the image to; enter `a:`. Finally,
`rawrite` asks for confirmation that a formatted diskette is in the drive you've
selected. After pressing [Enter] to confirm, `rawrite` copies the image file onto
the diskette. If you need to make another diskette, label another diskette, and run
`rawrite` again, specifying the appropriate image file.

A.2   Making a Diskette Under a Linux-like O/S

To make a diskette under Linux (or any other Linux-like operating system), you
must have permission to write to the device representing a 3.5-inch diskette drive
(known as `/dev/fd0` under Linux). First, label a blank, formatted diskette appropriately (eg. "Boot Diskette", "Supplemental Diskette", etc). Insert it into the
diskette drive (but don't issue a `mount` command). After mounting the Red Hat
Linux CD, change directory to the directory containing the desired image file, and
use the following command (changing the name of the image file and diskette device as appropriate):

```
# dd if=boot.img of=/dev/fd0 bs=1440k
```

If you need to make another diskette, label another diskette, and run `dd` again,
specifying the appropriate image file.

B

Package List

This appendix lists the packages that make up Red Hat Linux. In each entry, you'll find the following information:

- The name of the package
- The packaged software's version number
- The size of the packaged software, in kilobytes
- A short description of the software

In addition, some packages will have one or more of the following icons alongside the package name:

[B] This package is part of the Red Hat Linux *base*, meaning that it is always installed.

[W] Workstation-class installations include this package.

[S] Server-class installations include this package.

Please Note: This package list was automatically generated right before Red Hat Linux 5.2 went into production. Because of the short timeframes involved, you might find minor typesetting problems in the package lists. However, we felt that an up-to-date package list was more important than a picture-perfect package list. We hope you'll agree...

You may also notice that some packages have different versions, and that packages listed here are not mentioned in the installation program (and vice versa). Any differences in package versions are normally due to the normal bug fixing process. It's possible that "missing" or "extra" packages are the result of last-minute changes prior to pressing CDROMs. Also note that all the packages in the "Base" group (and subgroups) are always installed, therefore you will not see them mentioned explicitly during the installation process.

Using the Package List After Installation   This list can come in handy even after you've installed Red Hat Linux. You can use it search for documentation. Here's how:

1. Find the package in this list.

2. Note the package name (The very first thing listed in bold at the start of each package description).

3. Enter the following command, taking care to enter the package name *exactly* as it is shown in the list (the package name is case-sensitive):

```
rpm -qd package-name
```

(Replacing package-name with the actual name of the package, of course.)

If you installed the package, you should get a list of filenames. Each file contains documentation relating to the package you specified. Here are some of the types of filenames you'll see:

- **/usr/man... something.n** – This is a man page. You can view it by using the man command (for example, man something. You might also need to include the file's ending number in the man command (as in man n something

- **/usr/X11R6/man... something.nx** – This is a man page for part of the X Window System. View these files the same way as a regular man page.

- **/usr/doc/something...** – Files under /usr/doc can be in any number of different formats. Sometimes the end of the filename can provide a clue as to how it should be viewed:

  - **.html** – An HTML file. View with the web browser of your choice.
  - **.txt** – A text file. View with cat or less.
  - **.ps** – A Postscript file. You can print it to a Postscript printer, or you can view it with gv.
  - **.gz** – A file compressed with gzip. If you make a copy of the original file, you can use gunzip to decompress it (you'll probably want to keep the original file compressed to save space). You can then view the file as you would normally. The zless command combines gunzip and less, and makes it possible to read compressed text files without

> making interim copies. There are other, more elegant ways to work with compressed files, but this approach will work for those just starting to use Linux.

In general, most of the documentation files you'll find will be one of those listed above. If in doubt, it's a good bet that the file is text. You can always try the file command to see if the file's contents can be identified.

- **/usr/info...** – Files in /usr/info are meant to be viewed using the info (or Emacs' Info mode). If you use Emacs, press (Ctrl)-(i), followed by (i) to view the main Info screen.

B.1 Applications

As this section's name implies, this is where you can find most of the applications available with Red Hat Linux. We've split the applications into several different categories to make finding things a bit easier.

(If you noticed that we said *"most* of the applications" above, you can find more apps by looking at X11's application section towards the end of the appendix.)

B.1.1 Communications

This section contains packages that help you communicate – either via fax, on-line chat, or simple terminal emulation.

efax – (Version 0.8a, 203K)

This is a program to send and receive faxes over class 1 or class 2 fax modems. It has a nice interface to help facilitate faxing.

ircii – (Version 4.4, 1,678K)

This is a popular Internet Relay Chat (IRC) client. It is a program used to connect to IRC servers around the globe so that the user can "chat" with others.

ircii-help – (Version 4.4, 441K)

This package contains the help files and other documentation for the ircii client package.

lrzsz – (Version 0.12.14, 322K) (W) (S)

This collection of commands can be used to download and upload files using the Z, X, and Y protocols. Many terminal programs (like minicom) make use of these programs to transfer files.

minicom – (Version 1.82, 289K) (W) (S)

Minicom is a communications program that resembles the MSDOS Telix some-what. It has a dialing directory, color, full ANSI and VT100 emulation, an (external) scripting language and more.

B.1.2 Databases

This section contains packages that provide basic database support for Red Hat Linux.

postgresql – (Version 6.3.2, 9,312K)   Ⓢ

PostgreSQL Data Base Management System (formerly known as Postgres, then as Postgres95).

PostgreSQL is an enhancement of the POSTGRES database management system, a next-generation DBMS research prototype. While PostgreSQL retains the power-ful data model and rich data types of POSTGRES, it replaces the PostQuel query language with an extended subset of SQL. PostgreSQL is free and the complete source is available.

PostgreSQL development is being performed by a team of Internet developers who all subscribe to the PostgreSQL development mailing list. The current coordinator is Marc G. Fournier (scrappy@postgreSQL.org). This team is now responsible for all current and future development of PostgreSQL.

The authors of PostgreSQL 1.01 were Andrew Yu and Jolly Chen. Many others have contributed to the porting, testing, debugging and enhancement of the code. The original Postgres code, from which PostgreSQL is derived, was the effort of many graduate students, undergraduate students, and staff programmers work-ing under the direction of Professor Michael Stonebraker at the University of Cali-fornia, Berkeley.

The original name of the software at Berkeley was Postgres. When SQL functional-ity was added in 1995, its name was changed to Postgres95. The name was changed at the end of 1996 to PostgreSQL.

PostgreSQL runs on Solaris, SunOS, HPUX, AIX, Linux, Irix, FreeBSD, and most flavours of Unix.

postgresql-clients – (Version 6.3.2, 1,131K)   Ⓢ

This package includes only the clients and client libraries needed to access an Post-greSQL server. The server is included in the main package. If all you need is to connect to another PostgreSQL server, the this is the only package you need to install.

In this package there are client libraries available for C, C++ and PERL, as well as several command-line utilities you can use to manage your databases on a remote PostgreSQL server.

postgresql-data – (Version 6.3.2, 780K)   Ⓢ

This packages includes an initial database structure directory for PostgreSQL. For a quick startup on PostegreSQL, it is recommended to install this package with your PostgreSQL backend server (altough it is not required).

If you choose to not install this package you will have to create the initial database yourself using 'initdb' command and possibly modify the postgresql startup script if you choose a directory other than /var/lib/pgsql for storing your databases.

B.1.3 Editors

In this section, we have an assortment of packages that provide basic (and in some cases not so basic) file editing capabilities.

ed – (Version 0.2, 103K)   [B]

This is the GNU line editor. It is an implementation of one of the first editors under *nix. Some programs rely on it, but in general you probably don't *need* it.

emacs – (Version 20.3, 17,337K)   [W] [S]

Emacs is the extensible, customizable, self-documenting real-time display editor. Emacs has special code editing modes, a scripting language (elisp), and comes with many packages for doing mail, news, and more, all in your editor.

This package includes the libraries necessary to run the emacs editor - the actual program can be found in either the emacs-nox or emacs-X11 packages, depending on whether you use X Windows or not.

emacs-X11 – (Version 20.3, 5,839K)   [W]

This package contains an emacs binary built with support for X Windows. It will still work fine outside of X Windows (on the console, for instance) but supports the mouse and GUI elements when used inside of X Windows.

emacs-el – (Version 20.3, 16,778K)

This package contains the emacs-lisp sources for many of the elisp programs included with the main emacs package. You do not need this package unless you want to modify these packages, or see some elisp examples.

emacs-nox – (Version 20.3, 2,443K)   [W] [S]

This package contains an emacs binary built without support for X Windows. While the emacs binary in the main emacs package will work fine outside of X Windows (on the console, for instance), the one in this package has a smaller memory image.

jed – (Version 0.98.4, 1,193K)

Jed is a fast compact editor based on the slang screen library. It has special editing modes for C, C++, and other languages. It can emulate Emacs, Wordstar, and other editors, and can be customized with slang macros, colors, keybindings, etc.

jed-xjed – (Version 0.98.4, 153K)

Xjed is the same editor as jed, it just runs in its own X Window.

joe – (Version 2.8, 282K)

Joe is a friendly and easy to use editor. It has a nice interface and would be a good choice for a novice needing a text editor. It uses the same WordStar keybindings which are also used by Borland's development enbironment.

vim-X11 – (Version 5.3, 1,306K)

The VIsual editor iMproved is an updated and feature-added clone of the 'vi' editor that comes with almost all UN*X systems. It adds multiple windows, multi-level undo, block highliting, and many other features to the standard vi program.

This package is a version of VIM with the X-Windows libraries linked in, allowing you to run VIM as an X-Windows application with a full GUI interface and mouse support. You just run 'gvim'.

vim-color – (Version 5.3, 427K)

The VIsual editor iMproved is an updated and feature-added clone of the 'vi' editor that comes with almost all UN*X systems. It adds multiple windows, multi-level undo, block highliting, and many other features to the standard vi program.

vim-common – (Version 5.3, 4,354K)   Ⓑ

The VIsual editor iMproved is an updated and feature-added clone of the 'vi' editor that comes with almost all UN*X systems. It adds multiple windows, multi-level undo, block highliting, and many other features to the standard vi program.

The vim-common package contains files (such as help) that are needed by any vim binary in order to run.

vim-enhanced – (Version 5.3, 1,214K)

The VIsual editor iMproved is an updated and feature-added clone of the 'vi' editor that comes with almost all UN*X systems. It adds multiple windows, multi-level undo, block highliting, and many other features to the standard vi program.

This package contains a version of vim which has many of the extra features that have recently been introduced to vim such as perl and python interpreters.

vim-minimal – (Version 5.3, 427K)   Ⓑ

The VIsual editor iMproved is an updated and feature-added clone of the 'vi' editor that comes with almost all UN*X systems. It adds multiple windows, multi-level undo, block highliting, and many other features to the standard vi program.

The vim-minimal package installs a version of vim into /bin/vi that is suitable for running when only the root partition is present.

B.1.4 Emulators

In this section are packages that let your Red Hat Linux system run programs meant for other operating systems.

dosemu – (Version 0.98.1, 1,721K)   ⟨w⟩

This package enables you to run a number of DOS programs under Linux. This package includes an image with DOS-C kernel (MS DOS 3.31 compatible) and FreeDos utilities. You should be able to start up the DOS emulator by logging in as root and typing 'dos' at the prompt.

dosemu-freedos – (Version 0.98.1, 8,194K)

This package includes a hdimage file that will be installed in /var/lib/dosemu directory if you need some version of DOS to start using dosemu.

Generally dosemu requires you to have some version of DOS available to bootstrap your hdimage files before first use, or to have partitions formatted and installed with DOS. If you have neither you can use this image that is already bootable with FreeDOS.

You will need to edit your /etc/dosemu.conf file to add this image to the list of "drives" used by dosemu.

xdosemu – (Version 0.98.1, 26K)   ⟨w⟩

This is a version of the DOS emulator that is designed to run in an X windows session. It provides VGA graphics support as well as mouse support.

B.1.5 Engineering

This section contains packages for those of you that are into engineering.

spice – (Version 2g6, 769K)

SPICE is a general-purpose circuit simulation program for nonlinear dc, nonlinear transient, and linear ac analyses. Circuits may contain resistors, capacitors, inductors, mutual inductors, independent voltage and current sources, four types of dependent sources, transmission lines, and the four most common semiconductor devices: diodes, BJT's, JFET's, and MOSFET's.

units – (Version 1.0, 24K)

The units program converts quantities expression in various scales to their equivalents in other scales. The units program can only handle multiplicative scale changes.

B.1.6 Graphics

This section contains packages that help you work with graphics-related material.

ghostscript – (Version 4.03, 2,737K)   Ⓦ Ⓢ

Ghostscript is a PostScript interpretor. It can render both PostScript and PDF compliant files to devices which include an X window, many printer formats (including support for color printers), and popular graphics file formats.

ghostscript-fonts – (Version 4.03, 3,679K)   Ⓦ Ⓢ

These fonts can be used by the GhostScript interpreter during text rendering.

giftrans – (Version 1.12.2, 20K)

This program can convert and manipulate GIF images from the command line. It is most useful for making a color transparent for web sites.

libgr-progs – (Version 2.0.13, 1,388K)   Ⓦ Ⓢ

This package includes various utility programs for manipulating JPEG files for use by libgr programs.

libungif-progs – (Version 3.0, 285K)

This package contains various programs for manipulating gif image files.

xfig – (Version 3.2.2, 2,241K)

This program gives you all the features you need to create basic- to intermediate-level vector graphics, including bezier curves, lines, rulers, and more.

zgv – (Version 3.0, 168K)

Zgv is a picture viewer capable of displaying GIF files as defined by CompuServe, with the exceptions listed in the RESTRICTIONS section. It is also capable of displaying JPEG/JFIF files using the Independant JPEG Group's JPEG software, PBM/PGM/PPM files as used by pbmplus and netpbm, Microsoft Windows and OS/2 BMP files, Targa (TGA) files, and the new PNG format.

B.1.7   Mail

This section contains several of the more popular e-mail-related programs.

elm – (Version 2.4.25, 476K)   Ⓦ Ⓢ

ELM is one of the most popular terminal mode mail handling programs. It is powerful, easy to use, and easy to find help on. It has all the mail handling features you would expect, including MIME support (via metamail).

exmh – (Version 2.0.2, 1,814K)   Ⓦ Ⓢ

exmh is a graphical interface to the MH mail system. It includes MIME support, faces, glimpse indexing, color highlighting, PGP interface, and more. Requires sox (or play) for sound support.

fetchmail – (Version 4.5.8, 549K)   Ⓦ Ⓢ

Fetchmail is a program that is used to retrieve mail from a remote mail server. It can use the Post Office Protocol (POP) or IMAP (Internet Mail Access Protocol) for this, and delivers the mail through the local SMTP server (normally sendmail).

mailx – (Version 8.1.1, 88K) $\boxed{B}$

The /bin/mail program can be used to send quick mail messages, and is often used in shell scripts.

metamail – (Version 2.7, 333K) $\boxed{W}$ $\boxed{S}$

Metamail is an implementation of MIME, the Multipurpose Internet Mail Extensions, a proposed standard for multimedia mail on the Internet. Metamail implements MIME, and also implements extensibility and configuration via the "mailcap" mechanism described in an informational RFC that is a companion to the MIME document.

mutt – (Version 0.93.2, 507K) $\boxed{W}$ $\boxed{S}$

Mutt is a small but very powerful full-screen Unix mail client. Features include MIME support, color, POP3 support, message threading, bindable keys, and threaded sorting mode.

nmh – (Version 0.27, 4,353K) $\boxed{W}$ $\boxed{S}$

nmh mail handling system (with POP support). nmh is a popular mail handling system but includes only a command line interface. It is an important base, however, for programs like xmh and exmh.

pine – (Version 4.04, 3,071K) $\boxed{W}$ $\boxed{S}$

Pine is a very full featured text based mail and news client. It is aimed at both novice and expert users. It includes an easy to use editor, pico, for composing messages. Pico has gained popularity as a stand alone text editor in it's own right. It features MIME support, address books, and support for IMAP, mail, and MH style folders.

B.1.8   Math

This section contains packages of interest to the mathematician in all of us.

bc – (Version 1.05a, 128K) $\boxed{B}$

bc is a text mode calculator of sorts. It has many extended features such as base translation. It can also accept input from stdin and return output. dc is the RPN version.

gnuplot – (Version 3.6, 940K)

This is the GNU plotting package. It can be used to graph data in an X window or to a file.

B.1.9   Networking

This section contains network-related packages.

arpwatch – (Version 2.1a4, 117K)

Arpwatch and arpsnmp are tools that monitors ethernet or fddi activity and maintain a database of ethernet/ip address pairings.

libpcap – (Version 0.4, 123K)

Libpcap is a system-independent interface for user-level packet capture. Libpcap provides a portable framework for low-level network monitoring. Applications include network statistics collection, security monitoring, network debugging, etc. Libpcap has system-independent API that is used by several applications, including tcpdump and arpwatch.

lynx – (Version 2.8.1, 2,031K)   (W)(S)

This a terminal based WWW browser. While it does not make any attempt at displaying graphics, it has good support for HTML text formatting, forms, and tables.

ncftp – (Version 2.4.3, 170K)   (W)(S)

Ncftp is a ftp client with many advantageous over the standard one. It includes command line editing, command histories, support for recurisive gets, automatic logins, and much more.

rsync – (Version 2.1.1, 188K)

rsync is a faster flexible replacement for rcp allowing rapid and network efficient synchronization of files or directories on different machines by transferring just the differences between those directories in a compressed form. It doesn't need either machine to have a copy of what is on the other.

A technical report describing the rsync algorithm is included in this package.

tcpdump – (Version 3.4, 215K)   (W)(S)

Tcpdump prints out the headers of packets on a network interface. It is very useful for debugging network problems and security operations.

wget – (Version 1.5.2, 352K)

GNU Wget is a freely available network utility to retrieve files from the World Wide Web using HTTP and FTP, the two most widely used Internet protocols. It works non-interactively, thus enabling work in the background, after having logged off.

The recursive retrieval of HTML pages, as well as FTP sites is supported – you can use Wget to make mirrors of archives and home pages, or traverse the web like a WWW robot (Wget understands /robots.txt).

Wget works exceedingly well on slow or unstable connections, keeping getting the document until it is fully retrieved. Re-getting files from where it left off works on servers (both HTTP and FTP) that support it. Matching of wildcards and recursive mirroring of directories are available when retrieving via FTP. Both HTTP and FTP retrievals can be time-stamped, thus Wget can see if the remote file has changed since last retrieval and automatically retrieve the new version if it has.

By default, Wget supports proxy servers, which can lighten the network load, speed up retrieval and provide access behind firewalls. However, if you are behind a firewall that requires that you use a socks style gateway, you can get the socks library and compile wget with support for socks.

Most of the features are configurable, either through command-line options, or via initialization file .wgetrc. Wget allows you to install a global startup file (/etc/wgetrc on RedHat) for site settings.

B.1.10   News

This section contains packages that you can use to read on-line newsgroups.

slrn – (Version 0.9.4.3, 302K)   Ⓦ Ⓢ

Slrn is an easy to use but powerful full-screen NNTP based newsreader. It relies extensively on the S-Lang programmer's library for many of its features. Slrn works particularly well over slow network connections.

tin – (Version 1.22, 537K)   Ⓦ Ⓢ

Tin is a full-screen easy to use Netnews reader. It can read news locally (i.e. /usr/spool/news) or remotely (rtin or tin -r option) via a NNTP (Network News Transport Protocol) server.

trn – (Version 3.6, 431K)   Ⓦ Ⓢ

'trn' is one of the original threaded news readers. this version is configured to read news from an NNTP news server.

B.1.11   Productivity

This section contains packages aimed at helping you keep track of time, and staying productive.

ical – (Version 2.2, 785K)   Ⓦ Ⓢ

ical is a popular X-based calendar/scheduler application which can help you keep track of single events and recurring events (daily, weekly, monthly, or yearly), and sets off alarms to warn you of appointments.

B.1.12   Publishing

This section contains packages that turn your Red Hat Linux system into a high-quality typesetting workstation. (In fact, the printed version of this document is produced using many of these tools!)

groff – (Version 1.11a, 2,941K)   Ⓑ

The groff text formatting system can be used to create professional looking documents on both paper and a computer screen. All the man pages are processed with groff, so you'll need this package to read man pages.

groff-gxditview – (Version 1.11a, 70K)

The package contains the gxditview program, which can be used to format and view groff documents in X Windows. For example, man pages can be read using gxditview.

lout – (Version 3.08, 3,427K)

The Lout system reads a high-level description of a document similar in style to LaTeX and produces a PostScript file which can be printed on many laser printers and graphic display devices. Plain text output is also available.

Lout offers an unprecedented range of advanced features, including optimal paragraph and page breaking, automatic hyphenation, PostScript EPS file inclusion and generation, equation formatting, tables, diagrams, rotation and scaling, sorted indexes, bibliographic databases, running headers and odd-even pages, automatic cross referencing, multilingual documents including hyphenation (most European languages are supported, including Russian), formatting of C/C++ programs, and much more, all ready to use. Furthermore, Lout is easily extended with definitions which are very much easier to write than troff of TeX macros because Lout is a high-level language, the outcome of an eight-year research project that went back to the beginning.

lout-doc – (Version 3.08, 2,069K)

This package includes the complete Lout documentation, including the "user" and "expert" manuals, written in Lout and with PostScript output. Good examples of writing large docs with Lout.

sgml-tools – (Version 1.0.7, 1,997K)

SGML-Tools is a SGML-based text formatter which allows you to produce a variety of output formats. You can create PostScript and dvi (with LaTeX), plain text (with groff), HTML, and texinfo files from a single SGML source file.

tetex – (Version 0.9, 41,786K)   Ⓦ

TeX formats a file of interspersed text and commands and outputs a typesetter independent file (called DVI, which is short for DeVice Independent). TeX capabilities and language are described in The TeXbook, by Knuth.

tetex-afm – (Version 0.9, 2,134K)   Ⓦ

PostScript fonts are (or should be) accompanied by font metric files such as Times-Roman.afm, which describes the characteristics of the font called Times-Roman. To use such fonts with TeX, we need TFM files that contain similar information. afm2tfm does that conversion.

tetex-doc – (Version 0.9, 24,455K)

This package contains the documentation files from the teTeX system. Because of their big size, the documentation is now separated in its own subpackage.

tetex-dvilj – (Version 0.9, 375K)   [W]

Dvilj and siblings convert TeX-output .dvi files into HP PCL (i.e. HP Printer Control Language) commands suitable for printing on a HP LaserJet+, HP LaserJet IIP (using dvilj2p), HP LaserJet 4 (using dvilj4), and fully compatible printers.

tetex-dvips – (Version 0.9, 831K)   [W]

The program dvips takes a DVI file file[.dvi] produced by TeX (or by some other processor such as GFtoDVI) and converts it to PostScript, normally sending the result directly to the laserprinter.

tetex-latex – (Version 0.9, 6,443K)   [W]

LaTeX is a TeX macro package. The LaTeX macros encourage writers to think about the content of their documents, rather than the form. The ideal, very difficult to realize, is to have no formatting commands (like "switch to italic" or "skip 2 picas") in the document at all; instead, everything is done by specific markup instructions: "emphasize", "start a section".

tetex-xdvi – (Version 0.9, 1,025K)   [W][S]

xdvi is a program which runs under the X window system. It is used to preview dvi files, such as are produced by tex and latex.

texinfo – (Version 3.12, 505K)   [W][S]

The GNU project uses the texinfo file format for much of its documentation. This package includes the tools necessary to create .info files from .texinfo source files, as well as an emacs interface to all these tools.

B.1.13   Sound

This section contains packages that let you use your Red Hat Linux system's sound capabilities.

aumix – (Version 1.13, 47K)   [W]

This program provides a tty based, interactive method of controlling a sound cards mixer. It lets you adjust the input levels from the CD, microphone, and on board synthesizers as well as the output volume.

cdp – (Version 0.33, 36K)

This program allows you to play audio CD's on your computers CDROM drive. It provides a version with a full screen interface as well as a command line version.

maplay – (Version 1.2, 70K)

This program plays MPEG 2 format audio files through your PC's sound card. MPEG audio files are popular for sending high fidelity music over the Internet, and http://www.iuma.com contains a large archive of MPEG 2 sound files.

mikmod – (Version 3.0.3, 362K)

One of the best and most well known MOD players around (for unix). Play MOD (and their brethren) songs.

MikMod is a portable modules player originally written by Jean-Paul Mikkers (MikMak) for DOS. It has subsequently been hacked by many hands and now runs on many platforms, this particular distribution intended to compile fairly painlessly in a Unix (Linux) environment. It uses the OSS /dev/dsp driver including in all recent kernels for output, and will also write wav files. Supported file formats include mod, stm, s3m, mtm, xm, and it. The player uses ncurses for console output and supports transparent loading from gzip/pkzip/zoo archives and the loading/saving of playlists.

playmidi – (Version 2.4, 145K)   [W]

Plays MIDI sound files through a sound card synthesizer. It includes basic drum samples for use with simple FM synthesizers.

playmidi-X11 – (Version 2.4, 46K)   [W]

X program for playing MIDI sound files through a sound card synthesizer. It includes basic drum samples for use with simple FM synthesizers.

sox – (Version 12.14, 349K)   [W]

The self described "swiss army knife of sound tools", sox can convert between many different digitized sound formats and perform simple sound manipulation functions.

B.2   Base

This section contains the packages that are consider basic to every Red Hat Linux system. You will normally will not see them during the installation process, but they're included here for your information.

B.2.1   Kernel

This section contains packages related to your Red Hat Linux system's kernel. This part of the Linux operating system is central to all system operations.

kernel – (Version 2.0.36, 4,726K) Ⓑ

This package contains the Linux kernel that is used to boot and run your system. It contains few device drivers for specific hardware. Most hardware is instead supported by modules loaded after booting.

kernel-headers – (Version 2.0.36, 1,551K) ⓌⓈ

These are the C header files for the Linux kernel, which define structures and constants that are needed when building most standard programs under Linux, as well as to rebuild the kernel.

kernel-ibcs – (Version 2.0.36, 219K)

This package allows you to run programs in the iBCS2 (Intel Binary Compatibility Standard, version 2) and related executable formats.

kernel-source – (Version 2.0.36, 30,727K)

This is the source code for the Linux kernel. It is required to build most C programs as they depend on constants defined in here. You can also build a custom kernel that is better tuned to your particular hardware.

basesystem – (Version 4.9, 0K) Ⓑ

While this package does not contain any files, it does perform an important function. It defines the components of a basic Red Hat system, as the package installation order to use during bootstrapping. It should be the first package installed on a system, and it should never be removed.

crontabs – (Version 1.7, 4K) Ⓑ

The root crontab file is used to schedule execution of various programs.

dev – (Version 2.5.9, 0K) Ⓑ

Unix and unix like systems (including Linux) use file system entries to represent devices attached to the machine. All of these entries are in the /dev tree (though they don't have to be), and this package contains the most commonly used /dev entries. These files are essential for a system to function properly.

etcskel – (Version 1.3, 5K) Ⓑ

This is part of the Base Red Hat system. It contains the files that go in /etc/skel, which are in turn placed in every new user's home directory when new accounts are created.

filesystem – (Version 1.3.2, 79K) Ⓑ

This package contains the basic directory layout for a Linux system, including the proper permissions for the directories. This layout conforms to the Linux Filesystem Standard (FSSTND) 1.3.

initscripts – (Version 3.72, 94K) Ⓑ

This package contains the scripts use to boot a system, change run levels, and shut the system down cleanly. It also contains the scripts that activate and deactivate most network interfaces.

mailcap – (Version 1.0, 29K)   [B]

This is the Red Hat Mailcap package. Installing it will allow programs like lynx to automatically use zgv to display pictures (provided zgv is installed).

pam – (Version 0.64, 2,747K)   [B]

PAM (Pluggable Authentication Modules) is a powerful, flexible, extensible authentication system which allows the system administrator to configure authentication services individually for every pam-compliant application without recompiling any of the applications.

pamconfig – (Version 0.51, 2K)   [B]

This package has been made obsolete by pam-0.56, and is provided for compatibility purposes only. If the command:

rpm -q –whatrequires pamconfig

returns no package names, you may remove this package with:

rpm -e pamconfig

passwd – (Version 0.50, 17K)   [B]

This password-changing program uses PAM (Pluggable Authentication Modules) to set or change a password. Like all PAM-capable applications, it can be configured using a file in the /etc/pam.d/ directory.

pwdb – (Version 0.54, 1,260K)   [B]

pwdb (Password Database Library) allows configurable access to and management of /etc/passwd, /etc/shadow, and network authentication systems including NIS and Radius.

redhat-release – (Version 5.2, 0K)   [B]

Red Hat Linux release file

rootfiles – (Version 5.2, 2K)   [B]

This package contains all the startup files for the root user. These are basically the same files that are in the etcskel package.

setup – (Version 1.9.1, 8K)   [B]

This package contains a number of very important configuration and setup files, including the passwd, group, profile files, etc.

termcap – (Version 9.12.6, 424K)   [B]

The /etc/termcap file is a database defining the capabilities of various terminals and terminal emulators. Programs use /etc/termcap to gain access to various features of terminals such as the bell, color, and graphics.

B.3 Daemons

This section contains packages for all the daemons available for your Red Hat Linux system. Daemons are programs that run automatically, and perform various system functions for you.

SysVinit – (Version 2.74, 141K)   B

SysVinit is the first program started by the Linux kernel when the system boots, controlling the startup, running, and shutdown of all other programs.

at – (Version 3.1.7, 60K)   B

at and batch read commands from standard input or a specified file which are to be executed at a later time, using /bin/sh.

bdflush – (Version 1.5, 9K)   B

This program flushes the disk buffers the kernel keeps to prevent them from growing too stale.

gpm – (Version 1.13, 193K)   B

GPM adds mouse support to text-based Linux applications such as emacs, Midnight Commander, and more. It also provides console cut-and-paste operations using the mouse. Includes a program to allow pop-up menus to appear at the click of a mouse button.

kernel-pcmcia-cs – (Version 2.0.36, 754K)   B

Many laptop machines (and some others) support PCMCIA cards for expansion. Also known as "credit card adapters", PCMCIA cards are small cards for everything from SCSI support to modems. They are hot swappable (they can be exchanged without rebooting the system) and quite convenient. This package contains support for numerous PCMCIA cards of all varieties and supplies a daemon which allows them to be hot swapped.

procmail – (Version 3.10, 179K)   B

Red Hat Linux uses procmail for all local mail delivery. In addition to regluar mail delivery duties, procmail can be used to do many different automatic filtering, presorting, and mail handling jobs. It is the basis for the SmartList mailing list processor.

sendmail-cf – (Version 8.8.7, 611K)

This package contains all the configuration files used to generate the sendmail.cf file distributed with the base sendmail package. You'll want this package if you need to reconfigure and rebuild your sendmail.cf file. For example, the default sendmail.cf is not configured for UUCP. If you need to send and receive mail over UUCP, you may need this package to help you reconfigure sendmail.

sendmail-doc – (Version 8.8.7, 1,219K)

This package includes release notes, the sendmail FAQ, and a few papers written about sendmail. The papers are available in PostScript and troff.

sysklogd – (Version 1.3, 105K) $\boxed{B}$

This is the Linux system and kernel logging program. It is run as a daemon (background process) to log messages to different places. These are usually things like sendmail logs, security logs, and errors from other daemons.

uucp – (Version 1.06.1, 2,012K) $\boxed{W}$ $\boxed{S}$

UUCP is a Unix to Unix transfer mechanism. It is used primarily for remote sites to download and upload email and news files to local machines. If you didn't already know that, you probably don't need this package installed. :-)

vixie-cron – (Version 3.0.1, 54K) $\boxed{B}$

cron is a standard UNIX program that runs user-specified programs at periodic scheduled times. vixie cron adds a number of features to the basic UNIX cron, including better security and more powerful configuration options.

B.4   Development

This section contains packages of interest to programmers. Red Hat Linux comes with a very powerful and rich set of tools for the programmer, so there are several different subsections here.

B.4.1   Building

This section contains packages that help programmers easily build programs.

autoconf – (Version 2.12, 524K) $\boxed{W}$ $\boxed{S}$

GNU's "autoconf" is a tool for source and Makefile configuration. It assists the programmer in creating portable and configurable packages, by allowing the person building the package to specify various configuration options.

"autoconf" is not required for the end user - it is needed only to generate the configuration scripts.

automake – (Version 1.3, 777K) $\boxed{W}$ $\boxed{S}$

Automake is an experimental Makefile generator. It was inspired by the 4.4BSD make and include files, but aims to be portable and to conform to the GNU standards for Makefile variables and targets.

libtool – (Version 1.2b, 485K)

GNU libtool is a set of shell scripts to automatically configure UNIX architectures to build shared libraries in generic fashion.

make – (Version 3.76.1, 247K)   Ⓦ Ⓢ

The program make is used to coordinate the compilation and linking of a set of sources into a program, recompiling only what is necessary, thus saving a developer a lot of time. In fact, make can do a lot more - read the info docs.

pmake – (Version 1.0, 123K)   Ⓦ Ⓢ

The program make is used to coordinate the compilation and linking of a set of sources into a program, recompiling only what is necessary, thus saving a developer a lot of time. In fact, make can do a lot more - read the info docs.

Pmake is a particular version of make which supports some additional syntax not in the standard make program. Some berkeley programs have Makefiles written for pmake.

B.4.2   Debuggers

This section contains a number of packages that make it easier to find bugs in a program.

ElectricFence – (Version 2.0.5, 44K)   Ⓦ Ⓢ

Electric Fence is a libary that can be used for C programming and debugging. You link it in at compile time and it will warn you of possible problems such as free'ing memory that doesn't exist, etc.

gdb – (Version 4.17.0.4, 1,251K)   Ⓦ Ⓢ

This is a full featured, command driven debugger. It allows you to trace the execution of programs and examine their internal state at any time. It works for C and C++ compiled with the GNU C compiler gcc.

strace – (Version 3.1, 114K)   Ⓦ Ⓢ

Strace prints a record of each system call another program makes, including all of the arguments passed to it and the system call's return value.

xxgdb – (Version 1.12, 95K)   Ⓦ

xxgdb is a graphical interface to GNU's debugger. It has the ability to display source files as they are executed, set breakpoints, and singlestep through or over commands - all with an easy-to-use graphical X Windows interface.

B.4.3   Languages

This section lists the packages containing various programming languages.

basic – (Version 1.20, 52K)

This is a BASIC language interpreter. You can use it to run programs written in

BASIC. For those who may not know, BASIC is an archaic language used only to learn early fundamentals of programming, and it isn't very good for that, either. :-)

bin86 – (Version 0.4, 70K) $\boxed{W}\boxed{S}$

This package provides an assembler and linker for real mode 80x86 instructions. Programs that run in real mode, including LILO and the kernel's bootstrapping code, need to have this package installed to be built from the sources.

blt – (Version 2.4f, 4,096K)

BLT provides extra widgets and commands for tk programs. It includes graphing widgets, table geometry management, and folder widgets.

ctags – (Version 2.0.3, 77K) $\boxed{W}\boxed{S}$

A better ctags which generates tags for all possible tag types: macro definitions, enumerated values (values inside enum...), function and method definitions, enum/ struct/ union tags, external function prototypes (optional), typedefs, and variable declarations. It is far less easily fooled by code containing #if preprocessor conditional constructs, using a conditional path selection algorithm to resolve complicated choices, and a fall-back algorithm when this one fails. Can also be used to print out a list of selected objects found in source files.

egcs – (Version 1.0.3a, 2,782K) $\boxed{W}\boxed{S}$

A compiler aimed at integrating all the optimizations and features necessary for a high-performance and stable development environment.

egcs-c++ – (Version 1.0.3a, 1,780K) $\boxed{W}$

This package adds C++ support to the GNU C compiler. It includes support for most of the current C++ specification, including templates and exception handling. It does not include a standard C++ library, which is available separately.

egcs-g77 – (Version 1.0.3a, 2,356K)

This apckage adds support for compiling Fortran 77 programs with the GNU compiler.

egcs-objc – (Version 1.0.3a, 1,490K)

This package adds Objective C support to the GNU C compiler. Objective C is a object oriented derivative of the C language, mainly used on systems running NeXTSTEP. This package does not include the standard objective C object library.

expect – (Version 5.26, 746K) $\boxed{W}\boxed{S}$

Expect is a tool for automating interactive applications such as telnet, ftp, passwd, fsck, rlogin, tip, etc. It makes it easy for a script to control another program and interact with it.

f2c – (Version 19970805, 819K)

f2c is a Fortran to C translation and building program. It can take fortran source code, convert it to C, and then use gcc to compile it into an executable.

fort77 – (Version 1.14a, 11K)

This is the driver for f2c, a fortran to C translator.

gcc – (Version 2.7.2.3, 2,041K) $\boxed{W}$ $\boxed{S}$

The GNU C compiler – a full featured ANSI C compiler, with support for K&R C as well. GCC provides many levels of source code error checking tradionaly provided by other tools (such as lint), produces debugging information, and can perform many different optimizations to the resulting object code. This contains the back end for C++ and Objective C compilers as well.

guavac – (Version 1.2, 2,564K)

Guavac is a standalone compiler for the Java programming language. It was written entirely in C++, and should be portable to any platform supporting Gnu's C++ compiler or a similarly powered system.

guile – (Version 1.2, 634K)

Guile, a portable, embeddable Scheme implementation written in C. Guile provides a machine independent execution platform that can be linked in as a library when building extensible programs.

guile-devel – (Version 1.2, 1,949K)

What's needed to develop apps linked w/ guile

kaffe – (Version 1.0.b1, 1,495K)

This is Kaffe, a virtual machine designed to execute Java bytecode. This machine can be configured in two modes. In one mode it operates as a pure bytecode interpreter (not unlike Javasoft's machine); in the second mode if performs "just-in-time" code conversion from the abstract code to the host machine's native code. This will ultimately allow execution of Java code at the same speed as standard compiled code but while maintaining the advantages and flexibility of code independence.

p2c-devel – (Version 1.20, 24K)

This is the development kit for the Pascal to C translator. It contains the header files and some other programs that might be useful to someone using the translator.

python – (Version 1.5.1, 5,320K) $\boxed{B}$

Python in an interpreted, object orientated scripting language. If contains support for dynamic loading of objects, classes, modules, and exceptions. Adding interfaces to new system libraries through C code is straightforward, making Python easy to use in custom settings.

This Python package includes most of the standard Python modules, along with modules for interfacing to the Tix widget set for Tk and RPM.

python-devel – (Version 1.5.1, 2,877K)

The Python interpreter is relatively easy to extend with dynamically loaded extensions and to embed in other programs. This packages contains the header files and libraries which are needed to do both of these tasks.

python-docs – (Version 1.5.1, 2,611K)

This package contains documentation on the Python language and interpretor as a mix of plain ASCII files and LaTeX sources.

tcl – (Version 8.0.3, 5,464K)   Ⓦ Ⓢ

TCL is a simple scripting language that is designed to be embedded in other applications. This package includes tclsh, a simple example of a tcl application. TCL is very popular for writing small graphical applications because of the TK widget set which is closely tied to it.

tclx – (Version 8.0.3, 1,942K)   Ⓦ Ⓢ

TclX is a set of extensions to make it more suitable for common Unix programming tasks. It adds or enhances support for files, network access, debugging, math, lists, and message catalogs. It can be used with both tcl and tcl/tk applications.

tix – (Version 4.1.0.6, 2,709K)   Ⓦ Ⓢ

Tix is a add on for the tk widget set which adds many complex widgets which are built from tk building blocks. The extra widgets include combo box, file selection, notebooks, paned windows, spin controls, and hierarchical list boxes.

tk – (Version 8.0.3, 5,227K)   Ⓦ Ⓢ

Tk is a X Windows widget set designed to work closely with the tcl scripting language. It allows you to write simple programs with full featured GUI's in only a little more time then it takes to write a text based interface. Tcl/Tk applications can also be run on Windows and Macintosh platforms.

tkinter – (Version 1.5.1, 639K)   Ⓦ Ⓢ

A graphical interface for Python, based on Tcl/Tk, and used by many of the configuration tools.

umb-scheme – (Version 3.2, 1,211K)

UMB Scheme is an implementation of the language described in the IEEE Standard for the Scheme Programming Language (December, 1990).

xlispstat – (Version 3.52.5, 2,847K)

An implementation of the Lisp programming language for X-Windows, with extensions for advanced statistics computations.

B.4.4   Libraries

This section contains packages of the various libraries. Some libraries are required for normal system operation, while others are only needed if you will be using their features in a program you're writing.

cracklib – (Version 2.7, 69K)   Ⓑ

Checks passwords for security related characteristics - length, uniqueness, whether they are in a word database, etc.

e2fsprogs-devel – (Version 1.12, 257K)

Libraries and header files needed to develop ext2 filesystem-specific programs.

faces-devel – (Version 1.6.1, 22K)   Ⓦ

This is the xface development environment. It contains the static libraries and header files for doing xface development.

gd-devel – (Version 1.3, 7K)   Ⓦ

This package contains the files needed for development of programs linked against GD.

gdbm-devel – (Version 1.7.3, 70K)   Ⓦ

These are the development libraries and header files for gdbm, the GNU database system. These are required if you plan to do development using the gdbm database.

glibc – (Version 2.0.7, 15,608K)   Ⓑ

Contains the standard libraries that are used by multiple programs on the system. In order to save disk space and memory, as well as to ease upgrades, common system code is kept in one place and shared between programs. This package contains the most important sets of shared libraries, the standard C library and the standard math library. Without these, a Linux system will not function It also contains national language (locale) support and timezone databases.

glibc-debug – (Version 2.0.7, 2K)

These libraries have the debugging information debuggers use for tracing the execution of programs. These are only needed when the shared libraries themselves are being debugged – they are not needed to debug programs which use them.

glibc-devel – (Version 2.0.7, 11,688K)   ⓌⓈ

To develop programs which use the standard C libraries (which nearly all programs do), the system needs to have these standard header files and object files available for creating the executables.

glibc-profile – (Version 2.0.7, 10,010K)

When programs are being profiled used gprof, they must use these libraries instrad of the standard C libraries for gprof to be able to profile them correctly.

gpm-devel – (Version 1.13, 23K)   Ⓦ

This package allows you to develop your own text-mode programs that take advantage of the mouse.

inn-devel – (Version 1.7.2, 128K)

This library is needed by several programs that interface to INN, such as newsgate or tin.

libgr-devel – (Version 2.0.13, 302K)   (W)

This package is all you need to develop programs that handle the various graphics file formats supported by libgr.

libjpeg-devel – (Version 6b, 228K)   (W)

This package is all you need to develop programs that manipulate jpeg images, including documentation.

libpng-devel – (Version 1.0.1, 332K)   (W)

The header files and static libraries are only needed for development of programs using the PNG library.

libstdc++-devel – (Version 2.8.0, 1,090K)   (W)

This is the GNU implementation of the standard C++ libraries. This package includes the header files and libraries needed for C++ development.

libtiff-devel – (Version 3.4, 1,372K)   (W)

This package is all you need to develop programs that manipulate tiff images.

libungif-devel – (Version 3.0, 237K)

Libraries and headers needed for developing programs that use libungif to load and save gif image files.

ncurses-devel – (Version 4.2, 6,418K)   (W)

This package includes the header files and libraries necessary to develop applications that use ncurses.

newt-devel – (Version 0.30, 116K)   (W)

These are the header files and libraries for developing applications which use newt. Newt is a windowing toolkit for text mode, which provides many widgets and stackable windows.

postgresql-devel – (Version 6.3.2, 1,000K)   (S)

This package contains header files and libraries required to compile applications that are talking directly to the PostgreSQL backend server.

pythonlib – (Version 1.22, 236K)   (B)(W)(S)

This package contains code used by a variety of Red Hat programs. It includes code for multifield listboxes and entry widgets with non-standard keybindings, among others.

readline-devel – (Version 2.2.1, 255K)   (W)

The "readline" library will read a line from the terminal and return it, using prompt as a prompt. If prompt is null, no prompt is issued. The line returned is allocated with malloc(3), so the caller must free it when finished. The line returned has the final newline removed, so only the text of the line remains.

rpm-devel – (Version 2.5.5, 232K) ⟨W⟩

The RPM packaging system includes a C library that makes it easy to manipulate RPM packages and databases. It is intended to ease the creation of graphical package managers and other tools that need intimate knowledge of RPM packages.

slang-devel – (Version 0.99.38, 472K) ⟨W⟩

This package contains the slang static libraries and header files required to develop slang-based applications. It also includes documentation to help you write slang-based apps.

svgalib-devel – (Version 1.3.0, 751K) ⟨W⟩

These are the libraries and header files that are needed to build programs which use SVGAlib. SVGAlib allows programs to use full screen graphics on a variety of hardware platforms and without the overhead X requires.

xpm-devel – (Version 3.4j, 217K) ⟨W⟩

Allows you to develop applications that display bitmaps in X-Windows.

zlib-devel – (Version 1.1.3, 162K) ⟨W⟩

The 'zlib' compression library provides in-memory compression and decompression functions, including integrity checks of the uncompressed data. This version of the library supports only one compression method (deflation) but other algorithms may be added later and will have the same stream interface.

This package contains the header files and libraries needed to develop programs that use these zlib.

B.4.5 System

This section lists the packages containing system-level development tools.

linuxconf-devel – (Version 1.12r5, 2,706K) ⟨W⟩

This package provides the components needed to develop linuxconf modules outside of the linuxconf source tree. The kit is also needed to develop standalone utilities using the linuxconf user interface toolkit.

B.4.6 Tools

This section contains packages that provide the usual assortment of tools that programmers require.

binutils – (Version 2.9.1.0.14, 4,537K)   ⒷⓌⓈ

Binutils is a collection of utilities necessary for compiling programs. It includes the assembler and linker, as well as a number of other miscellaneous programs for dealing with executable formats.

bison – (Version 1.25, 154K)   ⓌⓈ

This is the GNU parser generator which is mostly compatible with yacc. Many programs use this as part of their build process. Bison is only needed on systems that are used for development.

byacc – (Version 1.9, 52K)   ⓌⓈ

This is a public domain yacc parser. It is used by many programs during their build process. You probably want this package if you do development.

cdecl – (Version 2.5, 74K)   ⓌⓈ

This is a package to translate English to C/C++ function declarations and vice versa. It is useful for programmers.

cproto – (Version 4.4, 84K)   ⓌⓈ

Cproto generates function prototypes for functions defined in the specified C source files to the standard output. The function definitions may be in the old style or ANSI C style. Optionally, cproto also outputs declarations for variables defined in the files. If no file argument is given, cproto reads its input from the standard input.

flex – (Version 2.5.4a, 290K)   ⓌⓈ

This is the GNU fast lexical analyzer generator. It generates lexical tokenizing code based on a lexical (regular expression based) description of the input. It is designed to work with both yacc and bison, and is used by many programs as part of their build process.

gettext – (Version 0.10.35, 824K)   ⓌⓈ

The gettext library provides an easy to use library and tools for creating, using, and modifying natural language catalogs. It is a powerfull and simple method for internationalizing programs.

gperf – (Version 2.7, 245K)

GNU gperf generates perfect hash functions for sets of key words. A perfect hash function is simply:

A hash function and a data structure that allows recognition of a key word in a set of words using exactly 1 probe into the data structure.

indent – (Version 1.9.1, 80K)

This is the GNU indenting program. It is used to beautify C program source files.

xwpe – (Version 1.5.12a, 712K)

XWPE is actually a package of four programs: we, wpe, xwe, and xwpe. They are different versions of the same basic programmers editor and development environment. If you have used some of the Micro$oft Windows programming IDE's and longed for an X Windows equivalent, this is what you have been looking for! Also included are the text-mode equivalents of the X programs, enabling you to use xwpe no matter what your development environment may be.

This package includes the basic xwpe libraries and the text-mode programs; the X Windows programs are contained in the 'xwpe-X11' package.

B.4.7 Version Control

This section contains packages that allow the programmer to implement various forms of version control over their programs.

cvs – (Version 1.10.2, 3,024K) Ⓦ Ⓢ

CVS is a front end to the rcs(1) revision control system which extends the notion of revision control from a collection of files in a single directory to a hierarchical collection of directories consisting of revision controlled files. These directories and files can be combined together to form a software release. CVS provides the functions necessary to manage these software releases and to control the concurrent editing of source files among multiple software developers.

rcs – (Version 5.7, 487K) Ⓦ Ⓢ

The Revision Control System (RCS) manages multiple revisions of files. RCS automates the storing, retrieval, logging, identification, and merging of revisions. RCS is useful for text that is revised frequently, for example programs, documentation, graphics, papers, and form letters.

B.5 Documentation

This section lists packages that contain a variety of Linux-related information. There is a lot of good information here; unless you are low on disk space, you should install these packages. (Note, however, that you probably don't need all the HOWTO packages; in most cases howto and howto-html will probably suffice.)

faq – (Version 5.2, 1,116K)

This is a package of the Frequently Asked Questions (FAQ) about Linux from sunsite.unc.edu. It is one of the best sources of information about Linux.

gimp-manual – (Version 1.0.0, 17,979K)

This is release 1.0.0 of the GIMP User's Manual (GUM). This is the first stable release of the manual, a product of almost a year of work. It is available in HTML, PS, PDF and FM (FrameMaker) source code. Please read COPYING for the license terms of the manual.

The manual is about 590 pages long and there have been several imporvments over previous versions. Be sure to pay special attention to the new Gallery chaper which contains many nice images and a hints on how to make them. The Gallery is a good example of what you can do with the GIMP. All images in the manual is 100% pure GIMP images.

The HTML version is suitable for online manual, PS and PDF are suitable if you want to print it on a regular printer or have a nice looking online manual. The FM source code is only useful if you want to contribute to the Graphic Documentation Project. Submissions to the GIMP User's manual will follow under the license agreement in the COPYING file.

The HTML version of the manual, while convenient for an online manual, is not the same quality of the PDF or PostScript formats. Improvements will be made to the HTML version later. This release was under a time constraint.

For other formats of this manual check ftp://manual.gimp.org/pub/manual

howto – (Version 5.2, 9,803K)

This is the best collection of Linux documentation there is. It was put together on Apr 15 1998. If you want to find newer versions of these documents, see http://sunsite.unc.edu/linux. For the versions in this package, see /usr/doc/HOWTO

howto-chinese – (Version 5.2, 13,708K)

This package contains translated versions of the Linux HOWTO into chinese. Please note that not all the files have been translated, so you most likely will need the english version installed if you want to have a complete HOWTO install.

howto-croatian – (Version 5.2, 1,872K)

This package contains translated versions of the Linux HOWTO into croatian. Please note that not all the files have been translated, so you most likely will need the english version installed if you want to have a complete HOWTO install.

howto-dvi – (Version 5.2, 3,306K)

These are the dvi versions of the HOWTOs. Probably only useful to TeX hackers.

howto-french – (Version 5.2, 38,101K)

This package contains translated versions of the Linux HOWTO into french. Please note that not all the files have been translated, so you most likely will need the english version installed if you want to have a complete HOWTO install.

howto-german – (Version 5.2, 11,760K)

This package contains translated versions of the Linux HOWTO into german. Please note that not all the files have been translated, so you most likely will need the english version installed if you want to have a complete HOWTO install.

howto-greek – (Version 5.2, 2,822K)

This package contains translated versions of the Linux HOWTO into greek. Please note that not all the files have been translated, so you most likely will need the english version installed if you want to have a complete HOWTO install.

howto-html – (Version 5.2, 11,214K)

These are the html versions of the HOWTOs. You can view them with your favorite web browser.

howto-indonesian – (Version 5.2, 3,727K)

This package contains translated versions of the Linux HOWTO into indonesian. Please note that not all the files have been translated, so you most likely will need the english version installed if you want to have a complete HOWTO install.

howto-italian – (Version 5.2, 15,179K)

This package contains translated versions of the Linux HOWTO into italian. Please note that not all the files have been translated, so you most likely will need the english version installed if you want to have a complete HOWTO install.

howto-japanese – (Version 5.2, 25,676K)

This package contains translated versions of the Linux HOWTO into japanese. Please note that not all the files have been translated, so you most likely will need the english version installed if you want to have a complete HOWTO install.

howto-korean – (Version 5.2, 14,272K)

This package contains translated versions of the Linux HOWTO into korean. Please note that not all the files have been translated, so you most likely will need the english version installed if you want to have a complete HOWTO install.

howto-polish – (Version 5.2, 15,832K)

This package contains translated versions of the Linux HOWTO into polish. Please note that not all the files have been translated, so you most likely will need the english version installed if you want to have a complete HOWTO install.

howto-ps – (Version 5.2, 6,417K)

These are the PostScript versions of the HOWTOs. You can view them with ghostview or print them on PostScript printers.

howto-serbian – (Version 5.2, 37K)

This package contains translated versions of the Linux HOWTO into serbian. Please note that not all the files have been translated, so you most likely will need the english version installed if you want to have a complete HOWTO install.

howto-sgml – (Version 5.2, 8,498K)

These are the SGML versions of the HOWTOs. They are the "source" files that the HOWTOs are built from (using linuxdoc-sgml).

howto-slovenian – (Version 5.2, 2,137K)

This package contains translated versions of the Linux HOWTO into slovenian. Please note that not all the files have been translated, so you most likely will need the english version installed if you want to have a complete HOWTO install.

howto-spanish – (Version 5.2, 18,413K)

This package contains translated versions of the Linux HOWTO into spanish. Please note that not all the files have been translated, so you most likely will need the english version installed if you want to have a complete HOWTO install.

howto-swedish – (Version 5.2, 4,867K)

This package contains translated versions of the Linux HOWTO into swedish. Please note that not all the files have been translated, so you most likely will need the english version installed if you want to have a complete HOWTO install.

howto-turkish – (Version 5.2, 816K)

This package contains translated versions of the Linux HOWTO into turkish. Please note that not all the files have been translated, so you most likely will need the english version installed if you want to have a complete HOWTO install.

indexhtml – (Version 5.2, 6K)   W S

Red Hat html index page.

install-guide – (Version 3.2, 1,373K)

A general guide for installing and getting started with Linux. The installation sections should be ignored, in favor of the Red Hat Linux manual. Although, there is overlap, there is other useful information in this guide.

lpg – (Version 0.4, 1,739K)

This is a generic guide to the Programming on Linux systems. Check http://sunsite.unc.edu/LDP for more information about the Linux Documentation Project, and possible updates to this version.

man-pages – (Version 1.21, 1,575K)   W S

A large collection of man pages covering programming APIs, file formats, protocols, etc.

Section 1 = user commands (intro only) Section 2 = system calls Section 3 = libc calls Section 4 = devices (e.g., hd, sd) Section 5 = file formats and protocols (e.g., wtmp, /etc/passwd, nfs) Section 6 = games (intro only) Section 7 = conventions, macro packages, etc. (e.g., nroff, ascii) Section 8 = system administration (intro only)

nag – (Version 1.0, 1,217K)

This is a generic guide to the Network Administration of Linux systems. Check http://sunsite.unc.edu/LDP for more information about the Linux Documentation Project, and possible updates to this version.

rhl-alpha-install-addend-en – (Version 5.2, 196K)

This is a local copy of the HTML version of the Red Hat Linux 5.2 Alpha Installation Addendum.

rhl-install-guide-en – (Version 5.2, 1,472K)

This is a local copy of the HTML version of the Red Hat Linux 5.2 Installation Guide. An online copy can be found at http://www.redhat.com.

sag – (Version 0.6, 644K)

This is a generic guide to the System Administration of Linux systems. Check http://sunsite.unc.edu/LDP for more information about the Linux Documentation Project, and possible updates to this version.

B.6 Extensions

This section lists packages that provide language-specific extensions to Red Hat Linux.

B.6.1 Japanese

This section lists packages that provide Japanese-specific extensions to Red Hat Linux.

kterm – (Version 6.2.0, 147K)

kterm is the Kanji Terminal Emulator. It uses the Kanji character set instead of the normal english set for those who prefer Kanji.

B.7 Games

This section lists the packages that provide fun and entertainment to Red Hat Linux system owners the world over. Game packages that run under the X window system can be found in the X11 section near the end of this appendix.

bsd-games – (Version 2.1, 1,786K)

This is a bunch of games. Highlights include backgammon, cribbage, hangman, monop, primes, trek, and battlestar.

christminster – (Version 3, 223K)

This is a text adventure game for use with xzip.

colour-yahtzee – (Version 1.0, 19K)

This is a terminal mode version of the popular game, yahtzee. It is a dice and board game.

fortune-mod – (Version 1.0, 2,337K)

This is the ever popular fortune program. It will gladly print a random fortune when run. Is usually fun to put in the .login for your users on a system so they see something new every time they log in.

gnuchess – (Version 4.0.pl77, 1,328K)

This is the famous GNU chess program. It is text based, but can be used in conjunction with xboard to play X based chess.

mysterious – (Version 1.0, 163K)

Brian Howarth's Mysterious Adventure game series. This is a text based adventure game.

pinfocom – (Version 3.0, 170K)

'pinfocom' is an interpreter for those old Infocom-compatible text adventure games (remember those?).

scottfree – (Version 1.14, 31K)

'scottfree' is an interpreter for Scott-Adams-format text adventure games (remember those?).

trojka – (Version 1.1, 15K)

The aim of this game is to control and to place the falling blocks, so that at least three blocks horizontally or diagonally, or both, have matching patterns. This sequence is then removed, and the above blocks will coll you reach the top of the screen, the game is finished.

vga_cardgames – (Version 1.3.1, 110K)

A number of various card games for the Linux console, including Klondike, 'Oh Hell', Solitaire, and Spider, as well as some other popular time-wasters :)

vga_gamespack – (Version 1.3, 54K)

A number of various mind games for the Linux console using SVGAlib. The selection includes such favorites as Othello, Minesweeper, and Connect 4.

B.8   Libraries

This section lists packages that contain various libraries. These libraries are used by other program to support various functions, such as image manipulation, compatibility with older binary program formats, and screen handling.

aout-libs – (Version 1.4, 3,663K)

Old Linux systems used a format for programs and shared libraries called a.out while newer ones use the ELF format. In order to run old a.out format programs, you need the a.out format libraries which this package provide. With it, you are to run most a.out format packages for text, X, and SVGAlib modes.

gd – (Version 1.3, 312K)   [B]

This library allows you to easily create and manipulate GIF image files from your C programs.

gdbm – (Version 1.7.3, 25K)   [B]

This is a database indexing library. It is useful for those who need to write C applications and need access to a simple and efficient database or build C applications which use it.

glib – (Version 1.0.6, 54K)   [B]

Handy library of utility functions. Development libs and headers are in gtk+-devel.

gmp – (Version 2.0.2, 111K)

This is the GNU arbitrary precision library. Linking against it gives access to functions for handling arbitrarily large numbers with either a high level or a low level interface.

gmp-devel – (Version 2.0.2, 313K)

These are the static libraries, header files, and documentation for using the GNU arbitrary precision library in your own programs. With these, you can create your own own programs that use this library.

gsl – (Version 0.3b, 455K)

This is the GNU scientific library. Linking against it gives access to functions for handling many problems that arise in scientific computing.

ld.so – (Version 1.9.5, 246K)   [B]

This package contains the shared library configuration tool, ldconfig, which is required by many packages. It also includes the shared library loader and dynamic loader for Linux libc 5.

libc – (Version 5.3.12, 5,293K)   [B]

Older Linux systems (including all Red Hat Linux releases between 2.0 and 4.2, inclusive) were based on libc 5. This package includes these libraries and other libraries based on libc 5, allowing old applcications to run on glibc (libc 6) based systems.

libelf – (Version 0.6.4, 74K)

This library gives you access to the internals of the ELF object file format. It lets you poke around in the various different sections of an ELF file, check out the symbols, etc.

libg++ – (Version 2.7.2.8, 1,897K)   [B]

This is the GNU implementation of the standard C++ libraries, along with additional GNU tools. This package includes the shared libraries necessary to run C++ applications.

libgr – (Version 2.0.13, 206K) Ⓦ Ⓢ

This package is a library for handling various graphics file formats, including FBM, PBM, PGM, PNM, PPM, and REL.

libjpeg – (Version 6b, 243K) Ⓦ Ⓢ

This package is a library of functions that manipulate jpeg images, along with simple clients for manipulating jpeg images.

libjpeg6a – (Version 6a, 131K)

This package is a library of functions that manipulate jpeg images, along with simple clients for manipulating jpeg images.

libpng – (Version 1.0.1, 244K) Ⓦ Ⓢ

The PNG library is a collection of routines used to crate and manipulate PNG format graphics files. The PNG format was designed as a replacement for GIF, with many improvements and extensions.

libstdc++ – (Version 2.8.0, 366K) Ⓑ

This is the GNU implementation of the standard C++ libraries, along with additional GNU tools. This package includes the shared libraries necessary to run C++ applications.

libtermcap – (Version 2.0.8, 55K) Ⓑ

This is the library for accessing the termcap database. It is necessary to be installed for a system to be able to do much of anything.

libtermcap-devel – (Version 2.0.8, 11K) Ⓦ

This is the package containing the development libaries and header files for writing programs that access the termcap database. It may be necessary to build some other packages as well.

libtiff – (Version 3.4, 602K) Ⓦ Ⓢ

This package is a library of functions that manipulate TIFF images.

libungif – (Version 3.0, 37K) Ⓦ Ⓢ

GIF loading and saving shared library. (Saving uses an uncompressed gif algorithm that does not use LZW compression.)

ncurses – (Version 4.2, 2,334K) Ⓑ

The curses library routines give the user a terminal-independent method of updating character screens with reasonable optimization. This implementation is "new curses" (ncurses) and is the approved replacement for 4.4BSD classic curses, which is being discontinued.

ncurses3 – (Version 1.9.9e, 317K)

The curses library routines give the user a terminal-independent method of updating character screens with reasonable optimization. This implementation is "new curses" (ncurses) and is the approved replacement for 4.4BSD classic curses, which is being discontinued.

newt – (Version 0.30, 122K) *B*

Newt is a windowing toolkit for text mode built from the slang library. It allows color text mode applications to easily use stackable windows, push buttons, check boxes, radio buttons, lists, entry fields, labels, and displayable text. Scrollbars are supported, and forms may be nested to provide extra functionality. This pacakge contains the shared library for programs that have been built with newt as well as a /usr/bin/dialog replacement called whiptail.

p2c – (Version 1.20, 495K)

p2c is the Pascal to C translation system. It is used to convert Pascal source code into C source code so that it can be compiled using a standard C compiler (such as gcc).

readline – (Version 2.2.1, 250K) *B*

The "readline" library will read a line from the terminal and return it, allowing the user to edit the line with the standard emacs editing keys. It allows the programmer to give the user an easier-to-use and more intuitive interface.

slang – (Version 0.99.38, 164K) *B*

Slang (pronounced "sssslang") is a powerful stack based interpreter that supports a C-like syntax. It has been designed from the beginning to be easily embedded into a program to make it extensible. Slang also provides a way to quickly develop and debug the application embedding it in a safe and efficient manner. Since slang resembles C, it is easy to recode slang procedures in C if the need arises.

sox-devel – (Version 12.14, 518K)

Libraries that can be used to compile applications using sox libraries.

svgalib – (Version 1.3.0, 718K) *W*

SVGAlib is a library which allows applications to use full screen graphics on a variety of hardware platforms. Many games and utilities are avaiable which take advantage of SVGAlib for graphics access, as it is more suitable for machines with little memory then X Windows is.

zlib – (Version 1.1.3, 57K) *B*

The 'zlib' compression library provides in-memory compression and decompression functions, including integrity checks of the uncompressed data. This version of the library supports only one compression method (deflation) but other algorithms may be added later and will have the same stream interface.

This library is used by a number of different system programs.

B.9   Networking

This section lists packages that are related to networking. It has been split into several subsections for easier browsing.

B.9.1   Admin

This section lists packages that provide basic network administrative functions.

anonftp – (Version 2.6, 1,046K)   Ⓢ

Contains the files needed for allowing anonymous ftp access to your machine. This lets any user get files from your machine without having an account, which is a popular way of making programs available on the Internet.

caching-nameserver – (Version 5.2, 3K)   Ⓢ

Includes configuration files for bind (the DNS nameserver) which make it behave as a simple caching nameserver. Many users on dialup connections use this package (along with bind) and make the it's own nameserver to speed up name resoultions.

net-tools – (Version 1.46, 190K)   Ⓑ

This is a collection of the basic tools necessary for setting up networking on a Linux machine. It includes ifconfig, route, netstat, rarp, and some other minor tools.

nfs-server-clients – (Version 2.2beta37, 10K)   Ⓦ Ⓢ

This package contains client programs that interact with NFS servers. It is not needed to mount NFS volumes. At the moment the only program in it is showmount, which can be used to show exported and mounted filesystems.

tcp_wrappers – (Version 7.6, 242K)   Ⓦ Ⓢ

With this package you can monitor and filter incoming requests for the SYSTAT, FINGER, FTP, TELNET, RLOGIN, RSH, EXEC, TFTP, TALK, and other network services.

B.9.2   Daemons

This section lists packages that provide various network-related daemons. Daemons are programs that are run automatically to perform various system functions.

am-utils – (Version 6.0a16, 1,978K)

Am-utils is the"next generation" of the popular BSD Automounter, Amd. Am-utils includes many additional updates, ports, programs, features, bug fixes, and more.

Amd is the Berkeley automount daemon. It has the ability to automatically mount filesystems of all types, including NFS filesystems, CD-ROM's, and local drives, and unmount them when they are not being used any more.

The default setup allows you to 'cd /net/[hostname]' and get a list of directories exported from that host.

apache – (Version 1.3.2, 1,904K) Ⓢ

Apache is a full featured web server that is freely available, and also happens to be the most widely used.

apache-devel – (Version 1.3.2, 257K)

This package includes the source code and for Apache 1.3.1, as well as the 'apxs' binary for building dynamic shared objects (DSOs). This package needs to be installed if you want to compile or develop additional modules for Apache.

autofs – (Version 3.1.1, 100K)

autofs is a daemon which automatically mounts filesystems when you use them, and unmounts them later when you are not using them. This can include network filesystems, CD-ROMs, floppies, and so forth.

bind – (Version 8.1.2, 496K) Ⓢ

Includes the named name server, which is used to define host name to IP address translations (and vice versa). It can be used on workstations as a caching name server, but is generally only needed on one machine for an entire network.

bootp – (Version 2.4.3, 101K)

This is a server for the bootp protocol; which allows network administrators to setup networking information for clients via an /etc/bootptab on a server so that the clients can automatically get their networking information. While this server includes rudimentary DHCP support as well, we suggest using the dhcpd package if you need DHCP support, as it is much more complete.

cleanfeed – (Version 0.95.7b, 107K) Ⓢ

Cleanfeed is an automatic filter for INN that removes spam from incoming newsfeeds.

dhcp – (Version 2.0b1pl6, 437K)

This is the second release of the dhcp package from the Internet Software Consortium. It provides a server and a relay agent.

dhcpcd – (Version 0.70, 34K) Ⓑ

dhcpcd is an implementation of the DHCP client specified in draft-ietf-dhc-dhcp-09 (when -r option is not speci- fied) and RFC1541 (when -r option is specified).

It gets the host information (IP address, netmask, broad- cast address, etc.) from a DHCP server and configures the network interface of the machine on which it is running. It also tries to renew the lease time according to RFC1541 or draft-ietf-dhc-dhcp-09.

gated – (Version 3.5.10, 2,248K)

GateD is a routing daemon that handles multiple routing protocols and replaces routed and egpup. GateD currently handles the RIP, BGP, EGP, HELLO, and OSPF routing protocols. The gated process can be configured to perform all routing protocols or any subset of them. It is curently maintained by Merit.

imap – (Version 4.4, 1,419K)

IMAP is a server for the POP (Post Office Protocol) and IMAP mail protocols. The POP protocol allows a "post office" machine to collect mail for users and have that mail downloaded to the user's local machine for reading. The IMAP protocol provides the functionality of POP, and allows a user to read mail on a remote machine without moving it to his local mailbox.

inn – (Version 1.7.2, 3,217K)   Ⓢ

INN is a news server, which can be set up to handle USENET news, as well as private "newsfeeds". There is a *LOT* of information about setting up INN in /usr/doc – read it.

intimed – (Version 1.10, 96K)

intimed is a server that will tell networked machines what time it currently has. It is useful for keeping networks of machines in sync with the proper time.

mars-nwe – (Version 0.99pl10, 533K)   Ⓢ

MARS is a NetWare compatible file and printer server. It lets you use a Linux machine as a file and print server for NetWare based clients using NetWare's native IPX protocol suite.

mod_perl – (Version 1.15, 1,407K)

mod_perl is a powerful Apache module that enables the use of the PERL language within HTML files and more.

mod_php – (Version 2.0.1, 667K)

PHP is a powerful apache module that adds scripting and database connection capabilities to the apache server.

mod_php3 – (Version 3.0.4, 2,935K)

PHP3 is a powerful apache module that adds scripting and database connection capabilities to the apache server.

nfs-server – (Version 2.2beta37, 155K)   Ⓢ

The NFS and mount daemons are used to create an NFS server which can export filesystems to other machines. This package is not needed to mount NFS filesystems – that functionality is already in the Linux kernel.

portmap – (Version 4.0, 43K)   Ⓦ Ⓢ

The portmapper manages RPC connections, which are used by protocols such as NFS and NIS. The portmap server must be running on machines which act as servers for protocols which make use of the RPC mechanism. This portmapper supports hosts.allow,deny type access control.

ppp – (Version 2.3.5, 275K)   [W] [S]

This is the daemon and documentation for PPP support. It requires a kernel greater than 2.0 which is built with PPP support. The default Red Hat kernels include PPP support as a module.

sendmail – (Version 8.8.7, 553K)   [B]

Sendmail is a Mail Transport Agent, which is the program that moves mail from one machine to another. Sendmail implements a general internetwork mail routing facility, featuring aliasing and forwarding, automatic routing to network gateways, and flexible configuration.

If you need the ability to send and receive mail via the internet you'll need sendmail.

squid – (Version 1.1.22, 919K)

Squid is a high-performance proxy caching server for web clients, supporting FTP, gopher, and HTTP data objects. Unlike traditional caching software, Squid handles all requests in a single, non-blocking, I/O-driven process.

Squid keeps meta data and especially hot objects cached in RAM, caches DNS lookups, supports non-blocking DNS lookups, and implements negative caching of failed requests. If you are tight on memory, check out the NOVM version of this package.

Squid supports SSL, extensive access controls, and full request logging. By using the lightweight Internet Cache Protocol, Squid caches can be arranged in a hierarchy or mesh for additional bandwidth savings.

Squid consists of a main server program squid, a Domain Name System lookup program dnsserver, a program for retrieving FTP data ftpget, and some management and client tools. When squid starts up, it spawns a configurable number of dnsserver processes, each of which can perform a single, blocking Domain Name System (DNS) lookup. This reduces the amount of time the cache waits for DNS lookups.

Squid is derived from the ARPA-funded Harvest project.

squid-novm – (Version 1.1.22, 911K)

The NOVM version of the squid will use less memory to do the proxy job, at the expense of file descriptors. (NOVM stands for NO Virtual Memory). If you are tight on memory on your proxy/cache server, this might be for you.

Squid is a high-performance proxy caching server for web clients, supporting FTP, gopher, and HTTP data objects. Unlike traditional caching software, Squid handles all requests in a single, non-blocking, I/O-driven process.

Squid keeps meta data and especially hot objects cached in RAM, caches DNS lookups, supports non-blocking DNS lookups, and implements negative caching of failed requests.

Squid supports SSL, extensive access controls, and full request logging. By using the lightweight Internet Cache Protocol, Squid caches can be arranged in a hierarchy or mesh for additional bandwidth savings.

Squid consists of a main server program squid, a Domain Name System lookup program dnsserver, a program for retrieving FTP data ftpget, and some management and client tools. When squid starts up, it spawns a configurable number of dnsserver processes, each of which can perform a single, blocking Domain Name System (DNS) lookup. This reduces the amount of time the cache waits for DNS lookups.

Squid is derived from the ARPA-funded Harvest project.

ucd-snmp – (Version 3.5.3, 2,105K)   🆆 🆂

This is a derivative of the original Carnegie Mellon University Simple Network Management Protocol version 2 (SNMPv2). It is useful for managing networks and doing accounting.

wu-ftpd – (Version 2.4.2b18, 297K)   🆂

wu-ftpd is the daemon (background) program which serves FTP files to ftp clients. It is useful if you wish to exchange programs between computers without running a network filesystem such as NFS, or if you want to run an anonymous FTP site (in which case, you will want to install the anonftp package).

xntp3 – (Version 5.93, 2,043K)

This package contains utilities and daemons to help synchronize your computer's time to UTC standard time. It includes ntpdate, a program similar to rdate, and xntpd, a daemon which adjusts the system time continuously.

ypserv – (Version 1.3.5, 261K)

ypserv is an implementation of the standard NIS/YP networking protocol. It allows network-wide distribution of hostname, username, and other information databases. This is the NIS server, and is not needed on NIS clients.

B.9.3   Development

This section lists packages that are related to the development of networking-related code.

bind-devel – (Version 8.1.2, 230K)

All the include files and the library required for DNS development for bind 8.x.x

B.9.4 News

This section lists packages related to Usenet news.

inews – (Version 1.7.2, 47K)

The inews program is used by some news readers to post news. It does some consistency checking and header reformatting, and forwards the article on to the news server specified in inn.conf.

B.9.5 Utilities

This section lists packages that provide handy utilities related to networking.

bind-utils – (Version 8.1.2, 471K)   Ⓦ Ⓢ

Collection of utilities for querying name servers and looking up hosts. These tools let you determine the IP addresses for given host names, and find information about registered domains and network addresses.

bootpc – (Version 061, 35K)   Ⓑ Ⓦ Ⓢ

bootpc is the bootp client for Linux that will allow a linux machine to retrieve it's networking information from a server via the network. It sends out a general broadcast asking for the information which is returned.

comanche – (Version 0.6a, 189K)

Comanche stands for COnfiguration MANager for apaCHE. It is a front end for the Apache Configuration Server Project Apache is the most popular, fast, reliable Web server on the internet. You can find more about Apache at www.apache.org

This package is working with RCS to provide you with accurate history of the changes for the apache config files.

dip – (Version 3.3.7o, 86K)   Ⓦ Ⓢ

dip is a program to allow for automatic scripting of modem dialing. It's useful for setting up PPP and SLIP connections, but isn't required for either. It is used by netcfg for setting up SLIP connections.

fwhois – (Version 1.00, 7K)   Ⓦ Ⓢ

This is the "whois" program. It will allow you to find out information on people stored in the whois databases around the world.

ipxutils – (Version 1.0, 44K)   Ⓢ

This package includes utilities necessary for configuring and debugging IPX interfaces and networks under Linux. IPX is the low-level protocol used by NetWare to transfer data.

ltrace – (Version 0.3.4, 70K)

ltrace is a program that simply runs the specified command until it exits. It intercepts and records the dynamic library calls which are called by the executed process and the signals which are received by that process. It can also intercept and print the system calls executed by the program.

mgetty – (Version 1.1.14, 1,166K)

This package contains an intelligent getty for allowing logins over a serial line (such as through a modem). It allows automatic callback and includes fax support (though mgetty-sendfax needs to be installed to make full use of it's fax support).

mgetty-sendfax – (Version 1.1.14, 271K)

This package includes support for FAX Class 2 modems to send and receive faxes. It also includes simple FAX queueing support.

mgetty-voice – (Version 1.1.14, 622K)

This package includes support for some modems which have voice mail extensions.

nc – (Version 1.10, 104K)

NetCat is a minimal network client. It can be used to make terminal TCP connections to arbitrary ports and can fake connections over UDP. It can also listen on ports.

ncpfs – (Version 2.2.0, 446K) $\boxed{S}$

This package contains tools to help configure and use the ncpfs filesysten, which is a linux filesystem which understands the NCP protocol. This protocol is used by Novell NetWare clients use to talk to NetWare servers.

rdate – (Version 0.960923, 5K) $\boxed{W}$ $\boxed{S}$

rdate is a program that can retrieve the time from another machine on your network. If run as root, it will also set your local time to that of the machine you queried. It is not super accurate; get xntpd if you are really worried about milliseconds.

rdist – (Version 1.0, 118K) $\boxed{W}$ $\boxed{S}$

Rdist is a program to maintain identical copies of files over multiple hosts. It preserves the owner, group, mode, and mtime of files if possible and can update programs that are executing.

traceroute – (Version 1.4a5, 29K) $\boxed{W}$ $\boxed{S}$

Traceroute prints the route packets take across a TCP/IP. The names (or IP numbers if names are not available) of the machines which are routing packets from the machine traceroute is running on to the destination machine are printed, along with the time is took to receive a packet acknowledgement from that machine. This tool can be very helpfull in diagnosing networking problems.

ucd-snmp-devel – (Version 3.5.3, 583K)

These are the development libraries and header files for UCD SNMP. This will allow the network administrator to write programs for use with network management.

ucd-snmp-utils – (Version 3.5.3, 731K) $\boxed{W}\boxed{S}$

These are the various utilities for use with UCD SNMP. Contains utils such as snmpwalk, snmptest, and more.

yp-tools – (Version 2.0, 153K) $\boxed{W}\boxed{S}$

This implementation of NIS for linux is based on the YP stuff for FreeBSD. It is a special port for glibc 2.x and libc ¿= 5.4.21.

This implementation only provides NIS _clients_. You must already have a NIS server running somewhere. You can find one for linux on http://www-vt.uni-paderborn.de/ kukuk/linux/nis.html. Please read the NIS-HOWTO, too.

biff – (Version 0.10, 16K)

The biff client and comsat server are an antiquated method of asynchronous mail notification. Although they are still supported, most users use their shells MAIL variable (or mail under csh variants) to check for mail, or a dedicated application such as xbiff or xmailbox.

bootparamd – (Version 0.10, 17K)

Some (notably Sun's) network boot loaders rely on special boot server code on the server, in addition to rarp and tftp servers. This server is compatible with the SunOS bootparam clients and servers.

finger – (Version 0.10, 30K) $\boxed{W}\boxed{S}$

Finger is a simple protocol which allows users to find information about users on other machines. This package includes a standard finger client and server. The server runs from /etc/inetd.conf, which must be modified to disable finger requests.

ftp – (Version 0.10, 83K) $\boxed{W}\boxed{S}$

This provides the standard Unix command-line ftp client. ftp is the standard Internet file transfer protocol, which is extremely popular for both file archives and file transfers between individuals.

netkit-base – (Version 0.10, 53K) $\boxed{W}\boxed{S}$

This package provides the ping and inetd programs, which are both used for basic networking.

ntalk – (Version 0.10, 31K) $\boxed{W}\boxed{S}$

This package provides a client and daemon for the Internet talk protocol, which allows one-on-one chatting between users on different systems.

pidentd – (Version 2.7, 116K) $\boxed{W}\boxed{S}$

identd is a program that implements the RFC1413 identification server. identd operates by looking up specific TCP/IP connections and returning the user name of the process owning the connection.

routed – (Version 0.10, 38K)   ⓦⓈ

A number of protocols are available for automatic updating of TCP/IP routing tables. RIP is the simplest of those, and this package includes a daemon which broadcasts RIP routing notification and handles incoming RIP packets.

rsh – (Version 0.10, 95K)   ⓦⓈ

Rsh, rlogin, and rcp are a suite of programs which allow users to run commands on remote machines, login into other machines, and copy files between machines. All of these commands use rhosts style authentication. This package includes the client and servers needed for all of these services, as well as a server for rexec, which is an alternate method of executing remote commands. All of these servers are run from inetd and configured through /etc/inetd.conf and PAM. The rexecd server is disabled by default, but the rest are enabled.

rusers – (Version 0.10, 36K)   ⓦⓈ

The rusers server and client, both included in this package, allow users to find out what users are logged into various machines on the local network.

rwall – (Version 0.10, 17K)

The rwall client sends a message to an rwall daemon running on a remote machine, which relays the message to all of the users on the remote machine. The rwall daemon is run from /etc/inetd.conf, and is disabled by default on Red Hat systems.

rwho – (Version 0.10, 23K)   ⓦⓈ

The rwho program displays what users are logged into all of machines on the local network which are running the rwho daemon. Both the rwho client and daemon are provided in this package.

samba – (Version 1.9.18p10, 3,248K)   Ⓢ

Samba provides an SMB server which can be used to provide network services to SMB (sometimes called "Lan Manager") clients, including various versions of MS Windows, OS/2, and other Linux machines. Samba also provides some SMB clients, which complement the built-in SMB filesystem in Linux. Samba uses NetBIOS over TCP/IP (NetBT) protocols and does NOT need NetBEUI (Microsoft Raw NetBIOS frame) protocol.

This release is known as the "Locking Update" and has full support for Opportunistic File Locking. In addition this update includes native support for Microsoft encrypted passwords, improved browse list and WINS database management.

Please refer to the WHATSNEW.txt document for fixup information. This binary release includes encrypted password support. Please read the smb.conf file and ENCRYPTION.txt in the docs directory for implementation details.

telnet – (Version 0.10, 175K)   ⓦⓈ

Telnet is a popular protocol for remote logins across the Internet. This package provides a command line telnet client as well as a telnet daemon which allows remote logins into the machine it is running on. The telnet daemon is enabled by default, and may be disabled by editing /etc/inetd.conf.

tftp – (Version 0.10, 32K)   [W] [S]

The trivial file transfer protocol (tftp) is normally used only for booting diskless workstations. It provides very little security, and should not be enabled unless it is needed. The tftp server is run from /etc/inetd.conf, and is disabled by default on Red Hat systems.

timed – (Version 0.10, 60K)   [W] [S]

This timed server allows remote machines to query the time-of day of the machine the server is running on. This allows for simple time syncronization across a network.

ypbind – (Version 3.3, 37K)

This is a daemon which runs on NIS/YP clients and binds them to a NIS domain. It must be running for systems based on glibc to behave as NIS clients.

ytalk – (Version 3.0.3, 72K)

ytalk is an extension of the standard Internet 'talk' protocol that allows more than two users per conversation, redirection of program output to others, as well as an easy-to-use menu of commands. It uses the same talk daemon as the standard talk program.

B.10   Shells

This section lists packages that provide a wide variety of shells for your Red Hat Linux system.

ash – (Version 0.2, 247K)   [B]

ash is a bourne shell clone from Berkeley. It supports all of the standard Bourne shell commands and has the advantage of supporting them while remaining considerably smaller than bash.

bash – (Version 1.14.7, 1,327K)   [B]

Bash is an sh-compatible command language interpreter that executes commands read from the standard input or from a file. Bash also incorporates useful features from the Korn and C shells (ksh and csh).

Bash is ultimately intended to be a conformant implementation of the IEEE Posix Shell and Tools specification (IEEE Working Group 1003.2).

mc – (Version 4.1.35, 869K)   [W]

Midnight Commander is a visual shell much like a file manager, only with way more features. It is text mode, but also includes mouse support if you are running GPM. Its coolest feature is the ability to ftp, view tar and zip files, and poke into RPMs for specific files. :-)

pdksh – (Version 5.2.12, 391K)

pdksh, a remimplementation of ksh, is a command interpreter that is intended for both interactive and shell script use. Its command language is a superset of the sh(1) shell language.

sash – (Version 2.1, 280K)   Ⓑ

Sash is a very simple, statically linked shell. It includes simplified versions built in commands like ls, dd, and gzip. Sash can be quite usefull for system recovery.

tcsh – (Version 6.07.09, 487K)   Ⓑ

'tcsh' is an enhanced version of csh (the C shell), with additional features such as command history, filename completion, and fancier prompts.

zsh – (Version 3.0.5, 953K)

zsh is an enhanced version of the bourne shell with these features: - very close to ksh/sh grammar, with csh additions - most features of ksh, bash, and tcsh - 75 builtins, 89 options, 154 key bindings - short for loops, ex: for i (*.c) echo $i - select - shell functions ...and many more

B.11   Utilities

This section lists packages that provide various utilities for your Red Hat Linux system. Because there are so many, we've split them into different subsections.

B.11.1   Archiving

This section lists packages that provide utilities for data archiving.

bzip2 – (Version 0.9.0b, 239K)

Bzip2 compresses files using the Burrows-Wheeler block-sorting text compression algorithm, and Huffman coding. Compression is generally considerably better than that achieved by more conventional LZ77/LZ78-based compressors, and approaches the performance of the PPM family of statistical compressors.

The command-line options are deliberately very similar to those of GNU Gzip, but they are not identical.

cpio – (Version 2.4.2, 68K)   Ⓑ

cpio copies files into or out of a cpio or tar archive, which is a file that contains other files plus information about them, such as their file name, owner, timestamps, and access permissions. The archive can be another file on the disk, a magnetic tape, or a pipe. cpio has three operating modes.

gzip – (Version 1.2.4, 227K)   Ⓑ

This is the popular GNU file compression and decompression program, gzip.

lha – (Version 1.00, 52K)   Ⓦ

This is an archiving and compression utility. It is mostly used in the DOS world, but can be used under Linux to extract DOS files from LHA archives.

ncompress – (Version 4.2.4, 30K)   Ⓑ

ncompress is a utility that will do fast compression and decompression compatible with the original *nix compress utility (.Z extensions). It will not handle gzipped (.gz) images (although gzip can handle compress images).

tar – (Version 1.12, 471K)   Ⓑ

GNU 'tar' saves many files together into a single tape or disk archive, and can restore individual files from the archive. It includes multivolume support, the ability to archive sparse files, automatic archive compression/decompression, remote archives and special features that allow 'tar' to be used for incremental and full backups. If you wish to do remote backups with tar, you will need to install the 'rmt' package as well.

unarj – (Version 2.41a, 25K)   Ⓦ

The unarj program is used to uncompress .arj format archives, which were somewhat popular on DOS based machines.

unzip – (Version 5.31, 335K)   Ⓦ

unzip will list, test, or extract files from a ZIP archive, commonly found on MS-DOS systems. A companion program, zip, creates ZIP archives; both programs are compatible with archives created by PKWARE's PKZIP and PKUNZIP for MS-DOS, but in many cases the program options or default behaviors differ.

zip – (Version 2.1, 206K)   Ⓦ

zip is a compression and file packaging utility for Unix, VMS, MSDOS, OS/2, Windows NT, Minix, Atari and Macintosh. It is analogous to a combination of the UNIX commands tar(1) and compress(1) and is compatible with PKZIP (Phil Katz's ZIP for MSDOS systems).

B.11.2   Console

This section lists packages that provide utilities that manage your Red Hat Linux system's console.

SVGATextMode – (Version 1.8, 845K)

SVGATextMode allows the screen mode of the Linux console to be controlled in detail. This allows more characters on screen, more stable text, less characters on screen, less stable text, etc. also, on badly designed hardware, you could sometimes achieve a melted monitor.

Extra fonts are required to work fully, though without them useful effects can still be achieved.

open – (Version 1.4, 12K)

This program runs a command on an given virtual console number. It can also run the program on the first virtual console which isn't already in use.

vlock – (Version 1.2, 9K)

vlock either locks the current terminal (which may be any kind of terminal, local or remote), or locks the entire virtual console system, completely disabling all console access. vlock gives up these locks when either the password of the user who started vlock or the root password is typed.

B.11.3   File

This section lists packages containing file-related utility programs.

file – (Version 3.25, 198K)   ⒝

This package is useful for finding out what type of file you are looking at on your system. For example, if an fsck results in a file being stored in lost+found, you can run file on it to find out if it's safe to 'more' it or if it's a binary. It recognizes many file types, including ELF binaries, system libraries, RPM packages, and many different graphics formats.

fileutils – (Version 3.16, 868K)   ⒝

These are the GNU file management utilities. It includes programs to copy, move, list, etc, files.

The ls program in this package now incorporates color ls!

findutils – (Version 4.1, 155K)   ⒝

This package contains programs to help you locate files on your system. The find program can search through a hierarchy of directories looking for files matching a certain set of criteria (such as a filename pattern). The locate program searches a database (create by updatedb) to quickly find a file matching a given pattern.

git – (Version 4.3.17, 698K)   ⒲

GIT is a file system browser for UNIX systems. An interactive process viewer/killer, a hex/ascii file viewer, an auto-mount shell script and a per file type action script are also available.

The standard ANSI color sequences are used where available. Manual pages and info documentation are also provided.

lslk – (Version 1.18, 33K)

The UNIX lock file lister, lslk, attempts to list all the locks held on the local files of the executing system – i.e., on the active inodes. The locks may come from local processes or remote ones on NFS clients, served by the executing system. Note: Linux and PTX 2.1.9 lslk don't report on locks held by remote NFS client processes.

lsof – (Version 4.37, 534K)

Lsof's name stands for LiSt Open Files, and it does just that. It lists information about files that are open by the processes running on a UNIX system.

macutils – (Version 2.0b3, 201K)

This is a set of utilities for manipulating files from the Macintosh. Popular utilities like macunpack, hexbin, and binhex are included.

mtools – (Version 3.9.1, 481K)   ⓦ

Mtools is a collection of utilities to access MS-DOS disks from Unix without mounting them. It supports Win'95 style long file names, OS/2 Xdf disks, ZIP/JAZ disks and 2m disks (store up to 1992k on a high density 3 1/2 disk).

sharutils – (Version 4.2, 217K)   ⓦ ⓢ

The shar utilities can be used to encode and package a number of files, binary and/or text, in a special plain text format. This format can safely be sent through email or other means where sending binary files is difficult.

smbfs – (Version 2.0.1, 50K)   ⓢ

This package includes the tools necessary to mount filesystems from SMB servers.

stat – (Version 1.5, 6K)   ⓑ

The stat program prints out filesystem level information about a file, including permissions, link count, inode, etc.

symlinks – (Version 1.2, 98K)

This program check for a number of problems with symlinks on a system, including symlinks which point to nonexistant files (dangling symlinks). It can also automatically convert absolute symlinks to relative symlinks.

tree – (Version 1.2, 18K)

This program is basically a UNIX port of the very useful DOS utility 'tree', which prints out a view of the specified directory tree, along with the files it owns. Includes support for 'color ls'-style listings.

which – (Version 1.0, 7K)   ⓑ

Give it a program name, and it tells you if it is on your 'PATH'.

For example, 'which ls' would print '/bin/ls', because the ls program, which is in one of the directories listed in your PATH environment variable, is located in the

/bin directory.

B.11.4 Printing

This section lists packages that provide utility programs related to printing.

mpage – (Version 2.4, 84K) $\boxed{W}\boxed{S}$

mpage formats multiple pages of ASCII text onto a single page of PostScript. It supports many different layouts for the final pages.

B.11.5 System

This section lists packages that provide utilities that perform various system-related functions.

MAKEDEV – (Version 2.3.1, 24K) $\boxed{B}$

The /dev tree holds special files, each of which corresponds to a type of hardware device that Linux supports. This package contains a script which makes it easier to create and maintain the files which fill the /dev tree.

adjtimex – (Version 1.3, 22K)

adjtimex is a kernel clock management system. It is useful in adjusting the system clock for accuracy.

apmd – (Version 2.4, 63K)

This is a Advanced Power Management daemon and utilities. It can watch your notebook's battery and warn all users when the battery is low.

I have added an unofficial patch for shutting down the PCMCIA sockets before a suspend.

awesfx – (Version 0.4.2, 251K) $\boxed{W}$

awesfx includes a couple of utilities for the AWE32 sound driver. You need to use these utilities to enable sounds on the driver properly. This package includes a soundfont that is a replacement for the SYNTHGM.SBK that comes with the SB AWE32.

chkconfig – (Version 0.9.4, 44K) $\boxed{B}$

chkconfig provides a simple command-line tool for maintaining the /etc/rc.d directory hierarchy by relieving system administrators of directly manipulating the numerous symbolic links in that directory.

control-panel – (Version 3.7, 177K) $\boxed{W}\boxed{S}$

The Red Hat control panel is an X program launcher for various configuration tools. Other packages provide information which allow them to show up on the control panel's menu of available tools.

cracklib-dicts – (Version 2.7, 227K) Ⓑ

Includes the cracklib dictionaries for the standard /usr/dict/words, as well as utilities needed to create new dictionaries.

dump – (Version 0.3, 123K)

dump and restore can be used to backup extended 2 (ext2) partitions in a variety of ways.

e2fsprogs – (Version 1.12, 843K) Ⓑ

This package includes a number of utilities for creating, checking, and repairing ext2 filesystems.

eject – (Version 1.5, 34K) Ⓡ

This program allows the user to eject media that is autoejecting like CD-ROMs, Jaz and Zip drives, and floppy drives on SPARC machines.

ext2ed – (Version 0.1, 283K)

This is a package to allow for hacking of your extended two file systems. It is for hackers *only* and should only be used by experienced personnel. If you aren't sure if this is you, it isn't. Also, do not smoke near this software. You have been warned. This is not a recording.

getty_ps – (Version 2.0.7j, 122K) Ⓑ

getty and uugetty are used to accept logins on the console or a terminal. They can handle answer a modem for dialup connections (although mgetty is recommended for that purpose).

glint – (Version 2.6.1, 227K) ⓌⓈ

Glint is a graphical interface to the RPM package management tool. It allows you to browse packages installed on your system, verify and query those package. It allows allows you to update packages with new versions and install new packages.

hdparm – (Version 3.3, 36K) Ⓑ

This is a utility for setting Hard Drive parameters. It is useful for tweaking performance and for doing things like spinning down hard drives to conserve power.

helptool – (Version 2.4, 23K) ⓌⓈ

The help tool provides a unified graphical interface for searching through many of the help sources available, including man pages and GNU texinfo documents.

info – (Version 3.12, 193K) Ⓑ

The GNU project uses the texinfo file format for much of its documentation. This package includes a standalone browser program to view these files.

ipfwadm – (Version 2.3.0, 85K) $\boxed{W}$ $\boxed{S}$

This is the IP firewall and accounting administration tool. It is useful if you need to run a firewall (a machine that acts as a secure gateway to the Internet).

isapnptools – (Version 1.15a, 175K) $\boxed{B}$

These programs allow ISA Plug-And-Play devices to be configured on a Linux machine.

This program is suitable for all systems, whether or not they include a PnP BIOS. In fact, a PnP BIOS adds some complications because it may already activate some cards so that the drivers can find them, and these tools can unconfigure them, or change their settings causing all sorts of nasty effects. If you have (for example) plug and play network cards that already work, I suggest you read section 4 on the format of the configuration file below very carefully.

kbd – (Version 0.96a, 1,080K) $\boxed{B}$

This package contains utilities to load console fonts and keyboard maps. It also includes a number of different fonts and keyboard maps.

kbdconfig – (Version 1.8.2, 23K) $\boxed{B}$

This is a terminal mode program for setting the keyboard map for your system. Keyboard maps are necessary for using non US default keyboards. Kbdconfig loads the selected keymap before exiting and configures your machine to use that keymap automatically after rebooting.

kernelcfg – (Version 0.5, 58K) $\boxed{W}$ $\boxed{S}$

Red Hat Linux kernelcfg provides a GUI interface which allows you to easily administrate your kerneld configuration.

ldconfig – (Version 1.9.5, 109K) $\boxed{B}$

ldconfig scans a running system and sets up the symbolic links that are used to load shared libraries properly. It also creates /etc/ld.so.cache which speeds the loading programs which use shared libraries.

lilo – (Version 0.20, 1,437K) $\boxed{B}$

Lilo is repsonsible for loading your linux kernel from either a floppy or a hard drive and giving it control of the system. It can also be used to boot many other operating sysetms, including the BSD variants, DOS, and OS/2.

linuxconf – (Version 1.12r5, 7,324K) $\boxed{B}$

Linuxconf has an easy-to-navigate user interface that is accessible from a text console, a web interface, and a GUI interface.

Linuxconf has the ability to manage:

Networking: Host information: IP Address, Hostname etc. IP Subnet allocation Resolving Name Servers Routing and Gateways NIS IPX Interface Setup PPP and Slip Dialout NFS File Systems Named (DNS) Zones and Secondaries Reverse Lookup

Sendmail Virtual Email Domains UUCP IP Aliasing DCHP/BOOTP Server RARP Server Input Firewalling Output Firewalling Blocking Firewalling IP Masquerading Packet Accounting Mail to Fax Gateway User Accounts: User and Group management PPP Acounts Slip Accounts UUCP Accounts POP Only Accounts Virtual Email Domain Accounts Email Aliases For Normal and Virtual Domains Policies For Passwords and User Accounts Available User Shells Crontab Management Shadow Management File Systems: Local Partition Management (/etc/fstab) NFS Volume Management (Samba Volume Management coming soon) Swap File and Partition Management User and Group Disk Quotas File Permissions Boot Mode: Lilo Configuration Default Boot Mode Runlevel Definitions

And more...

logrotate – (Version 2.6, 41K)   [B]

Logrotate is designed to ease administration of systems that generate large numbers of log files. It allows automatic rotation, compression, removal, and mailing of log files. Each log file may be handled daily, weekly, monthly, or when it grows too large.

losetup – (Version 2.8a, 7K)   [B]

Linux supports a special block device called the loopback device, which maps a normal file onto a virtual block device. This package contains programs for setting up and removing the mapping between files and loopback devices.

Block loopback devices should not be confused with the networking loopback device, which is configured with the normal ifconfig command.

lpr – (Version 0.33, 168K)   [W][S]

This package manages printing services. It manages print queues, sends jobs to local printers and remote pritners, and accepts jobs from remote clients.

man – (Version 1.5f, 89K)   [B]

The man page suite, including man, apropos, and whatis. These programs are used to read most of the documentation available on a Linux system. The whatis and apropos programs can be used to find documentation related to a particular subject.

mingetty – (Version 0.9.4, 31K)   [B]

mingetty, by Florian La Roche, is a lightweight, minimalist getty for use on virtual consoles only. mingetty is not suitable for serial lines (the author recommends using 'mgetty' for that purpose).

mkbootdisk – (Version 1.1, 5K)   [B]

This package creates a self-contained boot disk for booting a system. It assumes that the boot disk should use the root partition mentioned in /etc/fstab. The resultant boot disk includes all of the SCSI modules needed to use the system.

mkdosfs-ygg – (Version 0.3b, 15K)   [W]

This is the mkdosfs package. You can use this under Linux to create MS-DOS FAT file systems.

mkinitrd – (Version 1.8, 6K)   *B*

Generic kernels can be built without drivers for any SCSI adapters which load the SCSI driver as a module. To solve the problem of allowing the kernel to read the module without being able to address the SCSI adapter, an initial ramdisk is used. That ramdisk is loaded by the operating system loader (such as lilo) and is available to the kernel as soon as it is loaded. That image is resonsible for loading the proper SCSI adapter and allowing the kernel to mount the root filesystem. This program creates such a ramdisk image using information found in /etc/conf.modules.

mkisofs – (Version 1.12b4, 138K)

This is the mkisofs package. It is used to create ISO 9660 file system images for creating CD-ROMs. Now includes support for making bootable "El Torito" CD-ROMs.

mkkickstart – (Version 1.0, 4K)

This package writes kickstart descriptions from the current machine, allowing you to generate automatic builds of the machine and clone it.

mktemp – (Version 1.4, 7K)   *B*

mktemp is a small utility that interfaces to the mktemp() function call to allow shell scripts and other programs to use files in /tmp safely.

modemtool – (Version 1.21, 15K)   *W* *S*

The modem tool is a graphical simple configuration tool for selecting which of your serial ports is connected to a modem.

modutils – (Version 2.1.85, 577K)   *B*

The Linux kernel allows new kernel pieces to be loaded and old ones to be unloaded while the kernel continues to run. These loadable piecs are called modules, and can include device drivers and filesystems among other things. This package includes program to load and unload programs both automatically and manually.

mount – (Version 2.8a, 107K)   *B*

Mount is used for adding new filesystems, both local and networked, to your current directory structure. The filesystems must already exist for this to work. It can also be used to change the access types the kernel uses for already-mounted filesystems.

This package is critical for the functionality of your system.

mouseconfig – (Version 3.0.8, 61K)   *B*

This is a text based mouse configuration tool. You can use it to set the proper mouse type for programs like 'gpm'. It also can be used in conjunction with the Red Hat Xconfigurator to setup the mouse for the X Window System.

mt-st – (Version 0.5, 64K) Ⓑ

The mt program can be used to perform many operations on tapes, including rewind, eject, skipping files and blocks, etc.

netcfg – (Version 2.19, 165K) ⓌⓈ

Red Hat Linux netcfg provides a GUI interface which allows you to easily administrate your network setup.

ntsysv – (Version 0.9.4, 19K) Ⓑ

ntsysv provides a full-screen tool for updating the /etc/rc.d directory hierarchy, which controls the starting and stopping of system services.

popt – (Version 1.1.1, 10K)

Popt is a C library for pasing command line parameters. It was heavily influenced by the getopt() and getopt_long() functions, but it allows more powerfull argument expansion. It can parse arbitrary argv[] style arrays and automatically set variables based on command line arguments. It also allows command line arguments to be aliased via configuration files and includes utility functions for parsing arbitrary strings into argv[] arrays using shell-like rules.

printtool – (Version 3.29, 112K) ⓌⓈ

The printtool provides a graphical interface for setting up printer queue. It manages both local printers and remote printers. Windows (SMB) and NetWare (NCP) printers can also be configured.

procinfo – (Version 14, 41K)

procinfo is a package to allow you to get useful information from /proc. /proc is the kernel filesystem. This is a place you can go to acquire information from your running kernel.

procps – (Version 1.2.9, 210K) Ⓑ

A package of utilities which report on the state of the system, including the states of running processes, amount of memory available, and currently-logged-in users.

psacct – (Version 6.3, 80K)

The tools necessary for accounting the activities of processes are included here.

psmisc – (Version 17, 41K) Ⓑ

This package contains programs to display a tree of processes, find out what users have a file open, and send signals to processes by name.

quota – (Version 1.55, 80K) Ⓑ

Quotas allow the system administrator to limit disk usage by a user and/or group per filesystem. This package contains the tools which are needed to enable, modify, and update quotas.

raidtools – (Version 0.51beta6, 115K)

Raidtools description.

rhbackup – (Version 0.2, 29K)

rhbackup is a backup utility that can be used for local and remote backups. This should be considered alpha quality software and should be used with care.

rhmask – (Version 1.0, 9K)

rhmaskR is intended to allow the distribution of files as masks against other files. This lets new versions of software be freely distributed on public internet servers but limits their usefulness to those who already have a copy of the package. It uses a simple XOR scheme for creating the file mask and uses file size and md5 sums to ensure the integrity of the result.

rhs-hwdiag – (Version 0.30, 70K)   [B]

A package of utilities which report on the devices of the system. PnP probing of serial and parallel devices is supported. Useful for reporting errors to Red Hat concerning hardware.

rhs-printfilters – (Version 1.46, 90K)   [W][S]

The Red Hat print filter system provides an easy way to handle the printing of numerous file formats. Meant primarily to be used in conjuction with the Red Hat printtool.

rhsound – (Version 1.7, 11K)   [W]

The fake "service" created by rhsound allows sound modules to be loaded in contrallable runlevels and preserves mixer settings on shutdown/restarts

rmt – (Version 0.3, 12K)   [B]

rmt provides remote access to tape devices for programs like dump, restore, and tar.

rpm – (Version 2.5.5, 1,015K)   [B]

RPM is a powerful package manager, which can be used to build, install, query, verify, update, and uninstall individual software packages. A package consists of an archive of files, and package information, including name, version, and description.

setconsole – (Version 1.0, 4K)   [B]

setconsole sets up /etc/inittab, /dev/systty, and /dev/console for a new console. The console may be either the local terminal (directly attached to the system via a video card) or a serial console.

setserial – (Version 2.14, 40K)   [B]

Setserial is a program which allows you to look at and change various attributes of a serial device, including its port, its IRQ, and other serial port options.

setuptool – (Version 1.0, 9K)   Ⓑ

setup is a friendly text-mode menu program that gives you easy, instant access to all the text-mode configuration programs in Red Hat Linux.

sh-utils – (Version 1.16, 337K)   Ⓑ

The GNU shell utilities provide many of the basic common commands used (among other things) for shell programming, hence the name. Nearly all shell scripts use at least one of these programs.

shadow-utils – (Version 980403, 583K)   Ⓑ

This package includes the programs necessary to convert standard UNIX password files to the shadow password format, as well as programs for command-line management of the user's accounts. - 'pwconv' converts everything to the shadow password format. - 'pwunconv' unconverts from shadow passwords, generating a file in the current directory called npasswd that is a standard UNIX password file. - 'pwck' checks the integrity of the password and shadow files. - 'lastlog' prints out the last login times of all users. - 'useradd', 'userdel' and 'usermod' for accounts management. - 'groupadd', 'groupdel' and 'groupmod' for group management.

A number of man pages are also included that relate to these utilities, and shadow passwords in general.

shapecfg – (Version 2.0.36, 3K)

Configure and adjust traffic shaper bandwidth limiters. This package requires a kernel that has support for the shaper module. Currently this is the case with the 2.0.36 or later kernels and with late 2.1.X kernels.

sliplogin – (Version 2.1.1, 52K)

Attaches a SLIP interface to standard input. This is often used to allow dialin SLIP connections.

sndconfig – (Version 0.26, 148K)   Ⓦ

The Red Hat sound package includes the sndconfig tool whichs is a text based sound configuration tool. You can use it to set the proper sound type for programs which use the devices /dev/dsp, /dev/audio, and /dev/mixer. Sound settings are saved via the use of aumix and sysV runlevel scripts.

statserial – (Version 1.1, 169K)   ⓌⓈ

Statserial displays a table of the signals on a standard 9-pin or 25-pin serial port, and indicates the status of the handshaking lines. It can be useful for debugging problems with serial ports or modems.

swatch – (Version 2.2, 129K)

Swatch is used to monitor log files. When it sees a line matching a pattern you specify, it can highlight it and print it out, or run external programs to notify you through mail or some other means.

taper – (Version 6.9, 874K)

This is a tape backup and restore program that provides a friendly user interface to allow backing/restoring files to a tape drive. Alternatively, files can be backed up to hard disk files. Selecting files for backup and restore is very similar to the Midnight Commander interface and allows easy traversal of directories. Recursively selected directories are supported. Incremental backup and automatic most recent restore are defaults settings. SCSI, ftape, zftape, and removable drives are supported

time – (Version 1.7, 17K) $\boxed{B}$

The 'time' utility is used as a sort of 'stopwatch' to time the execution of a specified command. It can aid in the optimization of programs for maximum speed, as well as a number of other uses.

timeconfig – (Version 2.4, 44K) $\boxed{B}$

This is a simple tool for setting both the timezone and the way your system clock stores the time. It runs in text mode using a simple windowing system.

timetool – (Version 2.3, 22K) $\boxed{W}\boxed{S}$

Timetool is a graphical interface for setting the current date and time for your system.

tksysv – (Version 1.0, 35K) $\boxed{W}\boxed{S}$

This is a graphical tool for manipulating run levels. It allows you to control what services get started and stopped for every run level.

tmpwatch – (Version 1.5.1, 8K) $\boxed{B}$

This package provides a program that can be used to clean out directories. It recursively searches the directory (ignoring symlinks) and removes files that haven't been accessed in a user-specified amount of time.

tunelp – (Version 1.3, 9K)

'tunelp' aids in configuring the kernel parallel port driver.

usernet – (Version 1.0.7, 26K) $\boxed{W}\boxed{S}$

A program that makes it easy for users to bring user-controllable network devices up and down, and to check on the status of those devices.

util-linux – (Version 2.8, 752K) $\boxed{B}$

util-linux contains a large variety of low-level system utilities necessary for a functional Linux system. This includes, among other things, configuration tools such as fdisk and system programs such as login.

B.11.6 Terminal

This section lists packages that provide utilities related to terminal handling.

dialog – (Version 0.6, 88K)   ⟨W⟩

Dialog is a utility that allows you to build user interfaces in a TTY (text mode only). You can call dialog from within a shell script to ask the user questions or present with choices in a more user friendly manner. See /usr/doc/dialog-*/samples for some examples.

screen – (Version 3.7.4, 358K)

Screen is a program that allows you to have multiple logins on one terminal. It is useful in situations where you are telnetted into a machine or connected via a dumb terminal and want more than just one login.

B.11.7 Text

This section lists packages that provide utilities related to the handling and manipulation of text.

diffstat – (Version 1.25, 13K)

'diffstat' provides a number of statistics on a patch generated by diff, including number of additions, number of removals, and total number of changes. It can be useful, for example, to find out what changes have been made to a program, just by feeding the update patch to diffstat.

diffutils – (Version 2.7, 149K)   ⟨B⟩

The diff utilities can be used to compare files, and generate a record of the "differences" between files. This record can be used by the patch program to bring one file up to date with the other. All these utilities (except cmp) only work on text files.

faces – (Version 1.6.1, 139K)

The faces package is for use mainly with exmh. You can take a photo of something and turn it into a "face" which can be transmitted in all email and will show up in exmh and other mailers.

faces-xface – (Version 1.6.1, 20K)

These are the utilities to handle X-Face mail headers. They are called by mail readers to display an face from a message.

gawk – (Version 3.0.3, 2,288K)   ⟨B⟩

This is GNU Awk. It should be upwardly compatible with the Bell Labs research version of awk. It is almost completely compliant with the 1993 POSIX 1003.2 standard for awk.

Gawk can be used to process text files and is considered a standard Linux tool.

gecko – (Version 1.5, 66K)   ⟨B⟩

newt-based front end for the linuxconf system.

This is the default interface to linuxconf on a Red Hat system if the X Window System is not available (that is, if the DISPLAY environment variable is not set).

grep – (Version 2.2, 258K) $\boxed{B}$

This is the GNU implementation of the popular 'grep' *nix utility. It allows for the fast locating of strings in text files.

ispell – (Version 3.1.20, 2,386K) $\boxed{W}\boxed{S}$

This is the GNU interactive spelling checker. You can run it on text files and it will interactively spell check. This means it will tell you about words it doesn't know, and will suggest alternatives when it can.

less – (Version 332, 138K) $\boxed{B}$

less is a text file viewer much like 'more', only better.

m4 – (Version 1.4, 117K) $\boxed{W}\boxed{S}$

This is the GNU Macro processing language. It is useful for writing text files that can be parsed logically. Many programs use it as part of their build process.

mawk – (Version 1.2.2, 126K)

Mawk is a version of awk, which is a powerful text processing program. In some areas mawk can outperform gawk, which is the standard awk program on Linux.

nenscript – (Version 1.13++, 24K)

nenscript is a print filter. It can take ASCII input and format it into PostScript output and at the same time can do nice transformations like putting 2 ASCII pages on one physical page (side by side).

patch – (Version 2.5, 94K) $\boxed{W}\boxed{S}$

Patch is a program to aid in patching programs. :-) You can use it to apply 'diff's. Basically, you can use diff to note the changes in a file, send the changes to someone who has the original file, and they can use 'patch' to combine your changes to their original.

perl – (Version 5.004m4, 12,155K) $\boxed{B}\boxed{W}\boxed{S}$

Perl is an interpreted language optimized for scanning arbitrary text files, extracting information from those text files, and printing reports based on that information. It's also a good language for many system management tasks. The language is intended to be practical (easy to use, efficient, complete) rather than beautiful (tiny, elegant, minimal).

perl-MD5 – (Version 1.7, 29K) $\boxed{S}$

Provides access to the md5 algorithm from RSA.

sed – (Version 3.02, 68K) $\boxed{B}$

Sed copies the named files (standard input default) to the standard output, edited according to a script of commands.

textutils – (Version 1.22, 683K) $\boxed{\mathcal{B}}$

These are the GNU text file (actually, file contents) processing utilities. They include programs to split, join, compare, and modify files.

words – (Version 2, 411K) $\boxed{\mathcal{B}}$

This package contains the english dictionary in /usr/dict. It is used by programs like ispell as a database of words to check for spelling and so forth.

rgrep – (Version 0.98.4, 16K)

a recursive 'grep' utility that can highlight the matching expression, by the author of Jed.

B.12   X11

This section lists packages related to the X Window System. If you'd like your Red Hat Linux system to have a spiffy graphical user interface, this is where you'll need to look. Since there are so many X-related packages, we've divided them into subsections to make it easier to browse.

B.12.1   Amusements

This section lists packages containing various amusing programs that run under X.

multimedia – (Version 2.1, 325K) $\boxed{\mathcal{W}}$

This package contains XPlaycd, XMixer and XGetfile. XPlaycd is a program to play audio cd's using a cdrom drive. XMixer is used to control the mixer on a soundcard. XGetfile is a versatile file browser, made for use in shell-scripts.

xbanner – (Version 1.31, 648K) $\boxed{\mathcal{W}}\boxed{\mathcal{S}}$

XBanner displays text, patterns, and images on the root window. This allows users to customize both their normal X background and the background used on xdm style login screens.

xearth – (Version 1.0, 188K)

Xearth displays a pseudo-3D globe that rotates to show the earth as it actually is, including markers for major cities and Red Hat Software :-).

xfishtank – (Version 2.0, 385K)

Enjoy an animated aquarium background on your screen, with a variety of tropical fish swimming in it.

xsnow – (Version 1.40, 28K)

A continual gentle snowfall is accompanied by Santa Claus flying his sleigh around your screen. Don't forget to shake the snow off those windows every now and then!

B.12.2   Applications

This section lists packages containing various applications that run under X.

ImageMagick – (Version 4.1.0, 2,427K)   Ⓦ Ⓢ

ImageMagick is an image display, conversion, and manipulation tool. It runs under X windows. It is very powerful in terms of it's ability to allow the user to edit images. It can handle many different formats as well.

gimp – (Version 1.0.1, 7,347K)   Ⓦ

The GIMP is an image manipulation program suitable for photo retouching, image composition and image authoring. Many people find it extremely useful in creating logos and other graphics for web pages. The GIMP has many of the tools and filters you would expect to find in similar commercial offerings, and some interesting extras as well.

The GIMP provides a large image manipulation toolbox, including channel operations and layers, effects, sub-pixel imaging and anti-aliasing, and conversions, all with multi-level undo.

This version of The GIMP includes a scripting facility, but many of the included scripts rely on fonts that we cannot distribute. The GIMP ftp site has a package of fonts that you can install by yourself, which includes all the fonts needed to run the included scripts. Some of the fonts have unusual licensing requirements; all the licenses are documented in the package. Get
ftp://ftp.gimp.org/pub/gimp/fonts/freefonts-0.10.tar.gz and
ftp://ftp.gimp.org/pub/gimp/fonts/sharefonts-0.10.tar.gz if you are so inclined. Alternatively, choose fonts which exist on your system before running the scripts.

gimp-data-extras – (Version 1.0.0, 7,825K)

Patterns, gradients etc. for gimp. This package isn't required, but contains lots of goodies for gimp.

gimp-devel – (Version 1.0.1, 268K)

Static libraries and header files for writing GIMP plugins and extensions.

gimp-libgimp – (Version 1.0.1, 164K)   Ⓦ

Libraries used to communicate between The GIMP and other programs which may function as "GIMP plugins".

gv – (Version 3.5.8, 411K)   Ⓦ Ⓢ

gv allows to view and navigate through PostScript and PDF documents on an X display by providing a user interface for the ghostscript interpreter. gv is based upon an earlier program known as ghostview.

mxp – (Version 1.0, 52K)

This is a very fast Mandelbrot set generator for X Windows. It lets you select regions to zoom in on and allows you to control other aspects of fractal generation.

netscape-common – (Version 4.06, 6,601K) Ⓦ Ⓢ

Files shared between the Netscape Navigator and Netscape Communicator web browsers.

netscape-communicator – (Version 4.06, 9,987K) Ⓦ Ⓢ

Netscape Communicator is the industry-leading web browser. It supports the latest HTML standards, Java, and JavaScript. It also includes full-featured Usenet news reader as well as a complete email client.

Information on the Netscape Communicator license may be found in the file /usr/doc/netscape-common-4.06/LICENSE.

netscape-navigator – (Version 4.06, 6,795K)

Netscape Navigator is the industry-leading web browser. It supports the latest HTML standards, Java, and JavaScript.

Information on the Netscape Navigator license may be found in the file /usr/doc/netscape-common-4.06/LICENSE.

transfig – (Version 3.2.1, 275K)

TransFig is a set of tools for creating TeX documents with graphics which are portable, in the sense that they can be printed in a wide variety of environments.

usermode – (Version 1.4.1, 539K) Ⓦ Ⓢ

Several graphical tools, including a tool to help users manage floppies (and other removable media) and a tool to help the user change his or her finger information.

x3270 – (Version 3.1.1.6, 553K)

This program emulates an IBM 3270 terminal, commonly used with mainframe applications, in an X window.

xanim – (Version 27070, 712K) Ⓦ

Viewer for various animated graphic formats, including QuickTime and FLiC.

xfm – (Version 1.3.2, 680K) Ⓦ

xfm is a file manager for X windows that allows you to manipulate files and directories in an intuitive, easy-to-understand manner, as well as allowing you to extend itself with other programs.

xgopher – (Version 1.3.3, 277K)

Gopher, a method of accessing information on the Internet, is made easy with this X-Windows gopher client. Although gopher is less up-to-date than the WWW, Xgopher can still open up a portal to the vast storehouse of information available on the Internet.

xloadimage – (Version 4.1, 235K)

Xloadimage displays images in an X11 window, loads them onto the root window, or writes them into a file. Many image types are recognized.

xmorph – (Version 1996.07.12, 123K)   ⟨W⟩

xmorph allows you to create fascinating "morphs" - animated changes between two different images - and provides the tools to do so in an intuitive and easy-to-comprehend manner.

xpaint – (Version 2.4.9, 407K)   ⟨W⟩

XPaint is a color image editing tool which features most standard paint program options, as well as advanced features such as image processing algorithms. It allows for the editing of multiple images simultaneously and supp

xpdf – (Version 0.7a, 745K)

Xpdf is a viewer for Portable Document Format (PDF) files. (These are also sometimes also called 'Acrobat' files, from the name of Adobe's PDF software.) Xpdf is designed to be small and efficient. It does not use the Motif or Xt libraries. It uses standard X fonts. Xpdf is quite usable on a 486-66 PC running Linux.

xrn – (Version 9.01, 234K)   ⟨W⟩⟨S⟩

This is an X program for reading USENET news. It allows point and click reading, replying, and posting or news as well as simple group selections.

xterm-color – (Version 1.1, 191K)   ⟨W⟩⟨S⟩

xterm-color displays the ANSI color codes in addition to performing as a standard xterm/VT100 terminal emulator.

xv – (Version 3.10a, 4,480K)   ⟨W⟩

This is the famous 'xv' by John Bradley. It is shareware, but we ship it with the permission of the authors. It is a graphics viewer for many file types, including gif, jpg, tiff, xwd, etc. It also have manipulation features such as cropping, expanding, etc.

xwpe-X11 – (Version 1.5.12a, 622K)

Includes the 'xwpe' and 'xwe' programs from the xwpe package that are specific to X Windows.

B.12.3   Games

This section lists packages that contain various games capable of running under X.

acm – (Version 4.7, 3,438K)

ACM is an X based flight simulator. It also have network cabailities for multiple player games.

cxhextris – (Version 1.0, 38K)

cxhextrix is a color version of the popular hextris. Both are a close of the popular T*tris video game, a game where one must try to stack odd shaped blocks together perfectly. This game requires X Windows to work properly.

flying – (Version 6.20, 212K)

This is a package of games that run under X Windows. It contains pool, snooker, air hockey, and other table games. WARNING: This software could become addictive and could cause serious levels of sleep deprivation or loss of mobility in the legs if used at extreme levels.

paradise – (Version 2.3p19, 413K)

Netrek is a very popular Internet based arcade game. You fly around with a team of players shooting at and capturing planets from the enemy (another team). A good way to drop out of college.

spider – (Version 1.0, 51K)

spider is a particularly challenging double-deck solitaire. Unlike most solitaires, it provides extraordinary opportunities for the skillful player to overcome bad luck in the deal by means of careful analysis and complex manipulations.

xbill – (Version 2.0, 183K)

This package has seen increased popularity with the dawn of the Linux age. Very popular at Red Hat.

The object of the game? To seek out and destroy all forms of Bill, to disestablish new and alien operating systems, and to boldly go where no geek has gone before.

xbl – (Version 1.0h, 176K)

A three dimensional version of a popular arcade game.

xboard – (Version 4.0.0, 588K)

xboard gives you an easy-to-use, graphical interface to the GNU chess program, allowing you to enjoy hours of mind-boggling chess action without having to learn complicated commands. It may also be used as a front end for playing chess with other people across the Internet.

xboing – (Version 2.4, 982K)

xboing is an X-Windows game in the tradition of the classic 'Breakout' arcade game. The object is to keep a ball bouncing on the bricks until they break down. Even more fun comes in later levels when you have to handle multiple balls and ball traps.

xchomp – (Version 1.0, 36K)

The classic arcade action game comes to your screen with xchomp, the PacMan-like game. Not as extensive as the original game, but still lots of fun!

xdemineur – (Version 1.1, 26K)

This is a game of intense concentration, where you must successfully determine the locations of mines through logic and deduction.

xevil – (Version 1.5, 527K)

An action/adventure game for X-Windows in which you, as a Ninja warrior, kill everything in sight, and explore if you survive.

xgalaga – (Version 1.6c, 366K)

A clone of the old space arcade game 'Galaga'. (It's Galaga, you know how to play Galaga! Ship follows the mouse, button fires. Auto-fire by holding it down, so no-one accuses us of breaking their mouse!)

xgammon – (Version 0.98, 3,276K)

This version of the popular card/board game 'backgammon' allows you to play either against the computer or another human.

xjewel – (Version 1.6, 49K)

Jewel is a game much like Domain/Jewelbox which is a puzzle game like Tetris.

It is played by controling the motion of blocks which continue to fall from the top of the screen. One can move them left and right, as well as rotate the jewel segements. The object is to get the most points before the grim reaper ends the fun.

xlander – (Version 1.2, 23K)

A very hard game, but lots of fun nonetheless. Try to manuver the lunar lander to a safe-and-nonviolent landing.

xpat2 – (Version 1.04, 459K)

In 1989, Dave Lemke, Heather Rose, Donald R. Woods and Sun Microsystems, Inc., created the xsol solitaire game (also known as klondike under DOS) and the rules of some other patience games. Its main features are variable rule sets and different card sets for different resolution monitors.

xpat2 (X Patience) is a collection of these assorted solitaire card games that will truly "try your patience".

xpilot – (Version 3.6.2, 1,574K)

xpilot is a fast-paced action game with multiplayer networking capabilities that make it full of hours of enjoyment. The basic object of them game is to kill and fly - need more be said?

xpuzzles – (Version 5.4.1, 497K)

An assortment of geometric puzzles and toys, including an electronic version of Rubik's cube, and a "dinosaur cube" program.

xtrojka – (Version 1.2.3, 181K)

Similar to xjewels or tetris, this game presents you with the challenge of keeping the playing area clear of falling blocks.

A variation on the addictive classic.

xzip – (Version 180, 105K)

Now all your favorite text adventure games can take on a new dimension with this X Windows interpreter for them.

B.12.4   Libraries

This section lists packages containing various X-related system libraries.

ImageMagick-devel – (Version 4.1.0, 1,415K)

This is the ImageMagick development package. It includes the static libraries and header files for use in developing your own applications that make use of the ImageMagick code and/or APIs.

Xaw3d – (Version 1.3, 278K)   Ⓦ Ⓢ

Xaw3d is an enhanced version of the MIT Athena Widget set for X Windows that adds a 3-dimensional look to the applications with minimal or no source code changes.

Xaw3d-devel – (Version 1.3, 644K)   Ⓦ

Xaw3d is an enhanced version of the MIT Athena Widget set for X Windows that adds a 3-dimensional look to the applications with minimal or no source code changes. This package includes the header files and static libraries for developing programs that take full advantage of Xaw3d's features.

gnome-core – (Version 0.20.1, 1,019K)

Basic programs and libraries that are virtually required for any GNOME installation.

GNOME is the GNU Network Object Model Environment. That's a fancy name but really GNOME is a nice GUI desktop environment. It makes using your computer easy, powerful, and easy to configure.

gtk+ – (Version 1.0.6, 1,175K)   Ⓦ Ⓢ

The X libraries originally written for the GIMP, which are now used by several other programs as well.

gtk+-devel – (Version 1.0.6, 1,688K)   Ⓦ

Static libraries and header files for the GIMP's X libraries, which are available as public libraries. GLIB includes generally useful data structures, GDK is a drawing toolkit which provides a thin layer over Xlib to help automate things like dealing with different color depths, and GTK is a widget set for creating user interfaces.

imlib – (Version 1.8, 342K) $\boxed{W}\boxed{S}$

Imlib is an advanced replacement library for libraries like libXpm that provides many more features with much greater flexability and speed.

imlib-cfgeditor – (Version 1.8, 337K)

The imlib_config program allows you to control the way imlib uses color and handles gamma correction/etc.

imlib-devel – (Version 1.8, 504K)

Headers, static libraries and documentation for Imlib.

nls – (Version 1.0, 4K) $\boxed{W}\boxed{S}$

This is a package of files used by some older X11R5 binaries such at Netscape. It isn't required by versions of Netscape greater than 3.0, however.

xpm – (Version 3.4j, 56K) $\boxed{W}\boxed{S}$

Allows applications to display color, bitmapped pictures. Used by a large number of popular X Windows programs to enhance the user interface.

B.12.5   Shells

This section lists packages containing various graphically-oriented shells.

mcserv – (Version 4.1.35, 19K)

mcserv is the server program for the Midnight Commander networking file system. It provides access to the host file system to clients running the Midnight file system (currently, only the Midnight Commander file manager).

tkmc – (Version 4.1.35, 560K) $\boxed{W}$

Midnight Commander is a visual shell much like a file manager, only with way more features. It is tk X window wersion. Its coolest feature is the ability to ftp, view tar and zip files, and poke into RPMs for specific files. The tk version of Midnight Commander is not yet finished, though. :-(

B.12.6   Utilities

This section lists packages containing utilities related to the X window system.

Xconfigurator – (Version 3.79, 266K) $\boxed{W}\boxed{S}$

This is the Red Hat X Configuration tool. It is based on the sources for xf86config, a utility from XFree86. It has a nicer user interface added to make it easier for the end user.

NOTE - use mouseconfig to change your mouse type, then re-run Xconfigurator to set X up for your new mouse type.

ee – (Version 0.3, 654K)

The Electric Eyes image viewer lets you view and manipulate images in a variety of formats.

gnome-linuxconf – (Version 0.14, 96K) $\boxed{W}$ $\boxed{S}$

Graphical user interface for the linuxconf configuration system.

mgetty-vlewfax – (Version 1.1.14, 93K)

This package includes an X11 fax viewer with zooming facilities.

mkxauth – (Version 1.7, 15K) $\boxed{W}$ $\boxed{S}$

'mkxauth' aids in the creation and maintenance of X authentication databases (.Xauthority files). Use it to create a /.Xauthority file or merge keys from another local or remote .Xauthority file. Remote .Xauthority files can be retrieved via ftp (using ncftp) or via rsh. For security, mkxauth does not create any temporary files containing authentication keys.

moonclock – (Version 1.0, 25K)

Displays the time of day and the current moon phase. Colors change depending on time of day (day/night) and the moon is displayed in a neat little wedge with a star field.

procps-X11 – (Version 1.2.9, 5K)

A package of X-based utilities which report on the state of the system. These utilities generally provide graphical presentations of information available from tools in the procps suite.

rxvt – (Version 2.4.7, 448K) $\boxed{W}$ $\boxed{S}$

Rxvt is a VT100 terminal emulator for X. It is intended as a replacement for xterm(1) for users who do not require the more esoteric features of xterm. Specifically rxvt does not implement the Tektronix 4014 emulation, session logging and toolkit style configurability. As a result, rxvt uses much less swap space than xterm - a significant advantage on a machine serving many X sessions.

xcpustate – (Version 2.5, 32K)

XCPUSTATE is a snapshot performance monitor. It was originally written by Mark Moraes to watch the load distribution on the CPUs on an Silicon Graphics Iris 4D/240. It has since been ported to a wide variety of multiprocessors and uniprocessors.

xdaliclock – (Version 2.10, 74K)

The xdaliclock program displays a digital clock; when a digit changes, it "melts" into its new shape.

It can display in 12 or 24 hour modes, and displays the date when a mouse button is held down. It has two large fonts built into it, but it can animate other fonts.

xlockmore – (Version 4.11, 975K)

An enhanced version of the standard xlock program which allows you to keep other users locked out of an X session while you are away from the machine. It runs one of many provided screensavers while waiting for you to type your password, unlocking the session and letting you at your X programs.

xmailbox – (Version 2.5, 30K)   ⒲Ⓢ

This program will notify you when new mail arrives. It is similar to xbiff, but offers more features and fancier notification options.

xosview – (Version 1.6.1.a, 99K)

xosview provides a convenient bar graph of the current system state - memory usage, CPU load, and network usage. Very useful for monitoring status.

xscreensaver – (Version 2.27, 2,453K)

Screen savers of every sort are included in this package, guaranteeing hours of enjoyment^H^H^H^H^H^H^H^H^Hmonitor saving[1]. And if you are bent on really saving your monitor, there's that old classic, the plain black screen.

xsysinfo – (Version 1.6, 21K)

Many aspects of system performance can be monitored with xsysinfo, including network traffic, CPU load, disk space, disk usage, and more. Displays a history of performance in a window so you can easily see changes.

xtoolwait – (Version 1.1, 9K)

Utility to start a program and wait for it to map a window. Not an end-user program, but useful for writing scripts that run X Windows programs.

xwpick – (Version 2.20, 44K)

Xwpick lets you pick an image from an arbitrary window or rectangular area of an X11-server and write it to a file in a variety of formats.

B.12.7   Window Managers

This section lists packages containing various window managers (and related files). Unlike other graphical user interfaces on other operating systems, your Red Hat Linux system lets you choose which window manager you'd like to run on top of X. The packages in this section let you choose from several window manager styles.

---

[1]This is a joke, not a typo!

AfterStep – (Version 1.5, 3,384K) Ⓦ Ⓢ

AfterStep is a continuation of the BowMan window manager which was originally put together by Bo Yang. BowMan was based on the fvwm window manager, written by Robert Nation. Fvwm was based on code from twm. And so on... It was originally designed to emulate some of the look and feel of the NEXTSTEP user interface, but has since taken steps towards adding more useful, requested, and neat features especially in 1.4 version ! The changes which comprise AfterStep's personality were originally part of bowman development, but due to a desire to move past simple emulation and into a niche as its own valuable window manager, AfterStep designers decided to change the project name and move on.

Important features of AfterStep include:

1. Wharf: a free-floating application loader which can "Swallow" running programs and also can contain "Folders" of more applications. 2. Gradient filled TitleBars with 5 button · help/zap, action/tasks, iconize/maximise, shade/stick & close/destroy buttons 3. Gradient filled root window PopUp menus which can be configured to accomodate different tastes and styles of management 4. NEXTSTEP style icons which give a consistent look to the entire desktop 5. Pixmapped Pager with desktop pixmmaping 6. Easy to use look files, to share you desktop appearance with your friends 7. Start menu entries in a hierarchy of directories 8. WinList : a tasklist which can be horizontal or vertical 9. Many modules & asapps to give a good look to your X window station

AfterStep-APPS – (Version 1.5, 715K) Ⓦ Ⓢ

This package includes some applets that can be used in the Wharf module used by window Managers like AfterStep and WindowMaker.

They all look very cool and will make your desktop look more appealing once you add them to your Wharf module.

AnotherLevel – (Version 0.7.2, 308K) Ⓦ Ⓢ

AnotherLevel is the next version of TheNextLevel. TheNextLevel desktop was created by Greg J. Badros and was the winning entry in the 1996 Red Hat Desktop Contest. It features a powerful and attractive fvwm configuration that works with fvwm2. That version suffered a number of enhancements and transformations, so we called it AnotherLevel. Some documentation is available in /usr/doc/AnotherLevel in html format.

This desktop is defined to be easily reconfigured. Most attributes may be redefined by copying /etc/X11/AnotherLevel/fvwm2rc.defines to a user's home directory as .fvwm2rc.defines and modifying the copied file appropriately.

WindowMaker – (Version 0.20.1, 2,977K)

WindowMaker is a window manager designed to emulate the look and feel of part of the NEXTSTEP (tm) GUI. It's supposed to be fast, relatively small, feature rich and easy to configure, with a simple and elegant appearance borrowed from NEXTSTEP(tm).

fvwm – (Version 1.24r, 550K) Ⓦ Ⓢ

fvwm is a small, fast, and very flexible window manager. It can be configured to look like Motif, and has a useful "button bar".

fvwm2 – (Version 2.0.46, 1,471K) Ⓦ Ⓢ

fvwm is a version of the popular "Feeble Virtual Window Manager"

fvwm2-icons – (Version 2.0.46, 599K) Ⓦ Ⓢ

This package contains icons, bitmaps and pixmaps for fvwm and fvwm2.

wmakerconf – (Version 1.1.1, 515K)

wmakerconf is a GTK+ based configuration tool for the window manager WindowMaker.

Support of all WindowMaker attributes: Font selection browser, pixmap preview browser, color selection dialog, shortcut dialog, file selection dialog, ...

Tooltips with short description of every attribute.

New attributes can be simply integrated by changing the wmakerconf proplist

wmconfig – (Version 0.5, 47K) Ⓦ Ⓢ

This is a program that will generate menu configurations for different window managers available for the X11 system. It is an attempt to gain some form of abstractization of the menu configuration across some window managers. Currently it supports: FVWM2, FVWM95, Afterstep, MWM, IceWM, KDE

B.12.8   XFree86

This section lists packages containing part of XFree86, a freely available version of the X Window System. In order to use X, you must install an X server capable of driving your Red Hat Linux system's video card. As you can see, XFree86 has a number of servers from which to choose.

X11R6-contrib – (Version 3.3.2, 446K) Ⓦ Ⓢ

This is a collection of X programs from X11R6's contrib tape, which contains programs contributed by various users. It includes listres, xbiff, xedit, xeyes, xcalcm, xload, and xman amoung others.

XFree86-100dpi-fonts – (Version 3.3.2.3, 1,228K)

The 100dpi fonts used on most Linux systems. Users with high resolution displays may prefer the 100dpi fonts available in a separate package.

XFree86 – (Version 3.3.2.3, 12,040K) Ⓦ Ⓢ

X Windows is a full featured graphical user interface featuring multiple windows, multiple clients, and different window styles. It is used on most Unix platforms, and the clients can also be run under other popular windowing systems. The X protocol allows applications to be run on either the local machine or across a network, providing flexibility in client/server mplementations.

This package contains the basic fonts, programs and documentation for an X work-station. It does not provide the X server which drives your video hardware – those are available in other package.

XFree86-75dpi-fonts – (Version 3.3.2.3, 1,060K) $\boxed{W}\boxed{S}$

The 75dpi fonts used on most Linux systems. Users with high resolution displays may prefer the 100dpi fonts available in a separate package.

XFree86-8514 – (Version 3.3.2.3, 3,413K)

X server for older IBM 8514 cards and compatibles from companies such as ATI.

XFree86-AGX – (Version 3.3.2.3, 3,580K)

X server for AGX based cards such as the Boca Vortex, Orchid Celsius, Spider Black Widow, and Hercules Graphite.

XFree86-I128 – (Version 3.3.2.3, 3,810K)

X server for the #9 Imagine 128 board.

XFree86-Mach32 – (Version 3.3.2.3, 3,544K)

X server for cards built around ATI's Mach32 chip, including the ATI Graphics Ultra Pro and Ultra Plus.

XFree86-Mach64 – (Version 3.3.2.3, 3,658K)

X server for ATI Mach64 based cards such as the Graphics Xpression, GUP Turbo, and WinTurbo cards. This server is known to have problems with some Mach64 cards which newer versions of XFree86 (which were only available as BETA re-leases at the time of this release) may fix. Look at http://www.xfree86.org for information on updating this server.

XFree86-Mach8 – (Version 3.3.2.3, 3,423K)

X server for cards built around ATI's Mach8 chip, including the ATI 8514 Ultra and Graphics Ultra.

XFree86-Mono – (Version 3.3.2.3, 3,668K)

Generic monochrome (2 color) server for VGA cards, which works on nearly all VGA style boards with limited resolutions.

XFree86-P9000 – (Version 3.3.2.3, 3,600K)

X server for cards built around the Weitek P9000 chips such as most Diamond Viper cards and the Orchid P9000 card.

XFree86-S3 – (Version 3.3.2.3, 4,042K)

X server for cards built around chips from S3, including most #9 cards, many Di-amond Stealth cards, Orchid Farenheits, Mirco Crystal 8S, most STB cards, and some motherboards with built in graphics accelerators (such as the IBM Value-

Point line).

XFree86-S3V – (Version 3.3.2.3, 3,793K)

X server for cards built around the S3 Virge chipset.

XFree86-SVGA – (Version 3.3.2.3, 4,585K)

X server for most simple framebuffer SVGA devices, including cards built from ET4000 chips, Cirrus Logic chips, Chips and Technologies laptop chips, Trident 8900 and 9000 chips. It works for Diamond Speedstar, Orchid Kelvins, STB Nitros and Horizons, Genoa 8500VL, most Actix boards, the Spider VLB Plus. It also works for many other chips and cards, so try this server if you are having problems.

XFree86-VGA16 – (Version 3.3.2.3, 3,594K)   Ⓦ Ⓢ

Generic 16 color server for VGA boards. This works on nearly all VGA style graphics boards, but only in low resolution with few colors.

XFree86-W32 – (Version 3.3.2.3, 3,458K)

X server for cards built around the ET4000/W32 chips, including the Genoa 8900 Phantom 32i, Hercules Dynamite cards, LeadTek WinFast S200, Sigma Concorde, STB LightSpeed, TechWorks Thunderbolt, and ViewTop PCI.

XFree86-XF86Setup – (Version 3.3.2.3, 575K)   Ⓦ Ⓢ

XF86Setup is a graphical configuration tool for the XFree86 family of servers. It allows you to configure video settings, keyboard layouts, mouse type, and other miscellaneous options. It is slow however, and requires the generic VGA 16 color server be available.

XFree86-Xnest – (Version 3.3.2.3, 1,985K)

X server which runs in a X window.

XFree86-Xvfb – (Version 3.3.2.3, 2,415K)

Virtual framebuffer X server.

XFree86-devel – (Version 3.3.2.3, 7,652K)   Ⓦ

Libraries, header files, and documentation for developing programs that run as X clients. It includes the base Xlib library as well as the Xt and Xaw widget sets. For information on programming with these libraries, Red Hat recommends the series of books on X Programming produced by O'Reilly and Associates.

XFree86-libs – (Version 3.3.2.3, 1,863K)   Ⓦ Ⓢ

This package contains the shared libraries most X programs need to run properly. They are in a separate package to reduce the disk space needed to run X applications on a machine w/o an X server (over a network).

B.12.9   gnome

This section contains packages that are related to the GNOME desktop environment.

gnome-libs – (Version 0.20, 556K)   Ⓦ Ⓢ

Basic libraries you must have installed to use GNOME.

GNOME is the GNU Network Object Model Environment. That's a fancy name but really GNOME is a nice GUI desktop environment. It makes using your computer easy, powerful, and easy to configure.

gnome-libs-devel – (Version 0.20, 1,888K)

Libraries, include files, etc you can use to develop GNOME applications.

urw-fonts – (Version 1.0, 2,181K)

Free versions of the 35 standard PostScript fonts. With newer releases of ghostscript quality versions of the standard 35 Type 1 PostScript fonts are shipped. They were donated and licenced under the GPL by URW. The fonts.dir was specially made to match the original Adobe names of the fonts, e.g. Times, Helvetica etc. With XFree86, these fonts are a must to have!

xinitrc – (Version 1.6, 9K)   Ⓦ Ⓢ

This package contains the basic X windows startup script used by the "startx" command.

General Parameters and Modules

This appendix is provided to illustrate *some* of the possible parameters that may be needed by certain drivers. It should be noted that, in most cases, these additional parameters are unnecessary. Also included is a list of network hardware and the associated modules required by that hardware.

Please keep in mind that if a device you are attempting to use requires one of these parameters, and support for that device is *not* compiled into the kernel, the traditional method of adding the parameter to the LILO boot command will not work. Drivers loaded as modules require that these parameters are specified when the module is loaded. The Red Hat Linux installation program gives you the option to specify module parameters when a driver is loaded.

For more information concerning the device support compiled into the kernel used by the Red Hat Linux installation program, please refer to Section 2.8 on page 25.

One of the more commonly used parameters, the hdX=cdrom parameter, *can* be entered at the boot prompt, as it deals with support for IDE/ATAPI CD-ROMs, which is part of the kernel.

C.1   CD-ROM parameters

Hardware	Parameter
Mitsumi CD-ROM	mcd=*port,irq*
Sony CDU 31 or 33 CD-ROM	cdu31a_port=*base_addr* cdu31a_irq=*irq*
Aztech CD268	aztcd=*port*
SB Pro or 16 compatible	sbpcd=*io_addr,sb_pro_setting*
ATAPI/IDE CD-ROM Drives	hd*x*=cdrom

Examples of the above would be:

Configuration	Example
non-IDE Mitsumi CD-ROM on port 340, IRQ 11	mcd=0x340,11
Sony CDU 31 or 33 at port 340, no IRQ	cdu31a_port=0x340 cdu31a_irq=0
Aztech CD-ROM at port 220	aztcd=0x220
ATAPI CD-ROM, jumpered as master on 2nd interface	hdc=cdrom
Panasonic-type CD-ROM on a SoundBlaster at port 230	sbpcd=0x230,1

Please Note: Most newer Sound Blaster cards come with IDE interfaces. You do not need to use sbpcd parameters, only use hd*x* parameters.

C.2   SCSI parameters

Hardware	Module	Parameters
Seagate ST0X	seagate.o	controller_type=1 base_address=*base_addr* irq=*irq*
F. Domain TMC-8xx	seagate.o	controller_type=2 base_address=*base_addr* irq=*irq*
F. Domain TMC-3260	fdomain.o	setup_called=1 port_base=*base_addr* interrupt_level=*irq*
AHA-2920	fdomain.o	setup_called=1 port_base=*base_addr* interrupt_level=*irq*
Trantor T128	t128.o	t128=*base_addr,irq*
NCR-5380 Based	g_NCR5380.o	ncr5380=*base_addr,irq,dma_channel*
AHA 152x	aha152x.o	aha152x=*base_addr,irq,scsi_id,reconnect,par*
AHA 1542	aha1542.o	bases=*base_addr*
Buslogic	BusLogic.o	buslogic=*base_addr*
PAS-16 SCSI	pas16.o	pas16=*base_addr,irq*
Zip Parallel Port	ppa.o	ppa_base=*base_addr*
Always In2000	in2000.o	setup_string="ioport:*base_addr* norese nosync:*x* period:*ns* disconnect:*x* debug: proc:*x*"

Some examples would be:

Configuration	Example
Adaptec AHA1522 at port 330, IRQ 11, SCSI ID 7	`aha152x=0x330,11,7`
Adaptec AHA1542 at port 330	`bases=0x330`
Future Domain TMC-800 at CA000, IRQ 10	`controller_type=2` `base_address=0xca000 irq=10`

When a parameter has commas, make sure you do not put a space after a comma.

C.3   Ethernet parameters

Most ethernet drivers accept parameters to specify a base IO address and an IRQ as follows:

```
io=base_addr irq=irq
```

For example, for a 3com 3c509 ethernet card located at IO address 210 (IO addresses are usually in hexadecimal) and IRQ 10, use the following parameters for the `3c509` driver:

```
io=0x210 irq=10
```

You can use multiple ethernet cards in one machine . If each card uses a different driver (e.g., 3c509 and a DE425), you simply need to add aliases (and possibly options) for each card to
`/etc/conf.modules`; for example:

```
alias eth0 3c509
options 3c509 io=0x210 irq=10
alias eth1 de4x5
options de4x5 io=0
```

See Section 8.2.2 on page 152 for more information.

However, if any two ethernet cards use the same driver (e.g., two 3c509's or a 3c595 and a 3c905), you will need to compile a custom kernel with the ethernet driver built in. In that case, you can use the "classic" LILO `boot:` parameters of the form:

```
ether=irq,base_addr,interface
```

For example:

```
LILO boot: linux ether=10,0x210,eth0 ether=11,0x300,eth1
```

(For more information about using more than one ethernet card, see the *Multiple-Ethernet* mini-HOWTO.)

C.4   Network Module Listing

The following table lists various network cards and the kernel modules that support them.

Cards	Driver Module
3Com 3c501	3c501.o
3Com EtherLink II	3c503.o
3Com EtherLink Plus	3c505.o
3Com EtherLink16	3c507.o
3Com EtherLink III	3c509.o
3Com EtherLink XL	3c515.o
3Com Vortex series (3c590, 3c592, 3c597, 3c595) 3Com Boomerang (3c900,3c905, 3c575) 3Com Cyclone (3c905B)	3c590.o
NS8390 and clones	8390.o
Ansel Communications EISA ethernet adaptor	as3200.o
Apricot 82596	apricot.o
Allied Telesis AT1700	at1700.o
RealTek pocket ethernet adaptor (RTL8002) RealTek pocket ethernet adaptor (RTL8012)	atp.o
EtherWORKS DE425, DE434, DE435, DE450, DE500, DC21040, DC21041, DC21142, DC21143	de4x5.o
D-Link DE-600 Ethernet pocket adapter	de600.o
D-Link DE-620 Ethernet pocket adapter	de620.o
DEPCA/EtherWORKS DEPCA, DE100,DE101, DE200, DE201, DE202, DE210, DE422	depca.o
Digi RightSwitch SE-X	dgrs.o
Cabletron E2100	e2100.o
Intel EtherExpress Pro/10	eepro.o
Intel EtherExpress Pro 100	eepro100.o
Intel EtherExpress	eexpress.o
SMC 83c170 EPIC/100	epic100.o
ICL EtherTeam 16i, EtherTeam 32 (EISA)	eth16i.o
EtherWORKS DE203, DE204, DE205	ewrk3.o
HP PCLAN/plus	hp-plus.o
HP Lan	hp.o
HP J2585B, J2585A, J2970, J2973 HP J2573 Compex ReadyLink ENET100-VG4 Compex FreedomLine 100/VG	hp100.o
IBM token ring	ibmtr.o
Allied Telesis AT1500 / HP J2405A / NE2100 / NE2500	lance.o
NE1000 / NE2000 (non PCI)	ne.o
NE2000 (PCI)	ne2k-pci.o

Cards	Driver Module
Rascal-Interlan NI5210	`ni52.o`
Rascal-Interlan NI6510	`ni65.o`
AMD PCnet/PCI 79C970 / PCnet32 / PCnet/PCI II 79C970A PCnet/PCI II 79C971A	`pcnet32.o`
Allied Telesyn AT2550 Genius GF100TXR (RTL8139) NDC Communications NE100TX-E RealTek RTL8129/8139 Fast	`rtl8139.o`
SMC Ultra / SMC UltraEZ / SMC Ultra32	`smc-ultra.o`
SMC 9000	`smc9194.o`
Compaq Netelligent 10 T PCI UTP Compaq Netelligent 10/100 TX PCI UTP Compaq Integrated NetFlex-3/P Compaq NetFlex-3/P Compaq Netelligent Integrated 10/100 TX UTP Compaq Netelligent 10/100 TX Embedded UTP Olicom OC-2183/2185 Olicom OC-2325 Olicom OC-2326 Compaq Netelligent 10/100 TX UTP Compaq Netelligent 10 T/2 PCI UTP/Coax	`tlan.o`
Accton EtherDuo PCI / Accton EN1207 Adaptec ANA6901/C / Adaptec ANA6911/TX C-NET CNE-935 Cogent EM100 / Cogent EM110 / Cogent EM400 Cogent EM960 / Cogent EM964 Quartet Danpex EN-9400P3 D-Link DFE500-Tx / D-Link DE-530CT Linksys EtherPCI Kingston EtherX KNT40T / Kingston EtherX KNE100TX Netgear FX310 TX 10/100 SMC EtherPower / SMC 8432BT / SMC EtherPower10/100 Surecom EP-320X Thomas Conrad TC5048 Znyx ZX312 EtherAction / Znyx ZX314/ZX315 Znyx ZX342 / ZX344 / ZX345 / ZX346 / ZX348 Znyx ZX351	`tulip.o`
WD8003, WD8013, various clones	`wd.o`
Packet Engines G-NIC (Yellowfin)	`yellowfin.o`

Red Hat Linux Installation Support FAQ

D.1   Introduction

This is the Official Red Hat Linux FAQ. It answers many commonly-asked questions concerning Red Hat Linux.

It is maintained by `faq-maintainer@redhat.com`; all comments or suggestions for this FAQ should be sent to that address. To get a more recent version of this FAQ see Section D.4 on the next page.

D.2   Errata

The single best source of information, especially with respect to bugs or problems with the Red Hat Linux distribution are the errata pages,available at `http://www.redhat.com/support/docs/errata.html`. Be sure to review both the general errata as well as the platform-specific errata specific to your version of Red Hat Linux. (See also Section D.4 on the following page for other ways to access the errata).

It may seem strange that we list this as the very first item, but the errata pages are perhaps the best resource for fixing 90% of the common problems with Red Hat Linux. In addition, security holes for which a solution exists are generally on the errata page 24 hours after Red Hat has been notified.

You should *always check there first*.

D.3   Contacting Red Hat Software

There are a number of different ways to contact Red Hat Software. We've listed them here as a handy reference.

- **General:**

      Red Hat Software
      PO Box 13588
      79 TW Alexander Dr.
      Research Triangle Park, NC 27709
      USA

      http://www.redhat.com
      ftp://ftp.redhat.com
      redhat@redhat.com

- **Sales:**

      tel: +1-888-RED-HAT1   (toll-free)
      tel: +1-919-547-0012   (toll call)
      fax: +1-919-547-0024

      http://www.redhat.com/products

- **Support:** http://www.redhat.com/support

- **Bugs:** Bugs should be entered via the Red Hat bug tracking system at
  http://developer.redhat.com/bugs/report.phtml

- **Suggestions and requests for new features:**suggest@redhat.com

- **Suggestions on improving Red Hat documentation:**docs@redhat.com

D.4   General Resources List

There are a large number of resources available for users of Red Hat Linux. Some are provided by Red Hat Software, and some are provided by other sources. Also, since a large number of questions about Red Hat Linux are comment to all Linux distributions, we've included pointers to other helpful resources, even if they don't mention Red Hat Linux by name.

- **Red Hat Linux Web Pages:**

- Main Red Hat Software Page `http://www.redhat.com`
- Errata Pages `http://www.redhat.com/support/docs/errata.html`
- Technical Support `http://www.redhat.com/support`
- Technical Support HOWTO
  `http://www.redhat.com/support/support-howto.html`
- Supported Hardware
  `http://www.redhat.com/support/docs/hardware.html`
- Mailing List Information `http://www.redhat.com/mailing-lists`
- Red Hat Linux Documentation:
  `http://www.redhat.com/support/docs/rhl/`

• **Generic Linux Web Pages:**

- Official home of Linux `http://www.li.org`
- Generic information on a number of topics
  * `http://www.redhat.com/linux-info`
  * `http://www.best.com/ aturner/RedHat-FAQ/`
- Excellent general Linux resources
  * `http://www.linuxnow.com`
  * `http://www.linuxhq.com`
  * `http://sunsite.unc.edu/LDP/`
- Excellent Linux developer sites
  * `http://news.freshmeat.net`
  * `http://developer.redhat.com`
- **Email Addresses:** (You can get documents from the following automated reply addresses)
  * Latest fixes for newest Red Hat release `errata@redhat.com`
  * Hardware list `hardware-compat@redhat.com`
  * How to get support `support-howto@redhat.com`
  * This FAQ document `faq@redhat.com`
  * Tips on getting PPP to work `ppp-tips@redhat.com`
- **FTP servers:** (There are also many Red Hat mirrors. Please see Section D.12.1 on page 341)
  * Red Hat FTP server `ftp://ftp.redhat.com`
  * RPM FTP server `ftp://ftp.rpm.org`
- **Usenet newsgroups:** For these newsgroups, pick **one** when asking a question; crossposting between multiple newsgroups is frowned upon.
  * For answers:
    · `comp.os.linux.announce`
    · `comp.os.linux.answers`
  * For questions:
    · `comp.os.linux.advocacy`
    · `comp.os.linux.development.apps`
    · `comp.os.linux.development.system`

- comp.os.linux.hardware
- comp.os.linux.m68k
- comp.os.linux.misc
- comp.os.linux.networking
- comp.os.linux.prog
- comp.os.linux.setup
- comp.os.linux.x

D.5   General Questions

D.5.1   How can I get Red Hat Linux?

Question

I am looking to acquire a copy of Red Hat Linux. How can I do this? Is there more than one way to do this?

Answer

Red Hat Linux is available on CD directly from Red Hat Software or from various Red Hat Linux resellers; it is also available via FTP from many sites around the world. (See Sections D.4 on page 298 and D.12.1 on page 341.)

D.5.2   How do I get new updates to Red Hat as they happen?

Question

I have a problem with a package. I would like to see if an update to that package has been made available from Red Hat. Where can I look for this?

Answer

Keep your eye on the Red Hat Linux Errata. (See Section D.2 on page 297)

Also check the `contrib` directory on our FTP mirrors for packages that users have contributed. We also make periodic announcements to the `redhat-announce-lis` mailing list.

D.5.3 Are mailing lists available for Red Hat Linux?

Question

I am looking for other people who use Red Hat Linux so that I can discuss a problem I would like to use Red Hat Linux to fix. Or I am having problems with Red Hat Linux that are outside of the installation support that was provided. Where can I turn to for answers?

Answer

In general, mailing lists and newsgroups are the best way of getting in touch with other Red Hat Linux users. Many of the applicable mailing lists and newsgroups are listed in Section D.4 on page 298.

D.5.4 Does Red Hat Linux include source code?

Question

I need to make changes to a program that came with Red Hat Linux. Does Red Hat Linux include source code for this program?

Answer

Yes. We include the exact source code that was used to build the distribution. From release 2.0 on, Red Hat Linux has been built with the RPM packaging system; RPM only uses pristine source (the same as what you'd find at the author's site), possibly including a Red-Hat-supplied patch. The sources (along with any patches) are contained in a source RPM file.

To install a source RPM, use the following command:

```
rpm -iv packagename-n.nn-r.src.rpm
```

RPM installs sources under the redhat source tree, which is /usr/src/redhat by default (you can configure the directory using the topdir command in /etc/rpmrc). Spec files (packagename-n.nn.spec) are installed in /usr/src/redhat/SPECS, while source archives and patch files go in /usr/src/redhat/SOURCES.

To unpack the source once it's installed, change to /usr/src/redhat/SPECS and use the following command:

```
rpm -bp packagename-n.nn.spec
```

RPM unpacks the source into /usr/src/redhat/BUILD/packagename-n.nn and applies any patches listed in the spec file.

For more information, please read the RPM manual page and visit the RPM website at:
`http://www.rpm.org/`.

D.5.5 What do I do if I have media (manual or CD) problems?

Question

I purchased the Red Hat Linux boxed set and have been having problems with the cd. It looks like it is scratched, or it just doesn't read. I even tried it on another system. What should I do?

Answer

If you are experiencing physical problems with the product you received (e.g., your manual is missing pages or your CD is scratched), please contact the Sales Office at Red Hat Software (Section D.3 on page 298)

We'll make sure the problem is rectified promptly. Please do not report these problems on the `redhat-list` or to Red Hat Support, as it is likely an isolated problem, and your product simply needs to be replaced.

(Note: This is not a common problem, but it does happen from time to time.)

D.6 Installation

D.6.1 How much disk space does Red Hat Linux Use?

Question

I am worried about how room Red Hat Linux will need to use on my hard drive. How much disk space do I need to reserve for Red Hat Linux?

Answer

As new features are added to software, that software grows in size. Red Hat Linux is no exception; it has grown an average of 20% with each release, due primarily to additional packages and libraries adding more features.

For Red Hat Linux version 4.2, the minimum disk space requirements include at least 16 MB for a swap partition, and 60 MB for basic installation with no X, development tools, or TeX. See `http://www.redhat.com/support/docs/hardware.html` for more information on disk space requirements.

Not suprisingly, with 5.2 the minimum disk space is larger. If you choose a custom install and deselect all automatically-selected packages, you will need at least a 16 MB swap partition, and 120 MB for a basic installation with no X, development tools, or Tex.

If you are installing via the workstation- or server-class installation methods, you will need to have 450MB free for a workstation install and 1620 MB free for a server install.

Of course, these installation methods may install many items an expert may not wish to install. In that case, a custom install is more flexible, as you can include or remove items at will. In general, the following is a good average for a typical custom install.

```
/boot (kernel partition)      20 MB
swap partition                16 - 127 MB
/                             500+ MB
/home        Depends on how many users you'll have on the
             system, and how much space each account needs.
```

Any additional space can be allocated to a partition which you can name whatever you like (ie `/stuff /private /test`).

If you plan to run a server, you should configure it a bit differently, adding a `/tmp` partition and a `/var` partition.

D.6.2 In what order should I install multiple operating systems?

Question

I have a blank hard drive and would like to install DOS (or Windows) and Linux onto it. What is the best method of doing this?

Answer

It is recommended to install the non-Linux operating system first, and then installing Linux. This allows the other OS to "get comfortable" with the hardware and possibly write values to the MBR that it would just over-write if Linux was installed first.

You will probably need to do this in a several step method, however. Start the install, but if the operating system allocates the entire drive for itself, see if you can "bail out" early and use the operating system's native fdisk to create a primary partition of the size you want to leave for the OS (150-500 megs is average, depending on your needs). Then reboot and go through the install again and normally the OS will just use the space that you've just set aside. Once the install is finished, you can then begin the Linux installation.

D.6.3   Are there alternate methods of installing Red Hat Linux?

Question

I do not have a cdrom that will work with Linux and I can not install from the network. Is there another method?

Answer

If you cannot use a CD-ROM or a network to install Red Hat Linux, you can install Red Hat Linux from a hard drive; just follow these steps.

You'll need a DOS partition that is formatted in FAT16; create a directory called \RedHat in it. From there you will need to copy the items from the cdrom (E: in our example) over to the hard-drive (C: in our example). Here's what you would do:

```
mkdir C:\RedHat
mkdir C:\RedHat\base
mkdir C:\RedHat\RPMS
copy E:\RedHat\base C:\RedHat\base
copy E:\RedHat\RPMS C:\RedHat\RPMS
```

If you do not have enough disk space for copying the entire RPMS directory tree over to your hard-drive, you will need to look in the file \RedHat\base\comps file for the RPMS that are needed in the base and in any other sections you feel you need.

Once you have done this, you can start the install and choose a Hard-Drive install. You will be asked to insert the supplemental floppy. Once the supplemental disk has been loaded, you will be presented with the next screen on the install. When asked to select the partition containing the Red Hat Linux files, do so, and the install will proceed from there.

D.6.4   Where are the floppies?

Question

My box didn't include floppy disks, or my floppy disks are bad. What can I do?

Answer

We are sorry for the problem. The cdrom contains all the data to make new boot and supplemental floppies for your system. To make new floppies under DOS, Win95, NT, or even Linux. Be aware that this process will overwrite any data on the 1.44 Megabyte floppies. Here's how it's done:

1. Boot DOS and change directory to the CD-ROM.

2. Enter the dosutils directory and run rawrite.

   ```
   cd \dosutils
   rawrite.exe
   ```

3. When prompted, for a disk, for the boot image enter:

   ```
   ..\images\boot.img
   ```

4. Then change floppies, and run 'rawrite' again. When prompted enter:

   ```
   ..\images\supp.img
   ```

If you are in Linux (or another Linux-like operating system), you can mount the CD-ROM and use dd to write the data to floppy. With Linux, you could do the following:

```
dd if=/mnt/cdrom/images/boot.img of=/dev/fd0 bs=72k
dd if=/mnt/cdrom/images/supp.img of=/dev/fd0 bs-72k
```

D.6.5   What is the difference between Linux and DOS disk names?

Question

I have an IDE system, and I am confused by how Linux sets up drives in comparison to DOS. Can you explain this?

Answer

Linux sets up the drive system in a very different manner than DOS, and this can be rather confusing. Instead of calling the first hard drive "C:", Linux uses a combination of letters signifying what kind of BUS (sd for SCSI, hd for IDE) and in which order the drive was detected. Finally a number is added onto the end to specify which partition on the drive is being referenced.

For IDE hard drives the layout depends on which IDE channel the drive is on and whether it is the master or slave on that channel.

```
Channel              Jumper          hdx
======================================
ide0                 master          hda
ide0                 slave           hdb
ide1                 master          hdc
ide1                 slave           hdd
ide2                 master          hde
ide2                 slave           hdf
ide3                 master          hdg
ide3                 slave           hdh

ide0 = primary
ide1 = secondary
ide2 = tertiary
ide3 = quaternary
```

The partition number follows an old PC standard that there are a limit of 4 primary partitions per hard drive. However, one of those partitions can be designated as an extended partition. Inside of this extended partition, logical partitions can be specified (for most drives you can have 12 logical drives in the extended partition for 16 partitions all together).

The numbering scheme is broken into the following:

- 1-4 primary partitions

- 5-16 logical partitions

D.6.6   Installation problems with IDE cdrom

Question

Linux is having trouble detecting my IDE CD-ROM drive during the install. Can I force the install to see it?

Answer

Sometimes IDE cdrom drives will not be detected either due to the fact that they are on a IDE channel the BIOS doesn't know about, or that when queried, replies back with data that Linux thinks is bogus (Early NEC IDE cdrom's respond with data saying that it is an IDE floppy drive instead of a cdrom.)

To solve your problem, you need to manually specify the the CD-ROM drive from the LILO boot prompt.

When you see:

```
boot:
```

or:

```
LILO:
```

You need to type in:

```
linux hdX=cdrom
```

where X is the IDE letter that Linux would specify for that drive depending on which IDE bus it is on.

D.6.7   Laptop Installation Problems

Question

I am having trouble getting linux installed on my Laptop computer.

Answer

Laptops are one of the hardest pieces of hardware to support in the industry. Many times the company that constructs the hardware has to tweak a chipset to make it fit in the confined structure or meet certain power requirements. These changes are usually only documented internally for trade secret reasons, leaving others to find work arounds.

When Red Hat support finds itself with a laptop question, our first and sometimes only reference is the Linux Laptop Pages, which can be found at:

```
http://www.cs.utexas.edu/users/kharker/linux-laptop/
```

D.6.8   Having trouble upgrading to 5.x from earlier Linux

Question

I am trying to upgrade my earlier Red Hat system to 5.x, but it complains that it can't find a valid RPM data base. What do I need to do?

Answer

The problem is that a few earlier versions of rpm would write the database in a way that seems corrupted to later versions. Rebuilding the database fixes this problem. To do this, we will need to upgrade rpm on your system to the one on the installation cdrom, and then rebuild the database.

First thing to do is mount the system CD on the system:

```
mount /mnt/cdrom
```

After doing this, upgrade 'rpm' from the CD like so:

```
cd /mnt/cdrom/RedHat/RPMS
rpm -Uvh --nodeps --force rpm-*rpm
```

When the new RPM is installed, rebuild the database using the following command:

```
rpm --rebuilddb
```

This will rewrite the database in a format that can be used by the version of RPM used during the installation (since they are now the same).

D.6.9   Installation problems with the Adaptec 2920

Question

I have an Adaptec 2920. During the install I do not see a choice for it, why is that, and what do I do? Or, I have a Future Domain TMC-3260, but when I specify options for it to be probed, it isn't found during the install.

Answer

The Adaptec 2920 does not use an Adaptec chip set, but actually uses the Future Domain TMC3260. If the card is not found with an auto-probe, you will need to specify options for it. When the installation menu asks you about SCSI, choose "options" and enter the following :

```
setup_called=1 port_base=<io base> interrupt_level=<irq>
```

An example of this would be:

```
setup_called=1 port_base=0xd000 interrupt_level=9
```

If the above options do not work, your card may have a newer BIOS that can't be probed correctly. We are working on the problem, but at this time do not have a satisfactory solution.

D.6.10 Problems with the Adaptec 274x/284x/294x cards

Question

I have an Adaptec SCSI card with the `aic7xxx` *chipset (2940/2840/2740/3940/etc). It is pretty common, so why is it not fully supported by Red Hat Linux?*

Answer

The problem is that in the past Adaptec was not open about how their hardware worked, which made it difficult to write a Linux driver for it.

However, Adaptec has recently changed their position on this matter, and Doug Ledford (the current writer of the aic7xxx.c SCSI code) has made significant headway in making the 2940 very functional. The problem currently is that this work is still in "catchup-mode" and may not work for people with the latest cards. Our current suggestion is to try the following when debugging Adaptec 2940 problems.

1. Try the latest boot images from
   `ftp://ftp.redhat.com/pub/redhat/updates`

2. The AHA-2940 is, like most Adaptec cards, extremely sensitive to termination issues (having active termination on BOTH ends of the bus can help a lot)

3. SCSI Hard drives that have on-drive termination seem (as a general rule) to supply *active* termination whereas SCSI CD-ROM drives and SCSI tape drives that can be configured for on-drive termination seem (as a general rule) to supply only *passive* termination. Therefore, try making a hard drive the last device on the bus.

4. If a SCSI-based system doesn't work when you have sync negotiation and disconnect enabled for your SCSI devices, but *DOES* work OK when you disable sync negotiation and/or disconnect for your SCSI peripherals, then suspect bad cables and/or bad (or less than adequate) termination.

5. HP C3725S SCSI drives do not work at all well with the AHA-2940AU, perhaps due to a problem with the drive, but just as likely due to some problem/problems with the AHA-2940 driver in the Linux 2.0.30 kernel.

6. For some large drives you have to disable the default option in the Adaptec-SCSI BIOS: "Extended BIOS translation for DOS drives > 1 GByte". This option causes the BIOS to use a translation scheme of 255 heads, 63 sectors per track. LILO does not like this. After disabling, everything works OK (windows95 installation, Linux and LILO installation, dual-boot).

7. Make sure that on a SCSI chain that the drive you are installing to is SCSI ID 0 (or 1 if you have no IDE drives in the system). Otherwise, your system may not be able to boot.

8. Others have found that using the conservative/slow settings "no tagged queuing", "5MB/s" etc, fixes problems.

9. Another problem found with some systems is that, if SCAM support is turned on, turning it off has solved the problem.

D.6.11   Signal 11 or Signal 7 problems during install

Question

During the install, I get a fatal signal 11 or signal 7. What does this mean and what can I do?

Answer

Signal 11's and signal 7's are errors indicating a hardware error in memory or on the bus. This can be due to problems in executables or with the hardware of the system. The Linux kernel uses more capabilities of the CPU, cache, and memory, and tends to expose marginally operating hardware.

The first thing to do is check to see if you have the latest installation and supplemental floppies from Red Hat. Check the errata for updates, and also the FTP site to see if newer versions are available. If the latest images still fail, it may be due to hardware. Common suspects are memory or CPU-cache. Try turning off the CPU-cache in the BIOS and see if the problem goes away. Also try swapping memory around in the motherboard slots to see if it is either slot or memory related.

The premier site on the net for this problem can be found at `http://www.bitwizard.nl/sig11/`

Answer

Filipe Custsdio reported the following as a solution from upgrading 4.2 and earlier releases to 5.1:

> I had a repeating sig 11 problem whenever I tried to upgrade my Red-hat 4.2 to 5.1. The problem was not with my hardware, but with my RPM database. A simple "rpm –rebuilddb" solved it.

To best accomplish this, you will should download the latest version of RPM from `ftp://ftp.redhat.com/pub/redhat/updates`. Boot into your older version of linux. Log in as root, upgrade to the new version of RPM you downloaded, and then rebuild the RPM database:

```
rpm -Uvh rpm*
rpm --rebuilddb
```

D.6.12   Is there a Live Filesystem with the Red Hat CD-ROM?

Question

I would like to be able to use the live file system on the cdrom to boot.

Answer

Red Hat Linux no longer supports the Live boot feature due to the change to a modular kernel. Because of this change, booting from read-only file system is not practical. The cdrom does contain data in its /live section that can be executed in rescue mode, but one needs to set the PATH and LD_LIBRARY_PATH environment variables.

D.6.13   Installing Linux and NT

Question

I have NT and would like to install Linux, but I have heard there are problems with booting both OS's. How can I avoid this?

Answer

The best instructions on dual-booting NT and Linux are to be found in the Linux+NT-Loader HOWTO. The latest version can be found at the Linux Documentation Project's website:
http://sunsite.unc.edu/LDP/HOWTO/mini/Linux+NT-Loader A possibly earlier one can also be found on the Red Hat Linux cdrom in \doc\HOWTO\mini\Linux+NT-Loader.

D.6.14   How to get around the "cylinder 1023" install problem?

Question

I can not install Linux below the 1023rd cylinder in my system. What can I do?

Answer

You will need to have the kernel below this limit, and use a different bootloader than LILO. The BIOS may not be able to reach it for one of the following reasons:

- The kernel is above the 1023 cylinder of the hard drive.

- The kernel is on a drive the BIOS can't boot to (not on Primary IDE or SCSI chain)

- Other esoteric kernel/BIOS problems.

- You have hardware that can only be initialized in DOS (Plug and Play, etc)

You will probably need to use the LOADLIN boot loader that is provided on the cdrom in \dosutils. You will need to copy this directory over to your DOS hard drive partition and edit the autoboot.bat file to point to its new position and remove the initrd= line. If your system is a SCSI system, you will need to go into rescue mode and copy the /mnt/boot/initrd.img from the hard drive over to the dos partition, and use it for booting.

D.6.15   Removing LILO

Question

For whatever reason, I want to remove LILO from the Master Boot Record (MBR) of my machine. How do I do this?

Answer

There are several methods to removing LILO from the master boot record of the machine. Inside of Linux, you can replace the MBR with an earlier saved version of the MBR using the /sbin/lilo command:

```
/sbin/lilo -u
```

In DOS, NT, and Windows 95 you can use the fdisk command to create a new MBR with the "undocumented" flag /mbr. This will rewrite the MBR to ONLY boot the primary DOS partition:

```
fdisk /mbr
```

D.6.16   Removing Linux from your hardware

Question

For whatever reason, I want to remove Linux from my hard-drive. I tried using DOS's fdisk, and it shows non-DOS partitions, but it can't remove them. What do I need to do?

Answer

If you need to remove linux from a hard drive, and have attempted to do this with the default DOS `fdisk`, you are having the "Partitions exist but they don't exist" problem. The best way to remove non-DOS partitions is with a tool that understands partitions other than DOS.

You can do this with the installation floppy by doing the following. Start the installation, select install (versus upgrade) and when it comes to partitioning the drive, choose `fdisk`. In `fdisk` type p to print out the partition numbers, and remove the Linux partitions with the d command. If satisfied with the changes you have made, you can quit with a w and the changes will be saved to disk. If you deleted too much, type q and no changes will occur.

Once you have removed the Linux partitions, you can reboot the box with `Control-Alt-Delete` instead of continuing with the install.

D.6.17   Using Loadlin

Question

I cant use LILO to boot my machine, and have heard of something called LOADLIN. How do I set it up to work?

Answer

At the DOS prompt you can type, for example:

```
C:\> CD \LOADLIN
C:\LOADLIN> LOADLIN zimage /dev/hdb1 ro vga=ask
```

Or, if you want to load a big kernel together with a RAM disk:

```
C:\LOADLIN> LOADLIN bzimage /dev/ram rw initrd=diskimage
```

or, if you have more parameters than will fit into the 128-byte DOS command line:

```
C:\LOADLIN> LOADLIN @params
```

An example params file is `test.par`. Please read it.

If "write-behind" caching is supported by the cache program, you should run smartdrv /C before LOADLIN is called:

```
C:\LOADLIN> smartdrv /C      do this to "sync" your disk
                             (usually not needed for DOS
                             6.2, but it doesn't hurt)
C:\LOADLIN> loadlin ....
```

It would be much smarter to use a batch file something like this:

```
SMARTDRV /C
C:\LOADLIN\LOADLIN C:\LOADLIN\ZIMAGE ↩
root=/dev/hdb2 ro vga=3
```

So you could simply type: LINUX.BAT and you are on the road!

A sample LINUX.BAT file is provided with the LOADLIN package.

D.6.18   Post Installation Problems with booting computer

Question

I have installed Linux without errors but on a reboot, I get only an L, LI, and some other items. What is happening and how can I recover?

Answer

If you have rebooted the system and have gotten an L, LI, or a combination of this and a lot of scrolling numbers, this indicates that LILO is having a problem bootstrapping itself due to one or more problems.

Write down the error codes that are being printed and what letter it stopped on (L, LI, LIL, etc). If you can access the cdrom (from DOS floppies or another machine), you can cd to (assuming DOS) \live\usr\doc\lilo-0.20\README and check to see what the error seems to indicate.

Most of the time, the LILO failures are due to the BIOS and the hard-drive mis-matching geometries or something similar:

- First the kernel (or parts of it) are above the 1023 cylinder so the BIOS can not bootstrap the information. If your BIOS has the capability to use LBA (Linear Block Addressing) mode and it isn't already enabled, you should enable it and then re-run lilo (either by reinstalling or using rescue mode). In most cases, you will probably have to repartition after enabling LBA.

- If you can reinstall and add more partitions, create a /boot partition and place it entirely below the 1023rd cylinder.

- You have placed the kernel on a drive the BIOS can't access. This can be an IDE drive that is not on the primary chain (IDE0 hda, hdb) or if you have placed Linux on a SCSI drive it is because the SCSI ID is not 0 (or 1 if you have NO IDE drives in the system).

If you need to gather more information for someone else (either for official support or from the mailing lists, newsgroups, friends, etc) you can use the rescue mode

Insert the installation floppy, and at the boot prompt type:

```
linux rescue
```

After a couple of screens that ask about hardware you will get a root prompt (#). You will need to mount the linux root partition like is done in this example which has the / partition as /dev/hda5:

```
mkdir /mnt
mount /dev/hda5 /mnt
```

Then do the following:

```
lilo -v -r /mnt
```

Record the output of the command. You can add more -v's if you need more information. If errors still occur, you can send that output to the appropriate support group.

D.7   Using Red Hat Linux

D.7.1   New to Linux

Question

I am totally new to linux and don't know anything about how to use it. or What is this root@localhost# *I am seeing?*

Answer

Many users new to Red Hat Linux need additional documentation on learning Linux. We are aware of this, and are continuing to expand our documentation, but should you require additional information, the following resources may be useful for you.

Books:

- Running Linux by Matt Welsh O'Reilly Books

- Linux for Dummies by various authors

- Red Hat Linux Unleashed Sams Publishing

- Teach Yourself Linux in 24 Hours Sams Publishing

Web Sites:

`http://www.redhat.com/linux-info/ldp/LDP/gs/node5.html`

`http://www.best.com/ aturner/RedHat-FAQ/`

For a complete description of supported hardware, please visit:

`http://www.redhat.com/support/docs/rhl/intel/`↩
`rh50-hardware-intel.html`

D.7.2   Running Quake and Quake II

Question

I heard I can run Quake on my linux system. How do I set this up?

Answer

In order to get Quake to run on your system, you need to download the Quake/Linux program from:

`http://www.idsoftware.com/archives/quakearc.html`

D.7.3   Getting colors with ls

Question

How come I don't see colors when I run ls? When I am using my old Linux, the filenames all have different colors.

Answer

In order to allow the color option, you must edit `.bashrc`. This line must be placed in the file:

```
alias ls='ls --color=auto'
```

D.7.4   Compiled programs dont run

Question

I have installed Red Hat Linux. When I attempt to run a simple program I compiled, the following happens:

```
$ a.out
bash: a.out: command not found
```

I have used other versions of Linux and never had such a problem in running programs. What is going on?

Answer

The problem is that, according to the computer shell, the program isn't there. The computer shell (the part of the OS that runs your commands) finds programs using a very strict path setting that figures out where items are. If you type the following, you will see what your PATH variable is set to:

```
echo $PATH
```

One of the items that should not be there is the current working directory [cwd] (sometimes called the present working directory). The cwd is known as ".", so to execute commands in the cwd, you need to either add the directory to your path, or type something like the following:

```
$ ./a.out
```

D.7.5   MacMillan Red Hat Linux Boxed Set Documentation

Question

I have purchased the MacMillan boxed set of Red Hat, and it says that it comes with extra on-line documentation. How do I install and read it?

Answer

The MacMillan Complete Red Hat Linux Operating System comes with several books (and parts of books) as an added value. These books are in PDF format, and require that you use a PDF document reader on them. The Linux Acrobat reader is included for this purpose.

To install the Reader, you will need to do the following while logged in as the user root.

Insert the installation cdrom and issue the following commands:

```
mount /mnt/cdrom
mkdir /tmp/acro
cd /tmp/acro
tar xzvf /mnt/cdrom/ebooks/acrobat.tar
# this will extract the files into the
# /tmp/acro directory

./INSTALL
# This will run the INSTALL script for your data.
# I usually install them into the default location
# of /usr/local
```

You can now run the command acroread and view the documentation in /mnt/cdrom/ebooks

D.8   X Window System

D.8.1   Missing server when using XFree86?

Question

When I try to start X with with the startx *command I get errors that no server was installed and I am left back at a shell prompt. What could be wrong?*

Answer

When you get an error about no servers installed, you should check to see if first the correct X server was installed and that the correct links have been set.

If you are using the latest Red Hat packages, you will be using the xserver-wrapper as a method to protect against various security problems.

/usr/X11R6/bin/X should be a symbolic link to xserver-wrapper and /etc/X11/X should be a symbolic link to the card-specific X server that you use, for example XF86_SVGA.

Here's an example of how you might create these symbolic links, as root:

```
cd /usr/X11R6/bin
ln -sf xserver-wrapper ./X
cd /etc/X11
ln -sf "../../usr/X11R6/bin/XF86_SVGA" ./X
```

This should set the symbolic links correctly for your system.

D.8.2 Starting X only get grey screen

Question

When I start X, all I see is a grey background and a X cursor.

Answer

One of the most common reasons is that you are not using the correct command to start the X server. The best command to start the X windows system is:

```
startx
```

If you are using this command, and only the gray screen is coming up, there can be some other explanations. First, are you waiting long enough? Due to either the speed of the processor, the amount of memory (less than 16 megs of ram), or network problems it may take up to 6 minutes before X windows is fully operational. In most cases this is an indication of a problem that can be solved (faster CPU, more memory, or finding out what is broken in networking).

Another problem can be that the starting scripts are not able to execute some command. You can try to get around this by creating a very simple ~/.xinitrc and running startx. You may also check /var/log/Xerrors for errors that might help you troubleshoot the problem.

D.8.3 Customizing the X window manager

Question

I would like to change the way Red Hat sets up my X window session. How do I customize the X window manager?

Answer

To customize any of the default window manager settings, add or remove programs from the menus, and/or change which programs start up automatically, you will need to change the files in

`/etc/X11/AnotherLevel`. Please see the man pages for `xinit`, `startx`, `AnotherLevel`, `fvwm2`, `FvwmM4`, and `wmconfig` for more details.

To try other window managers not included with Red Hat Linux, you may want ot look at:

`http://www.plig.org/xwinman/`

D.8.4   Alternate default window managers

Question

I don't like the Win95-like window manager configuration. How can I change it?

Answer

If you don't like the look or feel of the default window manager setup, you can select a different style from the `Preferences` menu, and then clicking on `WM Style` menu.

If you are interested in changing to other window managers, you will want to check out this web page:

`http://www.plig.org/xwinman/`

D.8.5   X window error 111

Question

I get an error about `errno=111`. *What does it mean and what can I do?*

Answer

Whenever the `XFree86` Xserver crashes, dies, ceases to exist or is inaccessible for any reason, you will see the error message `_X11TransSocketUNIXConnect: Can't connect:   errno = 111` or one similar to it.

It is a message from an X-client (any program running on your `XFree86` Xserver, for example the window manager) telling you that it tried to connect to the Xserver, but failed to do so for some reason.

To further debug this issue, you will need to look into the server output for what got this error. Normally you should see the real error message (why the server stopped to work) a few lines before the `error 111` message. If you still can't make head or tail from all those messages, make sure to quote the FULL server output in your problem report (to either technical support or a mailing list).

Obtaining the full server output is normally accomplished by redirecting both standard output and standard error to a file while starting the server. You can do this by running X like this:

```
startx &> startx.out
```

Other useful information to check are the symbolic links of X, the .xinitrc (if one exists) or what commands were running when the error occurred.

D.8.6   X Keyboard mapping problems

Question

My keyboard mappings don't work correctly in X. What can I do?

Answer

If you are using Metro-X you will need to do the following:

```
cd /usr/X11R6/lib/X11/xkb/keymap
cp xfree86 metro
```

This will solve many of the problems experienced. However it isn't a full solution due to the fact that some of the XFree86 mappings are out of date with modern keyboards. If you still experience problems with the keyboard settings, you will need to use the xmodmap and xev commands to correct the problems. Please send these corrections to bugs@xfree86.org so that they can be corrected in the main distributions.

D.8.7   X Library problems compiling or running programs

Question

I get an error message that libX can't be opened. or I can't compile X apps due to missing libraries.

Answer

More than likely, the required libraries are not installed. You will need to (re)install the packages to get them.

Insert the Red Hat Linux installation cdrom.

```
mount /mnt/cdrom
cd /mnt/cdrom/RedHat/RPMS
rpm -Uvh --force XFree86-devel* XFree86-libs* Xaw3d*
```

This should install most of the X libraries that you might need. If you still get the error, it may be due to the fact that the requested library is part of a package we do not provide (qt, xforms, motif, etc).

D.8.8 X and AGP video cards

Question

I have an AGP graphics card. Is it supported?

Answer

AGP cards were not supported in XFree86 before version 3.3.2. If you have 3.3.2 installed on your system, then Xconfigurator should show which AGP cards are supported.

If you do not already have 3.3.2, you may want to consider upgrading to this release. Please see their web page at http://www.xfree86.org/ for more details.

D.8.9 Having X start at boot up

Question

How do I have X start up at boot versus having to type startx everytime?

Answer

To enable X to run at boot time and using xdm to log in, you need to change the file /etc/inittab.

Edit your /etc/inittab file. Replace this line:

```
id:3:initdefault:
```

With this one:

```
id:5:initdefault:
```

Save your changes, and reboot the machine. (Note you could also manually change init levels to 5 but we find that rebooting the machine is actually less error prone.)

D.8.10   NeoMagic problems

Question

My computer has a NeoMagic graphics card chipset, how can I get X to work?

Answer

The NeoMagic cards are *NOW* supported by XFree86's X servers.

Red Hat worked with Precision Insight on making freely available servers for NDA hardware (like the NeoMagic) that people using any Linux distribution can download and use.

D.8.11   Problems with X after upgrading from RHL 4.1

Question

I upgraded from 4.1 (or earlier) and now when I use startx, the machine seems to hang at a grey screen.

Answer

The problem is that releases prior to 4.2 installed (.Xclients) in every user's home directory, which calls:

```
fvwm95-2 -cmd 'FvwmM4 -debug /etc/X11/TheNextLevel/...'
```

However, this window manager doesn't exist in 5.x. The proper workaround for this problem is to:

```
rm -f ~/.Xclients
```

(A more drastic work workaround is available to the root user):

```
rm -f /home/*/.Xclients
```

D.8.12   Problems with Netscape colors in X

Question

When I run netscape, the colors don't seem right, or When I run netscape, I get error messages and warnings about colors.

Answer

This problem often comes with the error:

```
Cannot allocate colormap entry for default background.
```

The reason is that X has run out of colors to allocate to applications (this shows up a lot on 16 and 256 color applications) To solve this problem you can try the following:

1. run netscape with -install switch. This can be *ugly* in that you'll see color flashes.

2. run X in 15bpp or higher. To obtain a higher bpp than 8 (default) run startx like:

    ```
    startx --bpp 16
    ```

   If it doesn't work, consult your X driver manuals, Xconfigurator or up-grade your videocard.

D.8.13   Problems with Accelerated X and Red Hat 5.x

Question

I am using Accelerated X, but when I try to start it I get this error: Fatal server error: could not open default font 'fixed'. *What can I do to fix this?*

Answer

In 5.x, the fonts come gzipped. Your version of AcceleratedX does not know how to handle this. What you need to do is gzip -d the fonts in your font directory, then run mkfontdir.

D.8.14   Problems with X and Microsoft Serial Mouse

Question

I have a Microsoft serial mouse, and Linux doesn't want to work with it. What can I do to fix it?

Answer

It has been found that the 2 button Microsoft Mouse of version 2.1A or greater is a "smart" mouse. It has been speculated that it is looking for wakeup signals from Windows, or it will not respond back to the computer.

This causes X and/or gpm to not work with Linux because the mouse is not responding in a way these programs are expecting. To "reset" the mouse to work with these programs, you can follow one of several methods. Use mouseconfig to set things up before running X:

```
mouseconfig --kickstart  --device cuaX
```

where X is either 0 (for com 1) or 1 (for com2).

Another solution is to get gpm-1.13, run as gpm -t pnp -R, and configure XFree86 for
MouseSystems Protocol with /dev/gpmdata as the device.

D.9   System Administration

D.9.1   Questions about PAM

Question

What is PAM? Why use it?

Answer

PAM is a standard adopted by other unices such as Solaris 2.6. For more information on PAM please read: http://www.redhat.com/linux-info/pam/

D.9.2   Questions about Secure Shell

Question

How can I setup Secure Shell (SSH) on my linux system?

Answer

Due to United States export restrictions on encryption technology, Red Hat Linux can not be shipped with ssh. The site ftp://ftp.replay.com has set up various downloads of ssh and PGP.

D.9.3   Problems with Linux finding all a machines RAM

Question

My machine has 128 Megs of RAM, however linux only sees 64 megs of it. What is going on, and how can I fix it?

Answer

There are a couple of things that could be causing Linux to not see all your memory. On some 386 systems you need to compile your kernel with 'Limit memory to 16M?" enabled.

On most systems, the reason is that the BIOS has a limit of how much memory it will tell the OS is present in the machine, even though the board can have more. Common limits seen with this problem are 16M, 32M, 64M, and 128M. To get around this, we need to explicitly specify the amount of memory to the kernel at boot time via the mem=< actual memory goes here > flag.

In the following example, we have a 32M machine but only 16M are being seen by Linux. At the LILO prompt, we type:

```
LILO: linux mem=32M
```

After the machine boots, we use the free command to see if the larger amount of memory was recognized by the kernel. If so, we can add an append line to the /etc/lilo.conf file and rerun lilo to make it happen permanently. The example from above could look like the following:

```
boot=/dev/sda
map=/boot/map
install=/boot/boot.b
prompt
timeout=50
image=/boot/vmlinuz-2.0.32
        label=linux
        root=/dev/sda1
        initrd=/boot/initrd-2.0.32.img
        read-only
        append="mem=32M"
```

Do not forget to run lilo after editing the file.

D.9.4   Problems with machine speed and large RAM

Question

I have over 64 Megs in my pentium or greater machine, however it seems sluggish when doing anything. If I tell Linux to use only 64Megs with the mem=64M machine, it seems to speed up. What is going on and can I do anything about it?

Answer

The most likely answer to this problem has to do with the motherboard of the computer. Many motherboards limit the L2 cache to be able to access up to 64 megs. The ones that we know of to be affected by this problem are the NX (I believe this was only for pentium 60-90), FX, VX, and TX boards from Intel. These are limited to a maximum of 512K of L2 cache. There may be other boards that have this problem, but these are our current canidates.

The following is from a user who researched the problem for us:

> ... typically have a maximum of 512k of L2 cache (either on the motherboard, or in a COAST module - looks a little like a DIMM, but a bit shorter) and can only cache up to 64 meg. If linux utilizes memory the same way as Microsoft OS's do, it goes from the top of the memory stack and works its way down. This can result in a pretty significant slowdown unless you really need the aditional memory. The exception to this was the HX chipset, which was also the only chipset (i think) that could handle dual or quad processor pentium boards (and even MMX). However, the vast majority of HX boards that I have seen also required a TAG-ram chip to cache over 64 meg, and still had a limit as to how much it could cache (the exact number escapes me at the moment).

> There were ways around this - the most obvious being a non-intel based motherboard. The VIA motherboards are a good option here, and very often can be found with 1 meg of cache (or even, a little more rarely, 2 meg). These boards can cache between 512 and 1 gig of memory, depending on the exact variation of the chipset.

D.9.5   Red Hat 5.X problems with old applications

Question

I am trying to use an old application that is compiled with libc5 libraries. When I run it, I immediately get SEGV errors or similar problems. What is going on, and what can I do?

Answer

The problem with crashing libc5 applications can be due to several items:

1. Before/after the upgrade, there was installed another version of libc that didn't get obsoleted by the upgrade process or placed libc5 libraries in a place that causes conflict.

   To find out if this is the case, do this:

   ```
   rpm -qa | grep libc
   ```

   It should produce output similar to this:

   ```
   glibc-devel-2.0.5c-12
   libc-5.3.12-24
   glibc-debug-2.0.5c-12
   rpm-2.4.10-1glibc
   rpm-devel-2.4.10-1glibc
   glibc-profile-2.0.5c-12
   glibc-2.0.5c-12
   ```

   If you see items like `libc-debug-5.3.12-18` or `libc-5.4.44-2`, you will need to remove these packages (for example, `rpm -e libc-debug`) and run `ldconfig -v`

2. Your `/etc/ld.so.conf` file has been changed from an optimal setting. For optimal loading, set your /etc/ld.so.conf file in the following order:

   ```
   /usr/i486-linuxaout/lib
   /usr/i486-linux-libc5/lib
   /usr/openwin/lib
   /usr/X11R6/lib
   ```

D.9.6   Problems with fstool

Question

When I run fstool, I get a message that says a partition seems to have been deleted and asks if I want to remove it from /etc/fstab.

Answer

The fstool program is not working properly with current versions of tcl and shouldn't be used. It should have been obsoleted, but slipped through the cracks.

First we will have to fix the /etc/fstab file since fstool may have corrupted it. The areas that seem to be changed by fstool are usually the cdrom and swap.

Here are sample lines (note that you will need to change the actual partitions to match those on your system):

```
/dev/sda2        swap           swap    defaults   0 0
/dev/cdrom       /mnt/cdrom     iso9660 noauto,ro  0 0
```

You should now remove the fstool program using rpm:

```
rpm -e fstool
```

If you are running 5.1 or later, please use the linuxconf program.

D.9.7   Configuring the Jaz drive and Linux

Question

How do I configure my Jaz drive under linux?

Answer

Documentation on using Jaz with Linux can be found on the cdrom in doc/HOWTO/mini/Jaz-Drive and on the system in /usr/doc/HOWTO/mini/Jaz-Drive.

D.9.8   Problems with Parallel Port Zip drive

Question

How do I use my parallel port zip drive?

Answer

Here's something you can try: edit /etc/conf.modules and add the following line to the others:

```
alias scsi_hostadapter ppa
```

If you need to send the ppa driver any options about which LP is being used etc, you would add the line:

```
options ppa ppa=<options go here.>
```

For more information, check http://www.torque.net/paraport.

D.9.9   Problems with IDE Zip drive

Question

I'm having problems getting my IDE zip drive to work. Can I make it work with Linux?

Answer

First check and make sure there is a disk in the drive. Also, make sure you are mounting it as partition 4 instead of 1. An example would be hdc4. The reason for this is that the Macintosh uses partition 4 for its data partition and has problems if data is on another partition.

D.9.10   Intel SMP

Question

How can I enable Intel SMP support?

Answer

Due to the experimental nature of Linux on a dual processor Intel machine, Red Hat Linux doesn't currently support this hardware without a recompile of the kernel.

However, we encourage you to investigate Linux for the dual processor systems at http://www.linux.org.uk/SMP/title.html

D.9.11   Problems with Red Hat 5.x, older applications and time

Question

Some of my older applications get the incorrect time.

Answer

Some libc5 apps want /usr/lib/zoneinfo, so you can either recompile them for libc6 or provide a symlink so that things will work:

```
ln -s ../share/zoneinfo /usr/lib/zoneinfo
```

Please also see check the Red Hat errata (http://www.redhat.com/errata) for other items.

D.9.12   More problems with time

Question

I have all the latest updates installed, but my programs still get the incorrect time.

Answer

If you have installed all the latest updates and you programs still get the incorrect time, try checking the settings in /etc/sysconfig/clock. They probably look something like this:

```
UTC=true
ARC=false
```

This means that Linux will assume that your BIOS clock is set to the UTC or GMT timezone. More than likely, the clock is set to your local timezone, and you need to change the UTC line to be:

```
UTC=false
```

D.9.13   What is on the 2nd cdrom

Question

During the install, I was not asked to use the 2nd cdrom. When I use the X program glint on it, it reports that there are no rpms, but when I look at the directories, I see lots of them. What is going on?

Answer

The 2nd cdrom in the Red Hat Linux boxed set contains the source code rpms (SRPM) for all of the Open Source applications that are on the first cdrom. From these source rpms, you can build all the Open Source applications we have in the distribution.

The reason that glint does not see source rpms is due to the fact that SRPMS are not stored in any of the RPM databases. This makes it almost impossible to tell if you have installed an src.rpm before or are over-writing an older version. Thus you will need to use the plain rpm command to install these items.

`rpm -ivh < filename >` will install the source code into the directory that the maintainer of that SRPM used. The data in src.rpms packaged by Red Hat are installed into `/usr/src/redhat` by default.

Rebuilding and improving on rpms is beyond the scope of this answer. The book Maximum RPM and the man pages are good sources of information on this.

D.9.14   Failure mounting CD-ROMS

Question

Linux recognizes my CDROM, but when I try to mount it, I get "mount failed" What do I do?

Answer

If your system was installed properly, simply typing `mount /mnt/cdrom` should work. If it does not, you must edit your `/etc/fstab` file. Here is an example of entry in `/etc/fstab`:

```
# For more details, see the fstab man page (ie, man fstab)
# CD-ROM device  directory   (filesystem type and options)
   /dev/hdc        /mnt/cdrom  iso9660 noauto,ro 0 0
```

To find out what the CD-ROM device is, type `dmesg | less` and scan it for information regarding your CD-ROM. If you wish to mount the CD-ROM without adding this to your `/etc/fstab`:

```
mount -t iso9660 /dev/hdc /mnt/cdrom
```

D.9.15   Booting Linux from floppy

Question

I have Linux installed on an IDE drive, and for whatever reason I need to boot from floppy. How can I boot my system from the install floppy?

Answer

If you have installed Linux onto an IDE hard-drive, you can boot from the installation floppy using the following method:

Insert the installation floppy and restart the machine. At the `boot:` prompt type the following:

```
vmlinuz root=/dev/hdXY
[Example: vmlinuz root=/dev/hdb5 ]
```

Where X = is the Linux drive letter and Y is the partition on the drive you installed the root (/) partition to.

D.9.16 Linux and Plug and Play

Question

I can't get my Plug and Play card to work.

Answer

The 2.0.xx kernels do not directly support the Plug and Play (PNP) protocol. You will need to either disable PNP on the card (via jumpers or card setup tools). You can also change your boot method to use Loadlin.exe from Windows (as windows would then have set up the PNP hardware).

Finally you can try using the isapnptools programs. First, type this:

```
pnpdump > /etc/isapnp.conf
```

This will create a configuration file that you will need to edit to choose the settings used for each card. Then type isapnp /etc/isapnp.conf to set up the devices.

See http://www.roestock.demon.co.uk/isapnptools/ for more information.

D.9.17 Problems with Sound Card

Question

I can't get linux to setup my sound card.

Answer

First make sure that your sound card is on the list of supported sound cards. Also, have you upgraded to the latest soundconfig, from here:

ftp://ftp.redhat.com/pub/sound/sndconfig/

You'll also need the latest kernel with sound module support. If you haven't already, you should download and install these packages.

The sound engineer recommends downloading the sound tools mentioned above and reporting problems to the `sound-list@redhat.com` (`http://archive.redhat.com/`) so that they can be worked on.

D.9.18   Unknown PCI messages

Question

When the system boots up, I see a message that says I have unknown PCI hardware. What does this mean?

Answer

The error "unknown PCI device" can occur for several reasons. The first and most harmless one is that PCI isn't responding to Linux's queries in a way it understands, but Linux is able to keep going. The more common occurrence is that the system hangs on querying PCI bus cards and cannot get any further.

Since this is a hardware problem in the kernel, there is not much that RedHat can do except point you to the maintainer of that section of the kernel. They may be able to let you know what is going on, and may want to look at what hardware you do have in your system so they can better handle it in the future. The maintainer can be reached at:

```
linux-pcisupport@cck.uni-kl.de
```

Please include the following information:

- /proc/pci

- your exact hardware description. Try to find out which device is unknown. It may be your main-board chip set, PCI-CPU bridge or PCI-ISA bridge.

- If you can't find the actual information in your hardware booklet, try to read the references of the chip on the board.

D.9.19   LILO and modules

Question

I used to be able to specify options to LILO: to get various hardware recognized. However, now those options don't seem to do anything. Why is this and what can I do?

Answer

Due to the fact that the kernels built by Red Hat after 4.0 use a modular kernel interface, many of the options that worked with either a different Linux or in Red Hat Linux prior to 4.0 no longer work. Instead you will have to supply items in the /etc/conf.modules file so that either kmod or kerneld will be able to load them correctly into kernel space.

D.9.20   Changing LILO default boot

Question

Currently when the machine boots, LILO defaults to running Linux. I would like it to boot my other operating system. How can I accomplish this?

Answer

To change the default OS that Linux boots into, you will need to edit the /etc/lilo.conf file and change the order of the OS's that LILO looks at. In the following example we change the order of booting so that DOS gets booted by default instead of Linux.

```
pico /etc/lilo.conf

# here is the old version

boot=/dev/hda
map=/boot/map
install=/boot/boot.b
prompt
timeout=50
image=/boot/vmlinuz-2.0.31
        label=linux
        root=/dev/hda2
        read-only
other = /dev/hda1
        label = dos
        table = /dev/hda

# change it to the following:

boot=/dev/hda
map=/boot/map
install=/boot/boot.b
prompt
```

```
timeout=50
other = /dev/hda1
        label = dos
        table = /dev/hda
image=/boot/vmlinuz-2.0.31
        label=linux
        root=/dev/hda2
        read-only
```

Save your changes to the file and leave the editor. Run the command:

```
/sbin/lilo -v
```

The updated lilo will then be written to the boot device. On a reboot, the machine
will boot into DOS as default now instead of Linux, with a 5 second delay to give
you time to choose linux at the boot prompt if you wish to boot to Linux.

D.9.21   Using RPM

Question

*How do I use rpm? What are some general commands that I will use with this command?
Also, for whatever reason, I think files have changed on my system but I don't know which
ones. Can RPM help?*

Answer

In general, normal usage of the rpm command can be summarized as follows:

Installation/Upgrading/Removal

To install a package: rpm -ivh < filename >

```
rpm -ivh somepackage.1.1-4.i386.rpm
```

To upgrade a package: rpm -Uvh < filename >

```
rpm -Uvh somepackage.1.1-5.i386.rpm
```

To remove a package: rpm -e < packagename >

```
rpm -ivh somepackage
```

Also for upgrading or installing some packages you may need to use additional flags to force the install happen. It is only recommended to use these if you know why these flags were needed:

```
--force  will overwrite files that are owned by other
         packages.
--nodeps will install even if the package needs packages
         that were not installed.
```

Querying

To see if a package is installed: rpm -q < packagename >

```
rpm -q somepackage
```

To get info on an installed package: rpm -qi < packagename >

```
rpm -qi somepackage
```

To list which files belong to a package: rpm -ql < packagename >

```
rpm -ql somepackage
```

To see what package a file belongs to: rpm -qf < path-to-filename >

```
rpm -qf /usr/bin/some_executable
```

One can usually join various query commands together, so rpm -qil will give info and list all the files in the package.

To look in a rpm file that isn't installed, simply add p to the query line:

```
rpm -qilp somepackage.1.1-4.i386.rpm
```

This example will list the information and the files contained in somepackage.

More Advanced

More advanced usage can be found in the man page for rpm and at the web site, http://www.rpm.org

Verification

To see what files on the system may have changed from their initial settings you can use RPM, to check up on them:

```
rpm -Va
```

will give you a list of all files that have changed in one form or another since the package it is associated was installed. This can be a lot of files (and a lot may be changed due to post installation work). To just see what packages have changed so that you can verify them more individually, you can do the following:

```
rpm -Va --pipe "awk 'print $2' | xargs rpm -qf | sort -u" &> ↵
/tmp/file1
```

Then look in the file /tmp/file1 for which packages have had changes from them.

D.10   Network Administration

D.10.1   Boot hangs during sendmail

Question

I have installed Linux, and it seems to initially start booting. However it gets down to something called sendmail and then the machine seems to hang. What is happening and what should I do?

Answer

If after the install the machine seems to hang when it reaches certain processes like sendmail, apache, or SMB there is probably a network problem. The most common cause is that Linux can not look up the name of the machine you have called the box (if you set up networking to have a machine name). The machine is currently paused waiting for the network timeout of DNS lookups, and will eventually bring up the login prompt. Login in as root and check the usual culprits for a problem.

If you are directly on a network with a DNS server, make sure the file /etc/resolv.conf has the correct values for your machine's DNS server. Check with your systems administrator that the values are correct.

If you are using Linux on a network without a DNS server (or this box is going to be the DNS server), then you will need to edit the /etc/hosts file to have the hostname and IP address so that the lookups will occur correctly. The format of the /etc/hosts file is:

```
127.0.0.1                    localhost localhost.localdomain
192.168.200.1                mymachine mymachine.mynetwork.net
```

Where the example machine is called mymachine.

D.10.2   Upgrade problems with Sendmail and 5.x

Question

I have upgraded to 5.x, and sendmail is no longer relaying email like it used to. What is going on?

Answer

Due to various email spammers using unknowing Red Hat boxes as email relayers and some other problems, we have turned this off by default in 5.x

You can add the names of systems that you want to be allowed to relay mail to the file
`/etc/relay_allow`. The web site
`http://www.informatik.uni-kiel.de/%7Eca/email/check.html` for more details on this.

If you are having problems with sites sending you UBE (Unsolicited Bulk Email), you can also deny them access to your machines with the new features of sendmail. Add the sites to the file `/etc/mail/deny` and then make a hash table for it.

The following command can be used to create the hash database version of this file:

```
makemap -v hash /etc/mail/deny < /etc/mail/deny
```

D.10.3   net-pf errors

Question

I have installed Linux, recompiled my kernel, and now I get errors when the network comes out about various net-pf modules not found. What is happening and what should I do?

Answer

This means that Linux was unable to find modules for various network protocols. The most common ones are `net-pf-4` (IPX) and `net-pf-5` (appletalk). It looks like that during a kernel recompile these were not included and some service is looking for it during the boot.

First check to see that you are not running a service that is wanting it (mars-nwe, netatalk, etc). If you are you will need to recompile the kernel with these items or turn off the service.

If you still get `net-pf` errors you can fix it by following these directions:

```
cd /etc
vi conf.modules
```

Add the following lines to the file:

```
alias net-pf-3 off
alias net-pf-4 off
alias net-pf-5 off
```

This should turn off the messages upon boot as it tells linux that these are OFF and should not be looked for.

D.11   Printer Administration

D.11.1   Basic Printer Configuration

Question

I am having trouble setting up my printer. My printer is not listed in the printer configuration tool.

Answer

Due to licensing problems, we can not ship the latest ghostscript. It is however available for download in the directory (having been contributed by another Red Hat user):

```
http://www.users.dircon.co.uk/~typhoon/
```

This later version of ghostscript supports many more printers.

D.11.2   Truncated Printout

Question

When I print, lines from my printout get truncated.

Answer

Some printers truncate ASCII lines when printing a page. This is how the printer handles lines that are too long. The text must be run through something that will format the text, like pr or mpage before sending it to the printer.

D.12   Appendix (Long answers)

D.12.1   The Red Hat FTP site is *slow*. Are there mirrors?

There are many mirrors of the Red Hat FTP site. An up-to-date list can always be found at:

```
ftp://ftp.redhat.com/pub/MIRRORS.html
```

D.12.2   What versions of Red Hat Linux are there?

There have been many now. Here's a rundown:

- Preview (or Beta) - Summer 1994
- Halloween - Fall 1994
- Mother's Day 1.0 - Summer 1995
- Mother's Day 1.1 - Late Summer 1995
- Red Hat Linux 2.0beta - Late Late Summer 1995
- Red Hat Linux 2.0 - Early Fall 1995
- Red Hat Linux 2.1 - Late Fall 1995
- Red Hat Linux/AXP 2.1-Beta - Late Fall 1995
- Red Hat Linux/AXP 2.1 - January 1996
- Red Hat Linux 3.0.3 (Picasso) - March 1996
- Red Hat Linux (Rembrandt beta) - August 1996
- Red Hat Linux 4.0 (Colgate) - October 1996
- Red Hat Linux 4.1 (Vanderbuilt) - January 1997
- Red Hat Linux 4.2 (Biltmore) - May 1997
- Red Hat Linux (Thunderbird beta) - May 1997
- Red Hat Linux (Mustang beta) - May 1997
- Red Hat Linux 5.0 (Hurricane) - December 1997
- Red Hat Linux 5.1 (Manhatten) - June 1998
- Red Hat Linux 5.2 - Oct 1998

The current version of Red Hat Linux is 5.2, and is available for Intel (386, 486, and various Pentiums), Alpha (various types), and SPARC.

Glossary

Alpha   A RISC (*Reduced Instruction Set Computer*) architecture developed by Digital Equipment Corporation.

IDE   An acronym for *AT Attachement Packet Interface*. ATAPI is the protocol by which CD-ROM drives communicate with a computer system over an IDE interface.

Binary   Although the base two numbering system used by computers is known as binary, the word often refers to the executable form of a program. Contrast with "source code".

BIOS   An acronym for *Basic Input/Output System*. On PC-compatible systems, the BIOS is used to perform all necessary functions to properly initialize the system's hardware when power is first applied. The BIOS also controls the boot process, provides low-level input/output routines (hence its name) and (usually) allows the user to modify details of the system's hardware configuration.

Boot Diskette   A diskette used to start most Red Hat Linux installations.

Bootstrap   See "Boot".

Boot   Short for "bootstrap". The process by which a computer starts running an operating system when power is applied.

CISC   An acronym for *Complex Instruction Set Computer*. A design philosophy for computers whereby the processor is designed to execute a relatively large number of different instructions, each taking a different amount of time to execute (depending on the complexity of the instruction). Contrast with RISC.

CMOS   Originally an acronym for *Complementary Metal Oxide Semiconductor* – a semiconductor technology used in many integrated circuits. Now often used to describe the low-level hardware that contains a personal computer's BIOS, and the computer's hardware clock.

Cylinder   When referring to disk drives, the number of different positions the disk drive's read/write heads can take over the unit's disk platters. When viewed from above the platters, each head position describes an imaginary circle of different diameters on the platter's surface, but when viewed from the side, these circles can be thought of as a series of cylinders nested within each other, hence the term. See also Geometry.

Daemon   A daemon is program that runs, without human intervention, to accomplish a given task. For example, lpd is a daemon that controls the flow of print jobs to a printer.

Dependencies   When referring to packages, dependencies are requirements that exist between packages. For example, package foo may require files that are installed by package bar. In this example, bar must be installed, or else foo will have unresolved dependencies. RPM will not normally allow packages with unresolved dependencies to be installed.

Device Driver   Software that controls a device that is connected to, or part of, a computer.

Disk Drive   See Hard Disk.

Disk Druid   Disk Druid is a component of the Red Hat Linux installation program that is used to partition disk drives during the installation process.

Diskette   A small mass storage device in a removable cartridge, and meant to be read/written in a compatible drive.

Distribution   An operating system (usually Linux) that has been packaged so as to be easily installed.

Domain Name   A domain name is used to identify computers as belonging to a particular organization. Domain names are hierarchical in nature, with each level in the hierarchy being separated from other levels with a period (pronounced "dot"). For example, Foo Incorporated's Finance department might use the domain name "finance.foo.com".

Driver   See Device Driver.

Dual Boot   The act of configuring a computer system to boot more than one operating system. The name is something of a misnomer, as it is possible to boot more than the two operating systems the word "dual" implies.

EIDE   An acronym for *Enhanced Integrated Drive Electronics*, which is a newer version of the IDE interface standard. EIDE makes larger and faster disk drives possible; most systems sold today use EIDE.

Errata   Errata is Latin for "Ooops"[1]. When software is found to have bugs, quite often the software is fixed, and released as errata. Red Hat Linux is no exception to the rule; we have an Errata web page at http://www.redhat.com/errata.

Extended Partition   A segment of a disk drive that contains other partitions. See Partition.

FAQ   An acronym for Frequently Asked Questions. Linux information is often presented in the form of lists of questions and answers called FAQs.

fdisk   fdisk is a utility program that is used to create, delete, or modify partitions on a disk drive.

Filesystem   A filesystem is the method by which information is stored on disk drives. Different operating systems normally use different filesystems, making it difficult to share the contents of a disk drive between two operating systems. However, Linux supports multiple filesystems, making it possible to, for example, read/write a partition dedicated to Windows.

Floppy   A somewhat historical term for a small mass storage device in a removable cartridge, and meant to be read/written in a compatible drive. See "diskette".

---

[1] Well, it should be. . .

Formatting   The act of writing a filesystem on a disk drive.

FQDN   An acronym for *Fully Qualified Domain Name*. An FQDN is the human-readable name that includes a computer's hostname and associated domain name. For example, given a hostname of "foo", and a domain name of "bar.com", the FQDN would be "foo.bar.com".

FTP   An acronym for *File Transfer Protocol*. Also the name of a program that, as the name implies, permits the copying of files from one system on a network to another.

Gateway   In networking terms, refers to a device that connects one or more computers on a network to other networks. The device may be specialized hardware (such as a router), or may be a general-purpose computer system configured to act as a gateway.

Geometry   When referring to disk drives, the physical characteristics of the disk drive's internal organization. Note that a disk drive may report a "logical geometry" that is different from its "physical geometry", normally to get around BIOS-related limitations. See also Cylinder, Head, and Sector.

GID   Short for *Group ID*. The means by which a user's membership in a group is identified to various parts of Red Hat Linux. GIDs are numeric, although human-readable names are stored in the /etc/group file.

Group   Groups are a way of assigning specific access rights to certain classes of users. For example, all users working on Project X could be added to group xproj. System resources (such as disk space) devoted to Project X could then be configured to permit only members of xproj full access.

Hard Disk   A hard disk contains rotating magnetic media (in the shape of a disk) that spin rapidly. Small heads float over the surface of each disk, and are used to write to and read from the disk as it rotates.

Head   When referring to disk drives, the number of read/write heads within a disk drive. For each platter in a disk drive, there are normally two heads for each platter – one for each surface – although one surface may go unused. See also Geometry.

Hostname   A hostname is a human-readable string of characters used to identify a particular computer system.

I18n   See Internationalization.

IDE   An acronym for *Integrated Drive Electronics*, which is the name of a standard interface used to connect primarily disk and CD-ROM drives to a computer system. See also "EIDE" and "ATAPI".

Intel   Company responsible for producing the microprocessors that most commonly appear in PC-compatible personal computers. These processors include the 80386, 80486, Pentium, Pentium Pro, and Pentium II.

Internationalization   The practice of designing and writing programs that can be easily configured to interact with the user in more than one language. Often referred to as "i18n" due to the number of letters between the starting "i" and the ending "n".

IP Address   IP addresses are the method by which individual computer systems (or from a more strictly accurate interpretation, the network interfaces on those computer systems) are identified on a TCP/IP network. All IP addresses consist of four numbers, each ranging from 0 to 255, and separated by periods.

Kernel   The central part of an operating system upon which the rest of the operating system is based.

Library   When speaking of computers, refers to a collection of routines that perform operations that are commonly required by programs. Libraries may be shared, meaning that the library routines reside in a file separate from the programs that use them. Library routines may also be "statically linked" to a program, meaning that copies of the library routines required by that program are physically added to the program. Such statically linked binaries do not require the existence of any library files in order to execute. Programs linked against shared libraries will not execute unless the required libraries have been installed.

LILO   A commonly used bootstrap loader for Linux systems based on an Intel-compatible processor.

Linus Torvalds   Created Linux in 1991 while a university student.

Linuxconf   A versatile system configuration program written by Jacques Gelinas. Linuxconf provides a menu-based approach to system configuration via several different user interfaces.

Linux   A full-featured, robust, freely-available operating system originally developed by Linus Torvalds.

Logical Partition   A partition that exists within an extended partition. See also "partition" and "extended partition".

Master Boot Record   The master boot record (or MBR) is a section of a disk drive's storage space that is set aside for the purpose of saving information necessary to begin the bootstrap process on a personal computer.

MBR   See "Master Boot Record".

Memory   When referring to computers, memory (in general) is any hardware that can store data for later retrieval. However, the term is usually used to specifically refer to RAM.

MILO   A commonly used bootstrap loader for Linux systems based on the Alpha processor.

Module   In Linux, a module is a collection of routines that perform a system-level function, and may be dynamically loaded and unloaded from the running kernel as required. Often containing device drivers, modules are tightly bound to the version of the kernel; most modules built from one version of a kernel will not load properly on a system running another kernel version.

Mount Point   The directory under which a filesystem is accessible after being mounted.

Mount   The act of making a filesystem accessible to a system's users.

Nameserver   In TCP/IP networking terms, a nameserver is a computer that can translate a human-readable name (such as "foo.bar.com") into a numeric address (such as "10.0.2.14").

Netmask   A netmask is a set of four numbers separated by periods. Each number is normally represented as the decimal equivalent of an eight-bit binary number, which means that each number may take any value between 0 (all eight bits cleared) and 255 (all eight bits set). Every IP address consist of two parts (the network address, and the host number). The netmask is used to determine the size of these two parts. The positions of the bits that are set in the netmask are considered to represent the space reserved for the network address, while the bits that are cleared are considered to represent the space set aside for the host number.

NFS An acronym for Network File System, NFS is a method of making the filesystem on a remote system accessible on the local system. From a user's perspective, an NFS-mounted filesystem is indistinguishable from a filesystem on a directly-attached disk drive.

Operating System A collection of software that controls access to various resources in a computer system.

Packages Files that contain software, and written in a particular format that enables the software to be easily installed and removed.

PAM An acronym for *Pluggable Authentication Modules*. PAM is an authentication system that controls access to Red Hat Linux.

Partition Table The partition table is a section of a disk drive's storage space set aside to define the partitions that exist on that disk drive.

Partition Type Partitions contain a field that is used to define the type of filesystem the partition is expected to contain. The partition type is actually a number, although many times the partition type is referred to by name. For example, the "Linux Native" partition type is 82. Note that this number is hexadecimal.

Partition A segment of a disk drive's storage space that can be accessed as if it was a complete disk drive.

PC Card See PCMCIA.

PCMCIA Acronym for *Personal Computer Memory Card International Association*. This organization produced a series of standards that define the physical, electrical, and software characteristics of small, credit card-sized devices that can contain memory, modems, network adapters, and more. Also known as PC Cards, these devices are mainly used in laptop computers (although some desktop systems can use PCMCIA cards, too).

Permissions The set of identifiers that control access to files. Permissions consist of three fields: user, group, and world. The user field controls access by the user owning the file, while the group field controls access by anyone matching the file's group specification. As the name implies, the world field controls access by everyone else. Each field contains the sme set of bits that specify operations that may or may not be performed, such as reading, writing, and executing.

PLIP   An acronym for *Parallel Line Internet Protocol*. PLIP is a protocol that permits TCP/IP communication over a computer's parallel port using a specially-designed designed cable.

POSIX   A somewhat mangled acronym for *Portable Operating System* Interface. A set of standards that grew out of the UNIX operating system.

Process   A process (in somewhat simplistic terms) can be considered to be one instance of a running program on a Linux system.

PS/2 Mouse   A PS/2 mouse gets its name from the original computer in which this type of mouse was first used – the IBM PS/2. A PS/2 mouse can be easily identified by the small, round connector at the end of its cable.

RAM   An acronym for *Random Access Memory*. RAM is used to hold programs while they are being executed, and data while it is being processed. RAM is also volatile, meaning that information written to RAM will disappear when the computer's power is turned off.

Reboot   To restart the boot process. See also "Boot".

Red Hat Software   A North Carolina software company. Produces and markets sofware for the Linux operating system, including Red Hat Linux.

Rescue Diskette   A diskette containing a rudimentary system environment. As the name implies, a rescue diskette is normally used in an attempt to "rescue" an ailing system from the necessity of re-installing the entire operating system.

RISC   An acronym for *Reduced Instruction Set Computer*. A design philosophy for computers whereby the processor is optimized to execute a relatively small number of different instructions in a predictably small amount of time. Contrast with CISC.

ROM   An acronym for *Read Only Memory*. ROM is used to hold programs and data that must survive the computer being turned off. This is because ROM is non-volatile; data in ROM will remain, unchanged, the next time the computer is turned back on. As the name implies, data cannot be easily written to ROM; depending on the technology used in the ROM, writing may require special hardware, or may be impossible. A computer's BIOS may be stored in ROM.

Root   The name of the login account given full and complete access to all system resources. Also used to describe the directory named "/"as in, "the root directory".

RPM   An acronym that stands for *Red Hat Package Manager*. RPM is also the name of a program that enables the installation, upgrading, and removal of packages.

SCSI   An acronym for *Small Computer System Interface*, SCSI is a standard interface for connecting a wide variety of devices to a computer. Although the most popular SCSI devices are disk drives, SCSI tape drives, scanners, and tape drives are also common.

Sector   When referring to disk drives, the number of fixed-size (normally 512 byte) areas that can be accessed by one of the disk drive's read/write heads, in one rotation of the disk, without that head changing position. See Also Geometry.

Serial Mouse   A serial mouse is a mouse that is designed to be connected to a computer's serial port. A serial mouse can be easily identified by the rectangular-shaped connector at the end of its cable.

setgid   A system call that can be used to set the GID of a process. Programs can be written using setgid such that they can assume the group ID of any group on the system.

setuid   A system call that can be used to set the UID of a process. Programs can be written using setuid such that they can assume the user ID of any process on the system. This is considered a possible security problem if a program is "setuid root".

Shadow Password   Normally, each user's password is stored, encrypted, in the file /etc/passwd. This file must be readable by all users so that certain system functions will operate correctly. However, this means that copies of user's encrypted passwords are easily obtained, making it possible to run an automated password-guessing program against them. Shadow passwords, on the other hand, store the encrypted passwords in a separate highly-protected file, making it much more difficult to crack passwords.

SILO   A commonly used bootstrap loader for Linux systems based on the SPARC processor.

SLIP   An acronym for *Serial Line Internet Protocol*. SLIP is a protocol that permits TCP/IP communication over serial line (typically over a dial-up modem connection).

SMB   Short for *Server Message Block*, SMB is the communications protocol used by Windows-based operating systems to support sharing of resources across a network.

source code   The human-readable form of instructions that comprise a program. Also known as "sources". Without a program's source code, it is very difficult to modify the program.

SPARC   A RISC (*Reduced Instruction Set Computer*) architecture developed by Sun Microsystems.

Supplemental Diskette   A diskette required for certain types of Red Hat Linux installations.

Swap   Also known as "swap space". When a program requires more memory than is physically available in the computer, currently-unused information can be written to swap, thereby freeing memory. Swap space is located on a hard disk; some operating systems support swapping to a file, but Linux swaps to a dedicated swap partition.

System Call   A system call is a routine that accomplishes a system-level function on behalf of a process.

TCP/IP   An acronym for *Transmission Control Protocol/Internet Protocol*, TCP/IP is the name given to the networking standard commonly used on the Internet today.

Torvalds, Linus   See Linus Torvalds.

UID   Short for *User ID*. The means by which a user is identified to various parts of Red Hat Linux. UIDs are numeric, although human-readable names are stored in the /etc/passwd file.

UNIX   A set of Linux-like operating systems that grew out of an original version written by some guys at a phone company.[2]

---

[2]Just kidding – thank you Ken Thompson and Dennis Ritchie for your inspired operating system design!

Unmount   The act of revoking access to a filesystem. (Note that the program that unmounts filesystems is called umount.)

Virtual Console   Virtual consoles provides multiple "screens" on which a user may log in and run programs. One screen is displayed on the computer's monitor at any given time; a key sequence is used to switch between virtual consoles.

Widget   A standardized on-screen representation of a control that may be manipulated by the user. Scroll bars, buttons, and text boxes are all examples of widgets.

X Window System   Also known as "X", this graphical user interface provides the well-known "windows on a desktop" metaphor common to most computer systems today. Under X, application programs act as clients, accessing the X server, which manages all screen activity. In addition, client applications may be on a different system than the X server, permitting the remote display of the applications graphical user interface.

XFree86   A free implementation of the X Window System.

Kickstart Installations

Due to the need for automated installation, Red Hat Software has created the *kick-start* installation method. With this method, a system administrator can create a single file containing the answers to all the questions that would normally be asked during a typical Red Hat Linux installation. The kickstart installation method is powerful enough that often a single kickstart file can be used to install Red Hat Linux on multiple machines.

Please Note: Kickstart installations can only be performed using the CD-ROM and NFS installation methods. FTP, local hard disk, or SMB installations cannot be automated using kickstart mode.

F.1   Where to Put A Kickstart File

To use kickstart mode, you must first create a kickstart file, and make it available to the Red Hat Linux installation program. Normally this is done by copying the kickstart file to the boot diskette, or making it available on the network. The network-based approach is most commonly used, as most kickstart installations tend to be performed on networked computers. This also makes it easier to install Red Hat Linux on many computers, as the kickstart files can be kept on single server system, and read by the individual computers during the installation.

Let's take a more in-depth look at the locations where kickstart file may be placed.

F.1.1   On Diskette

To perform a diskette-based kickstart installation, the kickstart file must be named `ks.cfg`, and reside in the boot diskette's top-level directory. Note that the Red Hat Linux boot diskettes are in MS-DOS format, making it easy to copy the kickstart file under Linux using the `mcopy` command (or, if you insist, you can also use Windows). Although there's no technological requirement for it, most diskette-based kickstart installations install Red Hat Linux from CD-ROM.

F.1.2   On the Network

Network installations using kickstart are quite common, because system administrators can easily automate the installation of many networked computers quickly and painlessly. In general, the approach most commonly used is for the administrator to have both a BOOTP/DHCP server and an NFS server on the local network. The BOOTP/DHCP server is used to give the client system its networking information, while the NFS server serves the actual files used during the installation. Often these two servers run on the same physical machine, but there is no requirement for this.

To do a network-based kickstart installation, you must have a BOOTP/DHCP server on your network, and it must include configuration information for the machine you are attempting to install. The BOOTP/DHCP server will be used to give the client its networking information as well as the location of the kickstart file. If a kickstart file is specified by the BOOTP/DHCP server, the client system will attempt an NFS mount of the file's path, and will copy the specified file to the client, using it as the kickstart file. The exact settings required vary depending on the BOOTP/DHCP server you use. Here's an example for the DHCP server shipped with Red Hat Linux:

```
filename "/usr/new-machine/kickstart/";
next-server blarg.redhat.com;
```

Note that you should use `filename` for the kickstart file's name (or the directory in which the kicstart file resides), and `next-server` to set the NFS server name.

If the filename returned by the BOOTP/DHCP server ends with a slash ("/"), then it is interpreted as a path only. In this case, the client system mounts that path using NFS, and searches for a specially-named file. The filename the client searches for is:

```
<ip-addr>-kickstart
```

The `<ip-addr>` section of the filename should be replaced with the client's IP address in dotted decimal notation. For example, the filename for a computer with an IP address of 10.10.0.1 would be `10.10.0.1-kickstart`.

Note that if you don't specify a server name, then the client system will attempt to use the server that answered the BOOTP/DHCP request as its NFS server. If you don't specify a path or filename, the client system will try to mount /kickstart from the BOOTP/DHCP server, and will try to find the kickstart file using the same *<ip-addr>*-kickstart filename as described above.

F.2   Starting a Kickstart Installation

To begin a kickstart installation, you must boot the system from a Red Hat Linux boot diskette, and enter a special boot command at the boot prompt. If the kickstart file resides on the boot diskette, the proper boot command would be:

```
boot: linux ks=floppy
```

If, on the other hand, the kickstart file resides on a server, the appropriate boot command would be:

```
boot: linux ks
```

F.3   The Kickstart File

Now that you have some background information on kickstart installations, let's take a look at the kickstart file itself. The kickstart file is a simple text file, containing a list of items, each identified by a keyword. You can create it by editing a copy of the README.ks file found in the docs/ directory of a Red Hat Linux CD-ROM, or you can create it from scratch. You should be able to edit it with any text editor or word processor that can save files as ASCII text.

First, some ground rules to keep in mind while creating your kickstart file:

- Items must be specified *in order*. It is not a good idea to try to change the order of the required items.

- Items that aren't required can be omitted.

- For kickstart *upgrades*, the following items are required:

  - language
  - installation method
  - device specification
  - keyboard setup
  - the upgrade keyword
  - LILO configuration

  If any other items are specified for an upgrade, those items will be ignored (note that this includes package selection).

- Omitting any required item will result in the installation process prompting the user for an answer to that question, just as during a normal installation. If this happens, once the answer is given the installation will continue unattended (unless it comes across another missing item).

- Lines starting with a pound sign ("#") are treated as comments, and are ignored.

Let's take a look at each item in order.

F.3.1   `lang` – Language Setting

The first item that must appear is the language setting. The language you specify will be used during the installation as well as to configure any language-specific aspect of the installed system. The language specification must be a two letter ISO language code, such as en for English, de for German, fr for French, and so on. For example, to set the language to English, the kickstart file should contain the following line:

```
lang en
```

F.3.2   `network` – Networking Configuration

The next item is the network configuration information. This line is used to tell the system how it should configure networking for itself. It is optional, and if omitted, the system will be configured for stand-alone operation.

There are three different methods of network configuration:

- DHCP
- BOOTP
- static

The DHCP method uses a DHCP server system to obtain its networking configuration. As you might guess, the BOOTP method is similar, requiring a BOOTP server to supply the networking configuration.

The static method requires that you enter all the required networking information in the kickstart file. As the name implies, this information is static, and will be used during the installation, and after the installation as well.

To direct a system to use DHCP to obtain its networking configuration, use the following line:

```
network --bootproto dhcp
```

To direct a machine to use BOOTP to obtain its networking configuration, use the following line in the kickstart file:

```
network --bootproto bootp
```

The line for static networking is more complex, as you must include all network configuration information on one line. You'll need to specify:

- IP address
- netmask
- gateway IP address
- nameserver IP address

Here's an example static line:

```
network --bootproto static ↩
--ip 10.0.2.15 ↩
--netmask 255.255.255.0 ↩
--gateway 10.0.2.254 ↩
--nameserver 10.0.2.1
```

Please Note: The entire network configuration *must appear on one line!* We've wrapped it here to make it easier to read.

Note that there are two restrictions you must keep in mind should you use the static method:

- All static networking configuration information must be specified on *one* line; you cannot wrap lines using a backslash, for example.
- You can only specify one nameserver here. However, you can use the kickstart file's %post section (described in Section F.3.19 on page 367) to add more nameservers, if needed.

F.3.3 Installation Methods

The next required item is the installation method. This item directs the installation program to the rest of the files required to install Red Hat Linux. There are two choices: NFS or CD-ROM. Let's look at both, starting with NFS.

F.3.4 `nfs` – The NFS Installation Method

For the NFS installation method, you must include the NFS server's name and the directory to be mounted. Here's an example:

```
nfs --server hostname.of.server --dir /path/to/RH/CD/image
```

F.3.5 `cdrom` – The CD-ROM Installation Method

For a CD-ROM-based kickstart installation, simply use the following line:

```
cdrom
```

F.3.6 `device` – Optional Hardware Information

The next set of items in the kickstart file are used to specify optional hardware information. For most PCI-based hardware you can omit this step, as this information can be obtained directly from the hardware. Note that IDE hard disks and common PCI cards fall into this category. Any other hardware may need to be specified here.

To specify a device, start with the `device` keyword, followed by the type of device:

- `ethernet` (for Ethernet cards)
- `scsi` (for SCSI cards)
- `cdrom` (for non-SCSI, non-IDE CD-ROM drives; usually sound cards with proprietary CD-ROM interfaces)

If a kernel module is required to support the device, the module name follows the device type.

Finally, if there are any parameters that are required by a device, they can be specified by using the `--opts` option. Enclose the parameters in quotes after `--opts`. We'll show you some examples below.

Note that you can specify more than one type of device in a given kickstart file. For example, if you know the machines you'll be kickstart-installing have either an Adaptec 1542 or a Buslogic SCSI card, you can enter both in the kickstart file. But be aware that the installation program uses only the first card found, so order the device entries appropriately.

An example for an ISA 3com Ethernet card would be:

```
device ethernet 3c509 --opts "io=0x330, irq=7"
```

Here's an example line for an Adaptec 1542 SCSI card:

```
device scsi aha154x
```

An example of a SoundBlaster CD-ROM might look like this:

```
device cdrom --opts "io=0x240"
```

F.3.7 `keyboard` – Keyboard Type

The next item you'll need to specify is the correct code for your keyboard type. For US keyboards, the type is us. For the others, please run the /usr/sbin/kbdconfig program on an already-installed Red Hat Linux system. An alternative approach would be to set the keyboard type to us and run kbdconfig on the installed system to set it properly after the installation completes).

An example of this would be:

```
keyboard us
```

F.3.8 Partitioning

The hard drive in the machine must be partitioned before Red Hat Linux can be installed. In this section, we will describe how to specify disk partitioning in the kickstart file.

F.3.9 `zerombr` – Partition table initialization

First, if you are installing Red Hat Linux on a new machine, you should use the zerombr keyword to clear the current partition information. This is a good idea, because the partition table on new hard drives is usually bogus. Here's an example of zerombr on a new system:

```
zerombr yes
```

On the other hand, if you are installing machines that have a valid partition table, even if you want to change part (or all) of it, you should use zerombr this way:

```
zerombr no
```

F.3.10 `clearpart` – Removing partitions based on partition type

The next command is optional, but can come in handy. If you'd like to remove all partitions, or just any Linux-related partitions, you can use `clearpart`. For example, to clear all partitions of type "Linux native" and "Linux swap", you could add this line:

```
clearpart --linux
```

To clear *all* partitions from a disk, this line would do the trick:

```
clearpart --all
```

The only options `clearpart` supports are `--linux` and `--all`.

F.3.11 `part` – Partition definition

The next step is to specify the partitions you want to create. These will only be created using the system's unpartitioned free space. In other words, if the machine had Windows-related partitions, and you had done `clearpart --linux` those Windows partitions would remain untouched). You must enter one partition per line using the following format:

```
part <mntpt> --size <size in megs> [--grow] ↵
[--maxsize <size in megs>]
```

(This `part` line was broken to make it more readable.)

`<mntpt>` is the location you are going to mount that partition in your installed system (for example, the root partition would have a mount point of `/`, while you may decide that another partition should have a mount point of `/home`).

`<size in megs>` is the size of the partition in megabytes. You can optionally specify that the partition is *growable* by adding the `--grow` option. Note that making a partition growable does *not* mean that you can later increase its size. Instead, a growable partition will be automatically resized to use all available unpartitioned free space (after all fixed-size partitions have been created).

Since the amount of unpartitioned free space can vary, and you probably want to use it all, by tagging partitions as growable you can easily make sure no space is wasted. If you have multiple partitions tagged as growable, the free space is split evenly among them.

Note that you can also limit the size of growable partitions with the optional `--maxsize` argument.

Here's an example of kickstart partitioning in action. Let's say you know the smallest disk out of a set of machines you plan to kickstart-install is 1GB. You'd like to use the same kickstart file. You could use the following partitioning scheme:

```
zerombr no
clearpart --all
part / --size 250
part swap --size 50
part /usr --size 500 --grow --maxsize 800
part /tmp --size 100 --grow
```

When defined this way, the installation program will first clear all partitions. It will then set up a 250MB root filesystem, followed by a 50MB swap partition. Next the installation program will create a /usr partition of at least 500MB (remember, it's growable), but it cannot grow beyond 800MB. Finally, the last line will create a /tmp partition of at least 100MB (again, it's growable).

So for that 1GB system, you would end up with a 250MB root, a 50MB swap, a 550MB /usr, and a 150MB /tmp partition. If another system has a 2GB drive, you would get a 250MB root, a 50MB swap, a 800MB /usr, and a 900MB /tmp.

F.3.12   install and upgrade – Install/Upgrade Selection

The next item to specify is whether you are doing a fresh install, or an upgrade of an already-installed system. For a fresh install, use:

```
install
```

For an upgrade of an existing system, use:

```
upgrade
```

Keep in mind that for upgrades, the only items that matter are:

- installation media (CD-ROM or NFS)
- device specification (if necessary)
- keyboard setup
- install/updgrade specification (which should be upgrade, of course!)
- LILO configuration

F.3.13 `mouse` – Mouse Configuration

To define the type of mouse your system has, you must use the `mouse` keyword. Run `mouseconfig --help` on an already-installed Red Hat Linux for a list of mouse types.

Depending on the type of mouse, you may also need to specify the device to which the mouse is attached. The default device is correctly set for bus mice. For serial mice, the default device is `/dev/cua0`, but can be overridden with the `--device` option followed by the device name, such as `cua1`.

For example, for a three-button PS/2 mouse, you would use:

```
mouse --kickstart generic3ps/2
```

For a two-button PS/2 mouse, use:

```
mouse --kickstart genericps/2
```

For a two-button Microsoft mouse on your second serial port, use:

```
mouse --kickstart microsoft --device cua1
```

F.3.14 `timezone` – Timezone Definition

Red Hat Linux is timezone-aware, so you'll need to specify the timezone in which the machine will operate. This is done using the `timezone` keyword. There are *many* different timezones; the best way to find yours is to run `/usr/sbin/timeconfig` on an already-installed Red Hat Linux system.

If you would like to have your system's hardware clock set to use GMT/UTC, add the `--utc` option to your timezone line. Here's an example that defines the timezone as US Eastern with the system clock set to GMT:

```
timezone --utc US/Eastern
```

F.3.15 `xconfig` – X Window Setup

The next item is the X Window setup line. The installation program will normally find common PCI video hardware and will know which X server to install. The keyword for X configuration is `xconfig`.

If your video card isn't probed properly, you can use the `--card` option to explicitly specify the card. You can use `Xconfigurator --help` on a running Red Hat Linux system to get a list of supported cards to choose from.

If your card isn't in the list but *is* supported by one of the existing servers, you can simply install the proper server by using the `--server` option. Again, use `Xconfigurator --help` to get the list of server names.

You also need to specify a monitor type. If you don't, the installation will assume a generic monitor capable of 640x480@60hz. Use the `--monitor` option to specify something other than the default. Again, `Xconfigurator --help` will list all valid monitor types.

If your monitor isn't listed, you can enter the actual monitor specifications by using the `--hsync` and `--vsync` options for horizontal and vertical sync rates, respectively. The rates may be single numbers (representing kilohertz and megahertz, as appropriate), groups of numbers separated by commas, or two numbers separated by a dash (signifying a range). For example:

```
xconfig --hsync "31.5,35.5,50-65" --vsync "50-70"
```

An example for a machine where the video card can be autoprobed properly would be:

```
xconfig --monitor "tatung cm14uhe"
```

An example for a machine where nothing is probed and the monitor isn't in the list might be:

```
xconfig --server "Mach64" --hsync "31.5,35.5,50-65" <
--vsync "50-70"
```

F.3.16 `rootpw` – Setting the Root Password

You can put the root passwd in a kickstart file in the clear (in which case it would go over the network in the clear on an NFS install) or you can specify that an encrypted password is to be used. To specify an unencrypted password in the kickstart file, use the `rootpw` keyword, followed by the cleartext password:

```
rootpw mypasswd
```

If you would rather use an encrypted password, grab it out of `/etc/passwd` (or wherever you have the encrypted version stored), and add the `--iscrypted` option:

```
rootpw --iscrypted encryptedpasswdstring
```

F.3.17 `lilo` – LILO Configuration

For machines that use LILO (Intel-based systems), you can specify the LILO configuration using the `lilo` keyword. The default line can be as simple as this:

```
lilo
```

This will install LILO in the hard drive's master boot record (MBR), and automatically configure boot entries for your Linux installation as well as a DOS or Windows installation (if one is present).

If you don't want LILO installed in the MBR, you can do so with by using the `--location` option. There are three possible places where LILO can be installed:

- `mbr` - put LILO on the master boot record (default)
- `partition` - put LILO on the beginning of the root partition
- `none` - don't install LILO at all (in which case you'll need your own method of booting the installed system)

You can also use the `--append` option to add an `append=` line to the Linux boot entry. This is handy if you need to do things like set memory sizes, etc. For example, to install LILO on the MBR on a machine with 128MB of RAM, you would add the following `lilo` line:

```
lilo --append "mem=128M" --location mbr
```

(Due to the new kernel in Red Hat Linux 5.2, the `mem` boot-time option shouldn't be necessary, but we needed an example.)

F.3.18 `%packages` – Package Selection

You can use the `%packages` keyword to start the beginning of a kickstart file section that lists the packages you'd like to install (Note that this is for installs only, as package selection during upgrades is not supported).

Packages can be specified by component or by individual package name. The installation program defines several components that group together related packages. See the `RedHat/base/comps` file on any Red Hat Linux CD-ROM for a list of components. The components are defined by the lines that begin with a number followed by a space, and then the component name. Each of the packages in that component are then listed, line-by-line, until the `end` keyword. Individual packages lack the leading number found in front of component lines.

In most cases, it's only necessary to list the desired components and not individual packages. Note that the `Base` component is always selected by default, so it's not necessary to specify it in the `%packages` section.

Here's an example `%packages` section:

```
%packages
@ Networked Workstation
@ C Development
@ Web Server
@ X Window System
bsd-games
```

As you can see, components are specified, one to a line, starting with an "@" symbol, a space, and then the full component name as given in the comps file. Specify individual packages with no additional characters (The bsd games line in the example above is an individual package).

Please Note: You can also direct the kickstart install to use the workstation- and server-class installation methods. To do this, simply add *one* of the following lines to the %packages section:

```
@ Workstation
@ Server
```

F.3.19 %post – Post-Installation Configuration Section

You have the option of adding commands to be run on the installed system after the installation is complete. This section must be at the end of the kickstart file and must start with the %post keyword. Note that you can access the network in the %post section; however, nameservice has not yet been configured at this point, so only IP addresses will work. Here's an example %post section:

```
%post

# add comment to /etc/motd
echo "Kickstart-installed Red Hat Linux '/bin/date'" > ↩
/etc/motd

# add another nameserver
echo "nameserver 10.10.0.2" >> /etc/resolv.conf
```

This section creates a message-of-the-day file containing the date the kickstart installation took place, and gets around the network keyword's one-nameserver-only limitation by adding another nameserver to /etc/resolv.conf.

Index

Symbols

A

B

C

S

Index of Packages